MW01626096

VIK MUNIZ

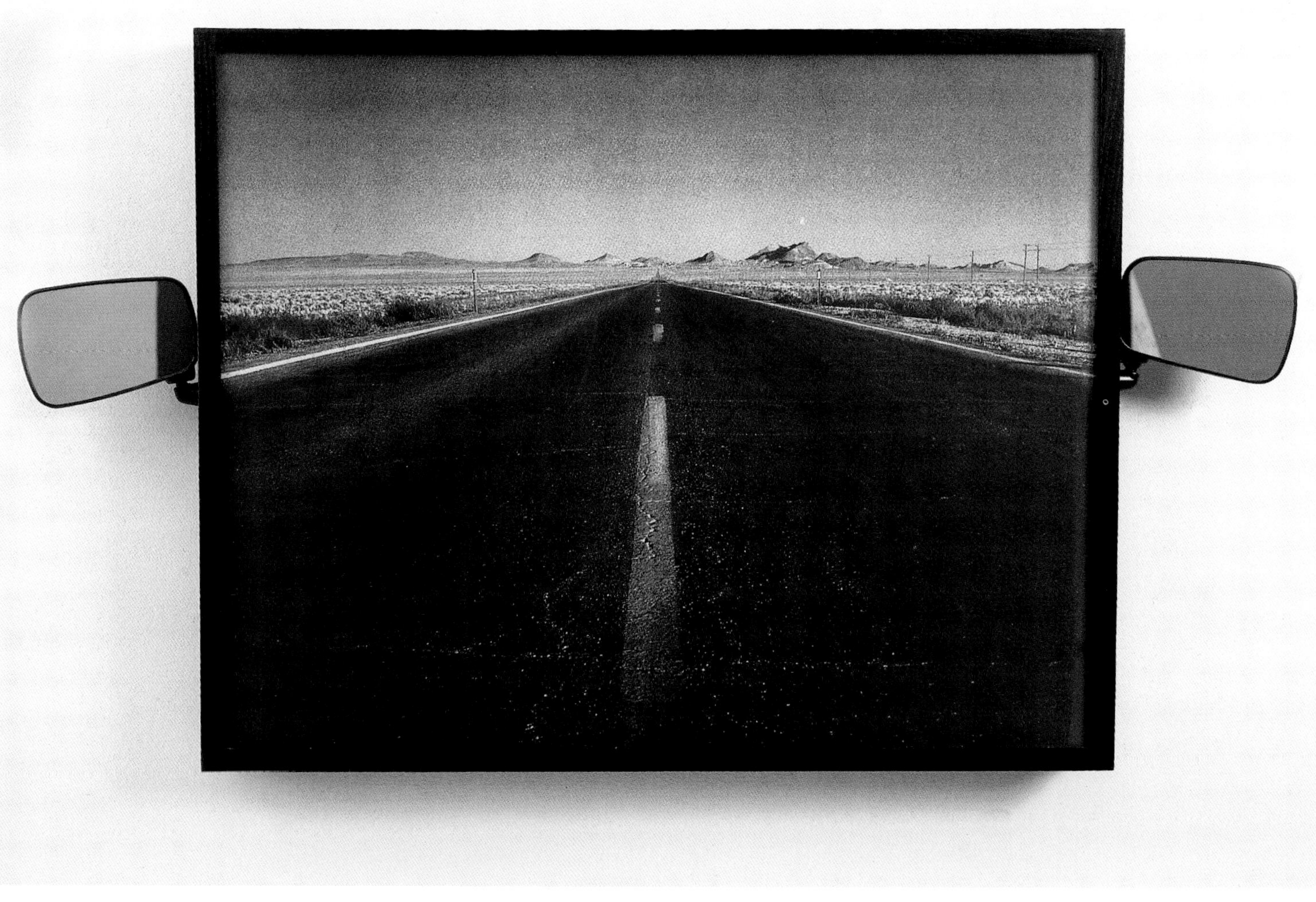

VIK MUNIZ

SEEING IS BELIEVING

Arena Editions

First edition published by Arena Editions
573 West San Francisco Street
Santa Fe, New Mexico 87501 USA
Telephone 505.986.9132
Fax 505.986.9138
www.arenaed.com

Concept by Charles Ashley Stainback and James Crump
Book design by Bethany Johns

Distribution by D.A.P./Distributed Art Publishers
155 Sixth Avenue, Second Floor
New York, NY 10013-1507
Telephone 212.627.1999
Fax 212.627.9484

This publication was produced in conjunction with the exhibition
Vik Muniz: Seeing Is Believing, curated by Charles Ashley Stainback
and on view at the International Center of Photography,
Midtown, New York, September 11 through November 15, 1998.

Printed by EBS, Verona, Italy
First edition 1998

ISBN 1-892041-00-6

Frontis: Vik Muniz, *Historical Photo*, 1989,
framed gelatin silver print with rearview mirrors, 30 x 40 inches.
Private Collection, New Jersey.

CONTENTS

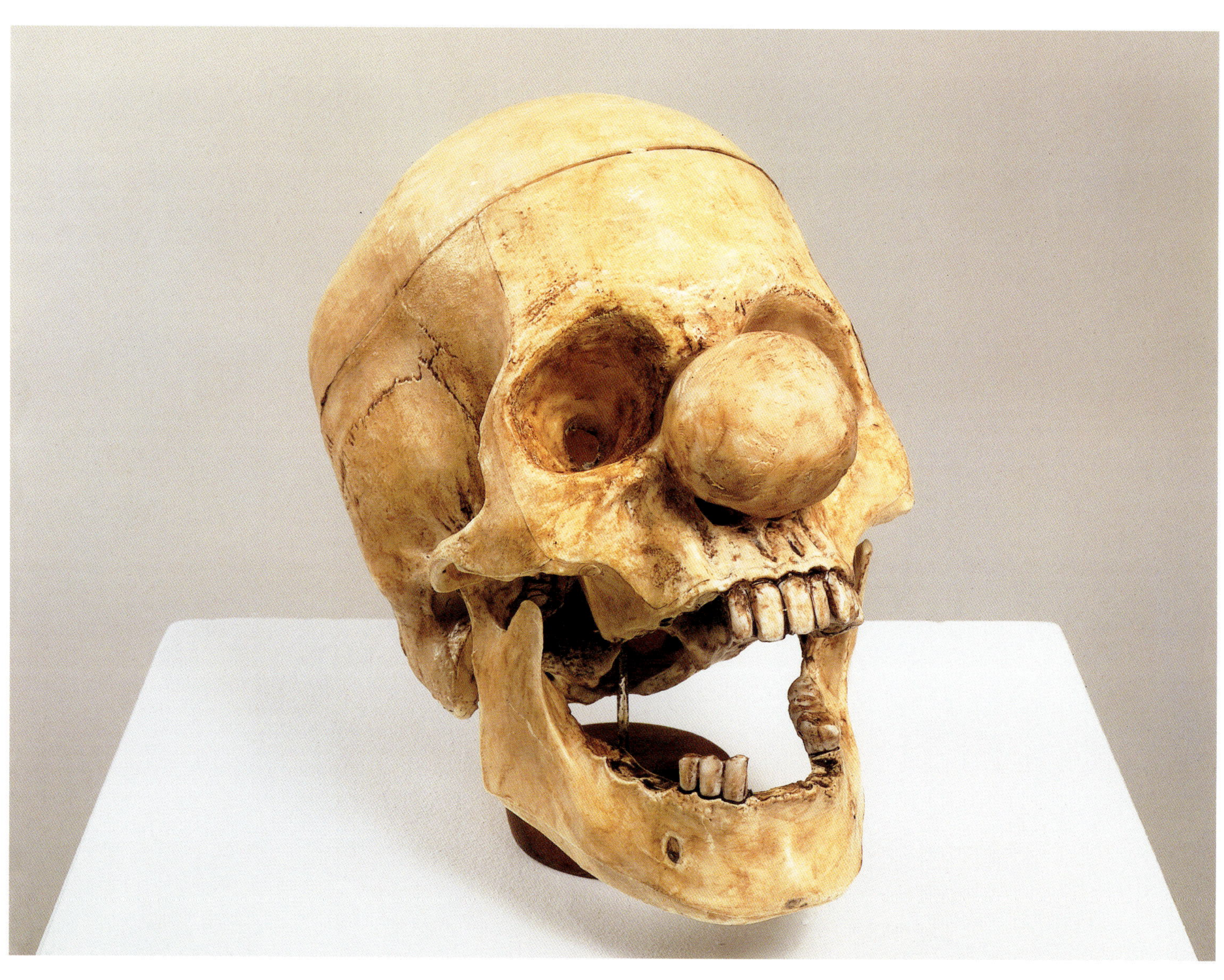

CHARLES ASHLEY STAINBACK

CRANIUM ENVY

OR TROMPE L'OEIL FOR THE IMAGE CONSCIOUS

Through a complicated process of superimposed exposures taken in different parts of the house, he was sure that sooner or later he would get a daguerreotype of God, if He existed, or put an end once and for all to the supposition of his existence.

—GABRIEL GARCÍA MÁRQUEZ, *ONE HUNDRED YEARS OF SOLITUDE*[1]

I mean, Bozo the Clown. I mean, does he really need "the Clown" in his title? ... Are we gonna confuse him with Bozo the District Attorney? Bozo the Pope? There's no other Bozo.

—JERRY SEINFELD[2]

We are inclined to believe what we see when it confirms something we already know. Over the last decade, Vik Muniz has produced a body of work that puts this basic question before us: Can we believe what we see? His photographs might appear to many as if the concept of "reality" has been transformed unexpectedly, a visual sleight-of-hand with the camera. What we see isn't what we get—"get," as in "get it?" Muniz's photographs invite, even beg, a second glance. In a similar way, a ventriloquist, mime, or celebrity impersonator shifts the notion of what is real from what we actually see (and hear) to what our mind perceives.

Taking his cue from seemingly disparate sources such as optical illusions, photorealist paintings, sight gags, abstractions, and real-life visual absurdities—the face of Jesus on a tortilla, for instance—Muniz's photographs are truly a hybrid of artistic technique, intellectual rigor, and youthful curiosity. With a keen ability to transform mundane yet atypical artistic materials into two-dimensional illusions, Muniz's photographs extend the notion of not only photography but artmaking in our post-postmodern age.

Ever since the proclamation "painting is dead" was made shortly after the invention of photography, painterly realism has been at odds with—if not an outright victim of—photographic veracity. Muniz understands this predicament all too well. By producing

Vik Muniz, *Clown Skull*, 1989, cast plastic, 12 x 8 x 9 inches. Collection Eileen Cohen, New York.

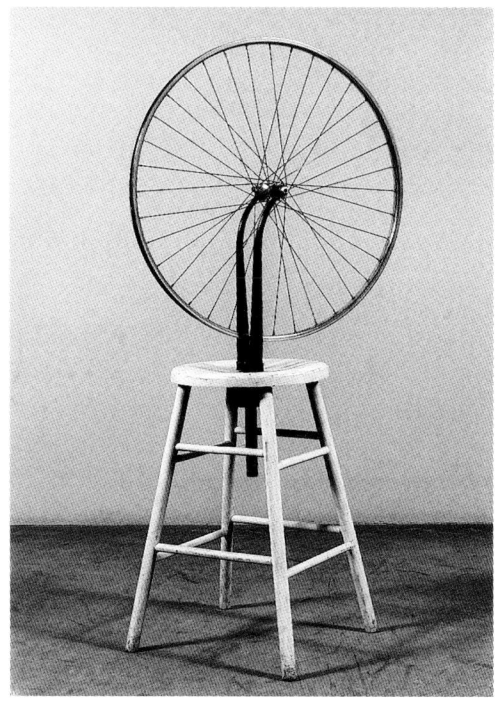

Marcel Duchamp, *Bicycle Wheel*, New York, 1951 (third version, after lost original of 1913). Assemblage: metal wheel 25 ½ inches diameter, mounted on painted wood stool 23 ¾ inches high; overall, 50 ½ x 25 ½ x 16 ⅝ inches. The Museum of Modern Art, New York. The Sidney and Harriet Janis Collection. Photograph © 1998 The Museum of Modern Art, New York.

photographs that merge the camera's precise translation of his handiwork in the three-dimensional world into two-dimensional artworks, Muniz elicits a drop-jaw response in our mind's eye. This perceptual cross-wiring, in which illusion short-circuits our notion of reality, is the result of our simultaneous certainty of what must have existed before the camera and the falsehood Muniz has created. Departing from the conventional, disrupting the barriers between disciplines and media, Muniz's sensibilities are directly linked to Pop, Fluxus, and Conceptual art of the 1960s, as well as Dada and Marcel Duchamp in the early part of the twentieth century. The playful contradictions of Muniz's images and his various series keep one on the edge of a slippery slope that delineates image and reality, fact and fiction, high art and kitsch, art-historical discourse and what he refers to as "talking about the history of old pictures."

With a smartalecky goofiness, Muniz embraces many of the photographic icons of our shared cultural and historical consciousness. Fascinated with copies, he often reworks specific images from our storehouse of pictures, for instance, *The Best of Life* volume or his own *Equivalents* (after the title given by Alfred Stieglitz to his series of "cloud interpretations"). In this way, Muniz asks us to rethink images and their meanings, a conceptual approach that on the surface appears rather simplistic but ultimately goes to the core of photographic representation.

Muniz's translations, performed with subtle wit and the spellbinding technique of the best magician, are the result of a transformation of various materials—dirt, sugar, chocolate syrup, wire—into what he calls "photographic delusions." These renderings always teeter on the edge: off-kilter photographic representations of Sigmund Freud or Jackson Pollock drawn with Bosco syrup, or even his own version of the nineteenth-century precursor of today's cable-television education channel, pseudo-scientific photographs of "vocal cords of a man saying 'buon giorno,'" actually closeup views of spaghetti presented as stereoviews.

In fact, Muniz fabricates all his images for the camera. His miniature setups might be done over several days. Or the exigencies of the medium force him to produce the work quickly, for instance, before heat from the lamps causes the syrup to run all over his latest rendition. Of course, fabrication is hardly a new idea in photography: creating illusions is what gave Louis Daguerre his first fifteen minutes of fame, prior to his invention of the process that would make his name known worldwide. As the builder of multifaceted dioramas,

Daguerre was the proprietor of the most popular spectacle in Paris during the early 1800s. These illusions usually consisted of a revolving floor and an enormous canvas (about half the size of a football field, i.e., 72 x 48 feet) with scenes painted on both sides. Through his own complicated process, Daguerre could make one scene dissolve into another – an Alpine village would become a midnight mass in a cathedral. The realism, the true-to-life likeness was so compelling that an art student set up an easel and began to paint one of the scenes. Daguerre is said to have told the aspiring and apparently awestruck artist, "Young man, come as often as you want, but don't work here, because you'll be making nothing but a copy of a copy. If you want to study seriously, go outdoors."[3]

It has been said that if it looks, walks, and sounds like a duck, it's a duck. This common-sense notion helps us avoid confusing a potato, let's say, with a duck. In other words, *looking* like a duck isn't sufficient: a thing must have all the essential attributes of a duck – mobility, the ability to quack – to *be* a duck. Vik Muniz confounds this common sense by giving us some, but not all, the inherent characteristics of a given subject – yet we are not confused. And that is the point. We've all seen countless images of ducks. We fill in the gaps, the missing attributes, just as we would when we view a movie at twenty-four frames per second. The mind adjusts and renders what it sees on the screen as fluid motion. We want to make sense of things that we see, even if they are nonsensical.

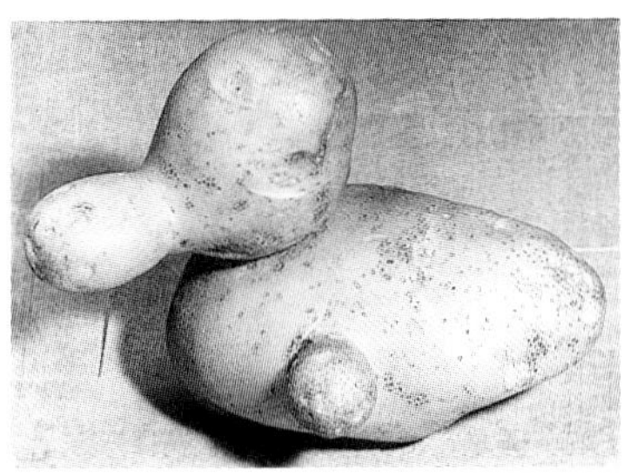

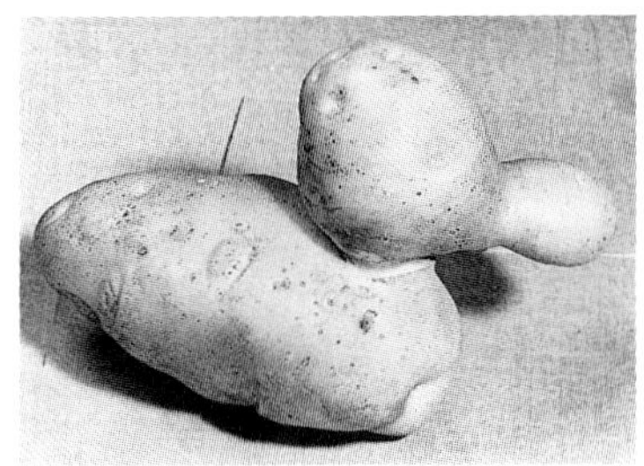

Potato Shaped Like Duck (photographer unknown). © 1998 Ripley Entertainment Inc.

But what are we to make of that gray area between reality and fiction, the illusion that we know to be make-believe yet has all the trappings of the real thing? They talk the talk, walk the walk, but something is a tad off in many of Muniz's photographs, leading us to question the very conditions that we have assumed were essential characteristics of a representation. By toying with these assumptions, by subverting the basic tenets of what a photograph is supposed to be, Muniz appears to be both shaman and heretic.

Muniz's approach to artmaking and his use of the photograph are part Duchampian, part trickster. And he enjoys the role. When Duchamp attached a bicycle wheel to a stool, he catalyzed a radical shift in artistic practice, a sensibility that Muniz embraces with vigor. Attaching round noses to human skulls, drawing *The Last Supper* with chocolate syrup, or making a closeup photograph of Cheese Doodles and titling it *Loser Gene*, Muniz tweaks artistic convention, good taste, and high-art seriousness. He also looks to the unconventional for inspiration. Pushing extremes, producing unlikely illusions, are at the heart of Muniz's work. His *Big Book* is presented in much the same spirit that produced the first Monster Truck, *Big Foot*, a Ford pickup with gigantic wheels that spawned a whole new form of

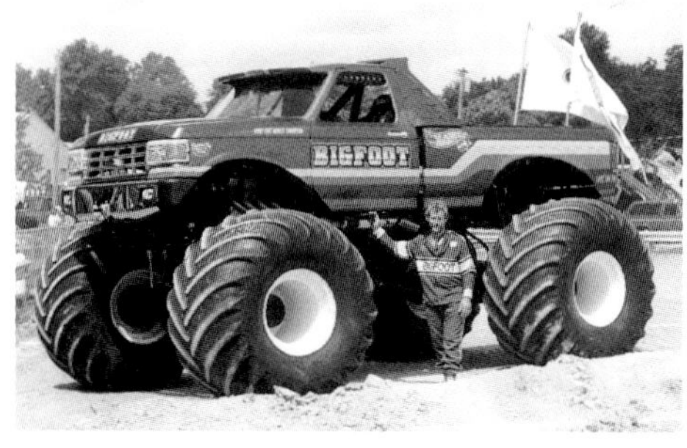

Big Foot **(the first Monster Truck). Photo © 1998 Eric Stern/Motorsports Photography Unlimited.**

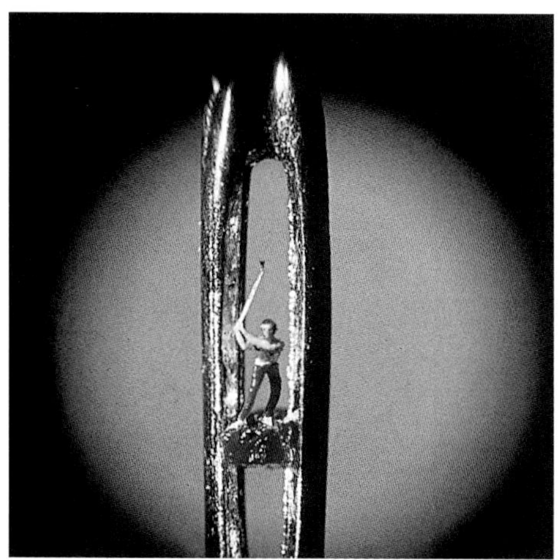

Hagop Sandaljian, *The Golfer*, 1984, micro-miniature sculpture in the eye of a needle. Courtesy of the Museum of Jurassic Technology, Los Angeles.

human expression (albeit testosterone-driven). By subverting an object's traditional function, both artists (yes, *artist*) suggest that we do judge the book by the cover, yet the ultimate test of quality is made when the rubber meets the road. Like Hagop Sandaljian's *Golfer*, a micro-sculpture set in the eye of a needle and created with the aid of a microscope, scale and content, artistic skill, and a disregard for conventions are butted side-by-side. And like Sandaljian's amazing ability to produce wondrous illusions, Muniz merges the skills of human creativity translated via an optical aid, the camera. Ultimately, Muniz's unique works suggest a radical reevaluation of the notion of artistic creation that has the genuine article rubbing alongside make-believe.

Captioned photographs are persuasive by their very nature. Consider Muniz's image of a "goosebump hormone" in the *Principia* series. As a "scientific" representation, this image seems reasonable enough. The text simply verifies our expectation. If we lived in a world full of clowns, pseudo-clowns, wannabe-clowns, and lookalike clowns, the designator following Bozo would be essential. Presented with someone calling himself Bozo, we immediately make the connection "the Clown," but do we just as instantly assume that a clown is Bozo? I'm not sure that I could pick Bozo out of a lineup of clowns (brought in for any number of felony convictions), or that I could distinguish between Bozo and Ronald MacDonald, for that matter. Seeing that many clowns could simply make one dizzy (or crazy). There are just those times when you must take things at face value and believe the caption.

Calling Vik Muniz's artwork "photography" might seem disingenuous. The idea of a photograph evokes snapshots, newspapers, or beautiful landscapes. Actually, painting, drawing, or sculpture might first come to mind when viewing a Muniz photograph. His works are like seeing Bozo without colorful clothes, makeup, and oversized shoes. With only the nose, he's still Bozo the Clown, yes? This paradox is the crux of our contemporary dilemma. We have known for quite some time that we can no longer simply assume that seeing is believing.

Notes

1. Gabriel García Márquez, *One Hundred Years of Solitude* (New York: Knopf, 1995), p. 57.
2. Quoted by permission of Castlerock Entertainment, Beverly Hills, California, from the *Seinfeld* episode, "The Fire," written by Larry Charles.

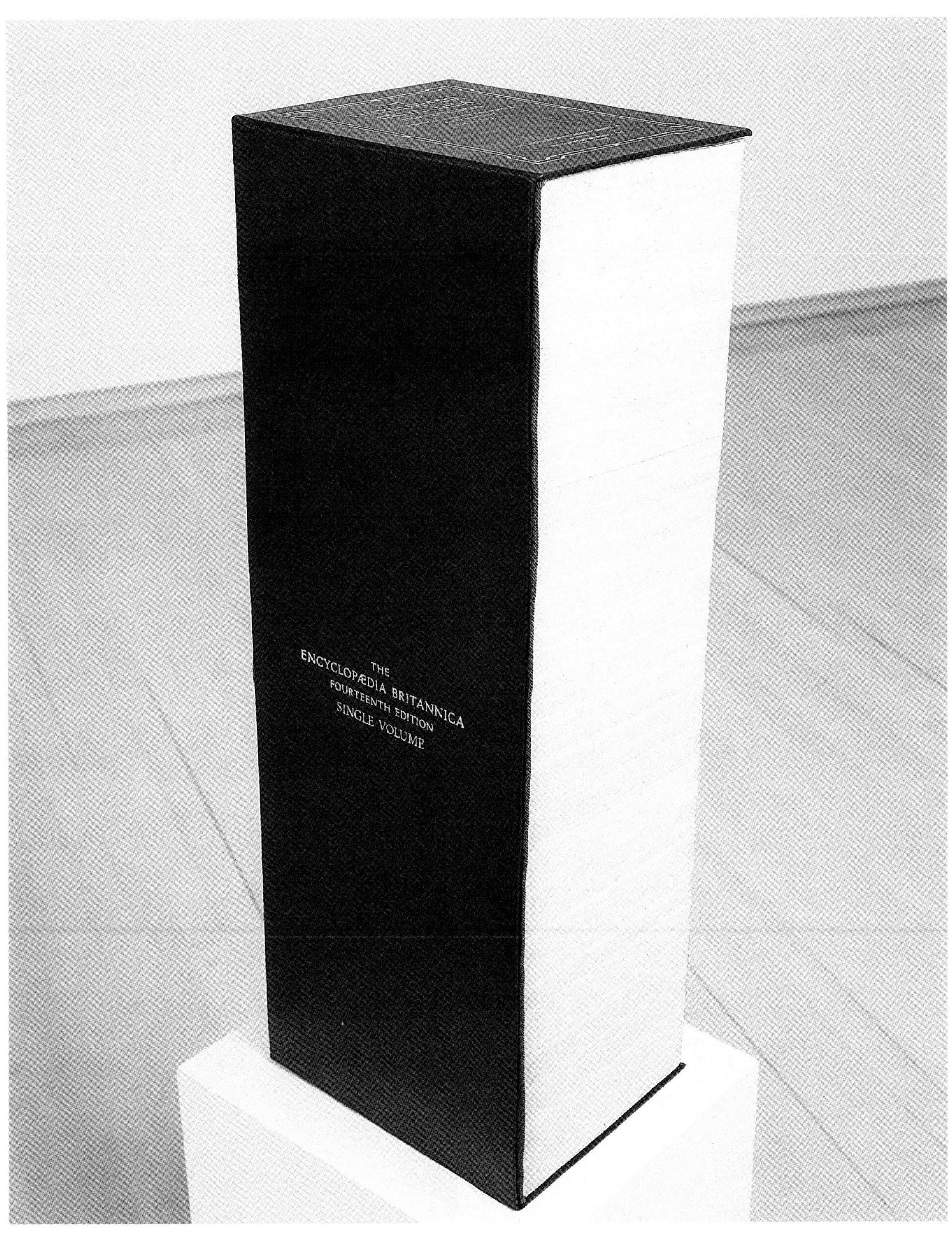

Vik Muniz, *Big Book*, 1989, leather-bound Encyclopaedia Britannica (entire set), 36 x 12 x 9 inches. Collection Randolfo Rocha, New York.

Overleaf:
Vik Muniz, eight works from *Displacements*, 1996, cibachrome prints, each 20 x 24 inches.

The quintuplets John, Paul, George, Ringo and Elvis Moreno from San Jacinto, TX

Emanuel Ungaro's glittering belted tunic dripping with jet paillettes

[VIK MUNIZ

White Blood Cells Clump Around an Invading Cell. Fritz Goro Studio, NJ

Karate champion Masayoshi Kato demonstrating how to shatter a 12" thick block of ice with a single blow of his elbow

Starving Sudanese child in a refugee camp near Mongoro

The Empire State Building, New York City

AND CHARLES ASHLEY STAINBACK: A DIALOGUE]

CHARLES STAINBACK: When did you start using photography? Let me rephrase that. When did you realize the power the photographic image could have in your work?

The Pope John Paul II kissing the American soil upon his arrival at Newark International Airport

The South Pole as photographed by Fuchs, January 19, 1958

VIK MUNIZ: Even though I have always been involved with photographic images, for a long time I was reluctant to make photographs myself. I guess I made a decision to stop producing images and concentrate on making real things right after I gave up a career in advertising. I became a sculptor so that I could work on the more material aspects of things. Those objects were somewhat successful and a gallery showed them in New York. The gallery also documented the work with slides and black-and-white reproductions. When I first saw those photographs, I liked them so much that I didn't care if the objects themselves were all set on fire. The photograph carried the code of the objects' tridimensionality without the baggage of weight and volume. The photograph also conveyed material information (a photograph of sandpaper, for example, "looks" coarse), but it was somehow bonded more firmly with the form of the objects portrayed. Ultimately, the photographs captured more of what the objects were as they first appeared in my mind, as an idea. I wanted to be involved with craft to the extent that it becomes invisible. This way the creative process goes full circle: you start with an idea and end up with something that resembles one.

CS: So your first use of the camera is similar to the intentions of artists in the 1960s who simply began making photographs to document happenings, earthworks, or performances?

VM: That's pretty accurate. I have always admired that kind of art for all the wrong reasons. My first reaction to finding *Spiral Jetty* in a book was, "Wow, what a great

---

Robert Smithson, *Spiral Jetty, April 1970, Great Salt Lake, Utah.* Photo: Gianfranco Gorgoni/Contact. Estate of Robert Smithson. Courtesy of John Weber Gallery, New York.

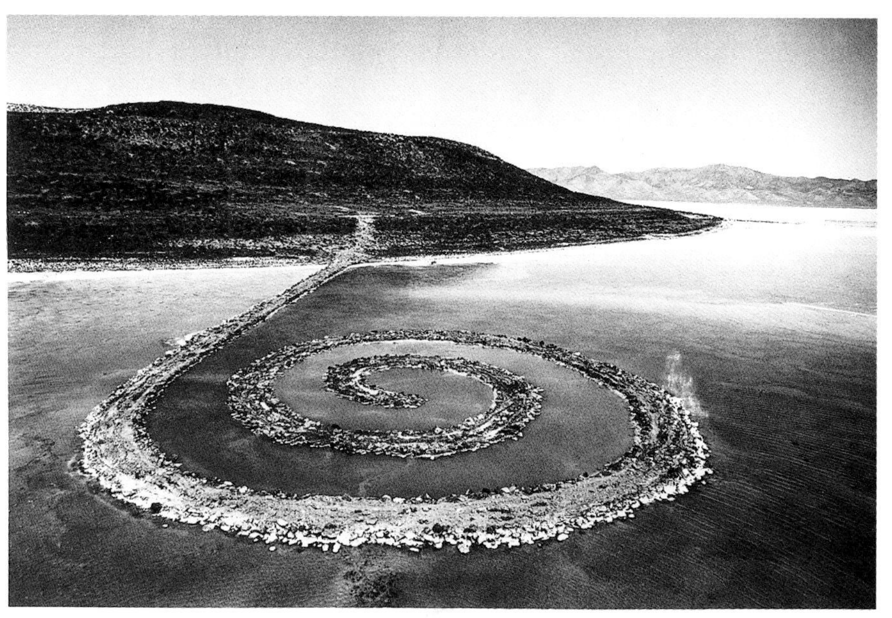

The scale of the Spiral Jetty tends to fluctuate depending on where the viewer happens to be. Size determines an object, but scale determines art. A crack in the wall if viewed in terms of scale, not size, could be called the Grand Canyon. A room could be made to take on the immensity of the solar system. Scale depends on one's capacity to be conscious of the actualities of perception. When one refuses to release scale from size, one is left with an object or language that appears to be certain. For me scale operates by uncertainty. To be in the scale of the Spiral Jetty is to be out of it.

— Robert Smithson, *The Writings of Robert Smithson*, edited by Nancy Holt (New York: New York University Press, 1979), p. 112.

photograph!" I could not believe someone had gone to so much trouble just to end up with a picture. I find quite paradoxical the fact that most of the art of the '60s has a "what you see is what you get" attitude, and because so much emphasis was placed on the physicality and evanescence of a work, most of what we're left with is documentation. Well, documentation can be art. Pictures of Mont Blanc taken by the Bisson Frères in the nineteenth century were records of a performance, but the performance was executed entirely with the record in mind. I am pretty sure artists like Smithson or Matta-Clark felt that a piece was complete only after a photograph had been taken of it. As for happenings, I have been to a few performances and I confess that I get very embarrassed and rarely enjoy them. Photographs of such events, however, are always fascinating. I am very interested in the ways a performance gets recorded and the way in which the record affects the performance. Japanese wood prints, for example, advertised Kabuki actors who embodied their own masked characters. Julia Margaret Cameron would title a male portrait *Iago* after the villainous character in *Othello*, ignoring the identity of the model. Jerry Seinfeld plays himself on his sitcom. How can a person *play* himself? These are things that interest me when I document my little private happenings.

CS: In a way, you are like a magician who reveals the workings of a trick to the audience – you want them to see how the illusion is created. Was that your intent when you started using photography as a part of your artwork?

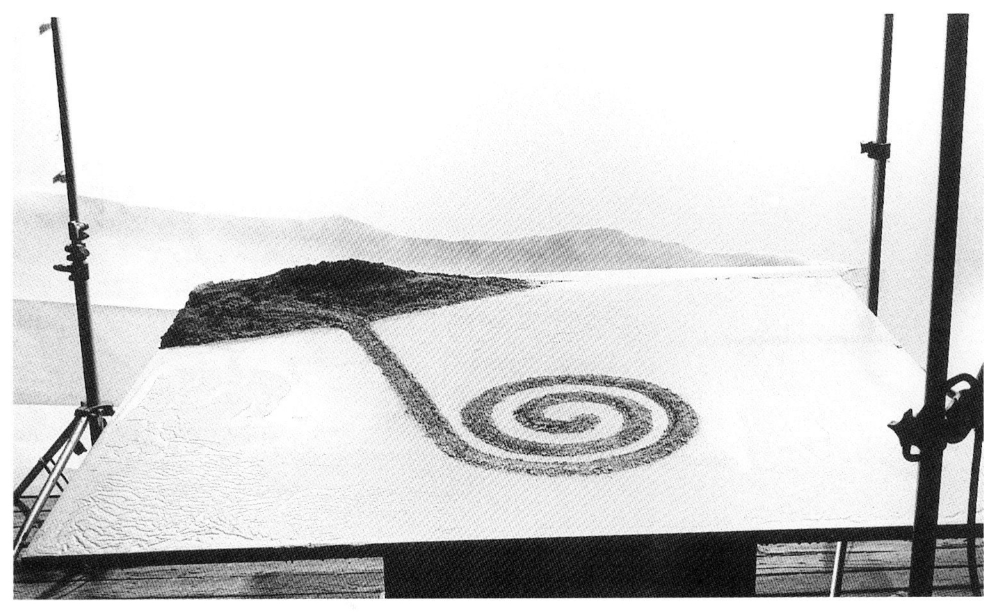

Vik Muniz, *Brooklyn, New York: Spiral Jetty*, 1998, reenactment of 1970s earthwork on a tabletop in the artist's studio.

VM: The magician as well as the artist makes a living by manipulating stuff people generally take for granted. The universe of knowledge has lots of black holes: the miraculous, the funny, the grotesque, the amazing, and even the truly beautiful are merely situations that occur in the gaps between mundane knowledge. I've always had an interest in this in-betweenness, these places where logic and common sense collapse, creating room for new experiences. Augustine once said that miracles exist not in relation to nature but in relation to what we *know* of nature. The difference is that with optical illusions, the magic is indelible. The optical cortex is truly a sucker of a mechanism.

No matter what people say, art – directly or indirectly – has always had to deal with illusion. The Paleolithic artist had to deal with it and so did Mondrian. Something happens when you experience an optical illusion that exchanges the experience of an object for the experience of vision itself. You don't simply see, you *feel* vision. I have neither the interest nor the means to produce illusions that expand the concept of what an illusion is – George Lucas and Steven Spielberg are doing that for us. My area of interest is in the opposite end of the spectrum of illusion: I want to make the worst possible illusion that will still fool the eyes of the average person. Something so rudimentary and simple that the viewer will think, "I don't believe what I'm seeing, I can't be seeing this, my mind is too sophisticated to fall for something as silly as this." Illusions as bad as mine make people aware of the fallacies of visual information and the pleasure to be derived from such fallacies. These illusions are made to reveal the architecture of our concept of truth. They are meta-illusions.

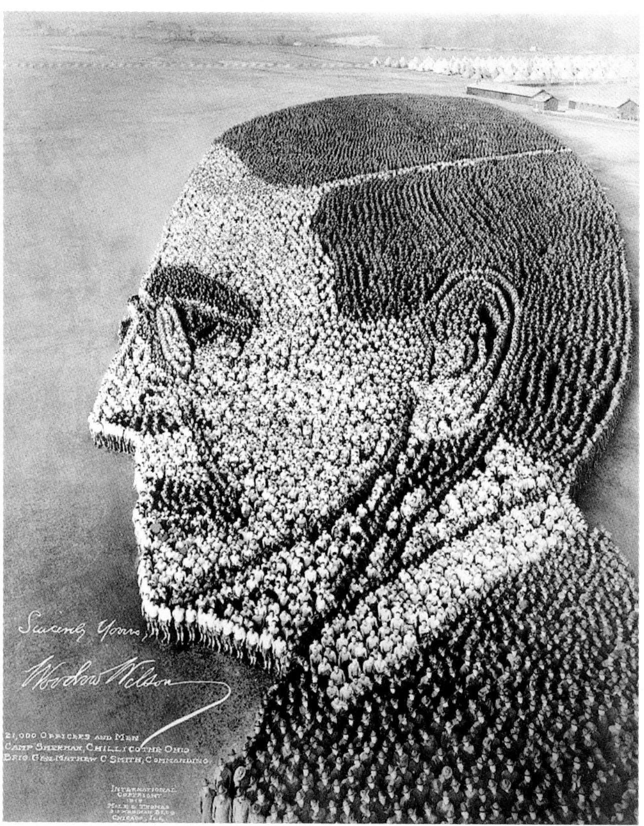

Arthur Mole (Mole & Thomas), *Woodrow Wilson (image of head formed by 21,000 men at Camp Sherman), Chillicothe (Ohio)*, 1919. Courtesy of the Chicago Historical Society (negative #ICHi-16304).

CS: Do people ever get confused by your work? Perhaps misinterpret your intentions? Or take your work too seriously? I assume you don't, by the way.

VM: No, I've never had the problem — or the pleasure — of being taken too seriously. My work is made not to confuse but to destabilize the viewer's notion of what a photograph is. In that respect, the viewer does get confused — and this is a good thing. The logical blur that one experiences in front of an illusionistic picture is similar to what one experiences after hearing a joke. Suddenly there is an enormous vacuum in your mind that the cognitive apparatus registers as pleasurable because that's what the mind likes to do: to fill these places with wild and abstract thoughts. The notion that separates entertainment and wonder from artistic merit was probably invented by some really sad people who could only measure the importance of the artwork against the fabric of history and society, forgetting entirely the role of the individual. The even sadder thing is that this notion endures, polluting the criteria of artistic appreciation at the level of art production: artists become serious and systematic, trying to make sense out of things. And if an artist creates illusions or makes "funny things," he is certainly bound to be taken lightly. I have elaborate opinions about race, gender, ecology, censorship, and economic distribution. I am just not confident enough to market these opinions as an artistic commodity. The subject of art is the study of the mechanisms responsible for conveying reality, and not the idea of reality itself. Only after you have emptied art of this responsibility can you actually make art that is "about" something.

Human knowledge relies on dualities and antagonisms in order to exist, making every notion entirely dependent on its negation to assert a significant meaning. In this respect, illusion becomes a way to improve our understanding of what reality is and humor becomes a subject for serious investigation.

CS: Your fakery, if I may use this description, *has* been taken seriously, more than once. For instance, the *Principia* series, in which you use stereoviews: works in which the line between fact and fiction is so blurred, there are no guide wires showing, no visible clues to your hoax.

VM: Well, there are actually two distinct bodies of work: one is about representation and the other is about interpretation. The *Pictures of Wire* series or *The Sugar Children*, for instance, are pretty much about whatever causes something to represent something else. Other series like *The Best of Life*, *Personal Articles*, and *Principia* are less about causes than they are about the *effects* of representation. They are ideas that developed from looking at mass-produced imagery and exploring how that imagery had affected me. *The Best of Life* fooled the viewer because the viewer thought he knew everything about the picture before he saw it. *Personal Articles* played with what people could not know about the pictures. And *Principia* tested how people would respond to very silly pseudo-scientific photos seen through an apparatus. In all these works, there is a process of digestion – or perhaps I should say indigestion – and regurgitation of media images. Their basic formal aspect is the stuff that is already part of our collective unconscious. More than 50 percent of the world comes to us in the form of halftones, electromagnetic waves, and distorted light.

> CS: After hearing you talk about your work, I must admit that Gerhard Richter comes to mind. Not so much because your work is similar, but more for the coalescing of extremes in the entire body of artwork. Besides the connection of the extreme from "realism to abstraction," have you ever thought about the similarities?

VM: What is very interesting in Gerhard Richter's work is that he is not trying to push the limits of realism or abstraction away from each other. His photo-based landscapes, still lifes, and portraits have the odd immateriality of an abstract painting, and his abstract works (in a way similar to Matta's) seem to create a notion of space within the brushstrokes. I have always been drawn to his work. The series of famous men at the Ludwig Museum and the *Bader Meinhof* paintings had an enormous impact on me. When I stop to think of what contemporary artists I am most likely to absorb ideas from, I can only think of painters who use photography in their work. Vija Celmins and Chuck Close, for example, are also people

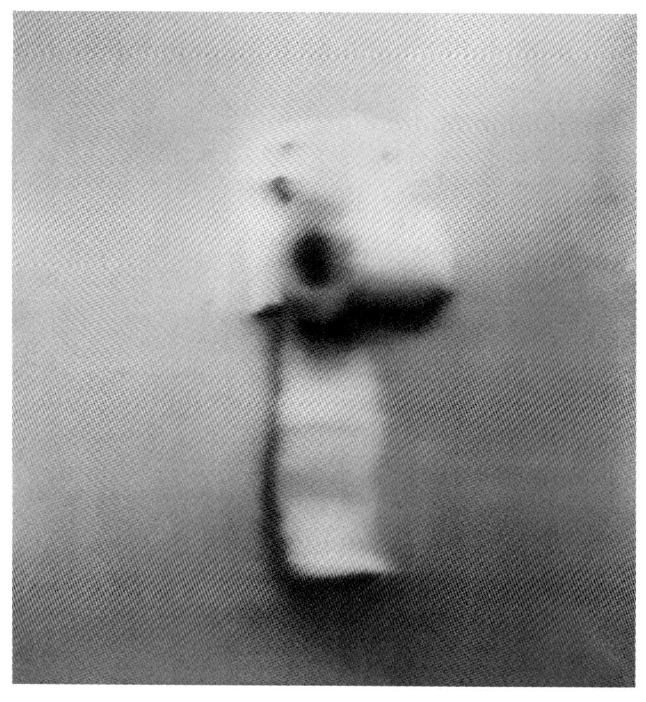

Gerhard Richter, *Loo Paper*, 1994, oil on canvas. Photo courtesy Marian Goodman Gallery, New York. © 1998 Gerhard Richter.

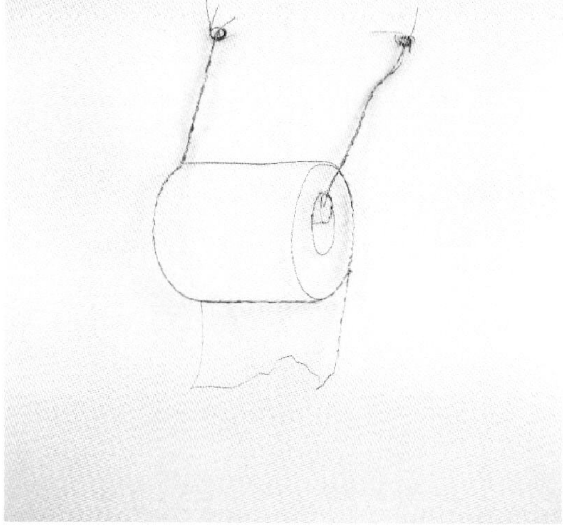

Vik Muniz, *Paper and Wire I*, 1995, gelatin silver print, 20 x 16 inches. Collection Gary Schneider, San Francisco.

whose work I am constantly studying. The only sculptors that come to mind when I think of what has always interested me are Robert Irwin and Charles Ray.

I had a similar discussion with someone else recently, and she was a bit disappointed that I am not influenced by younger artists. She even used a funny term – "more contemporary." I told her that I am sure I will love the art of today in about twenty years.

CS: You mention Vija Celmins and Chuck Close and their use of photography. However, what seems even more pronounced as an influence is the tremendous wealth of trompe l'oeil in art history. Since more than twenty years have passed for many of art history's great illusions of trompe l'oeil, I assume a few might spark your interest?

VM: There is a kind of trompe l'oeil that does a bit more than trompe the oeil. I like illusions that say something about reality or, at least, our ability to cope with it. Illusions of this kind are usually very understated and quiet. A painting by Peto, for example, is a nice and entertaining trick, but a landscape by Bierstadt or Church is a lesson in perception. For me, Ansel Adams is a more interesting illusionist than Jerry Uelsman.

CS: Your photographs are a hybrid of intellect, humor, and illusion. Can you explain your working method and the process of bringing these often incongruous ingredients together in one work or series?

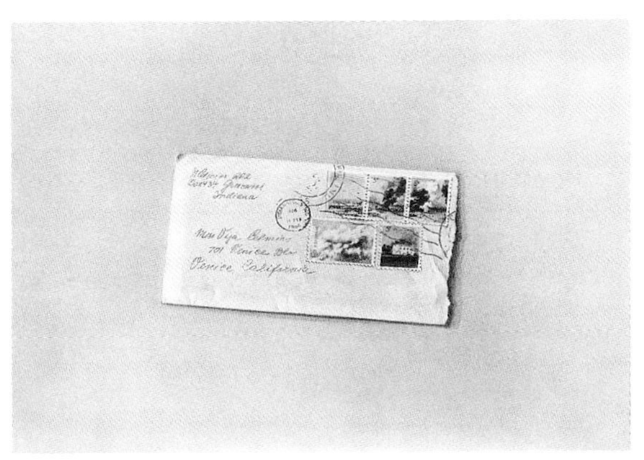

Vija Celmins, *Letter*, 1968, graphite on acrylic ground on paper, 13 ¼ x 18 ⅛ inches. Collection Donna O'Neill, Los Angeles. Courtesy of McKee Gallery, New York.

[A] microscopic approach to landscape is denoted in the exquisite drawing *Letter* (1968): its minute rendering of make-believe stamps features such vistas as the explosion of the atom bomb, in a laconic, trompe-l'oeil sendup of the standard missive from home—in this case, Box 434, Greenwood, Indiana.

— Brooks Adams, "Visionary Realist," *Art in America* (October 1993), p. 106.

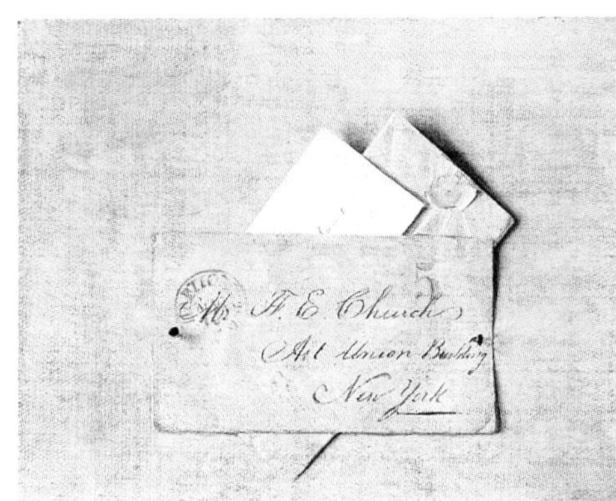

Frederic Edwin Church (1826–1900), *The Letter Revenge*, before 1892, oil on canvas, 21 x 26 cm. Allen Memorial Art Museum, Oberlin College, Ohio; Gift of Charles F. Olney, 1904.

[Church's painting] was presented in Oberlin College in 1904 by a gentleman named Olney who had acquired it from the artist and who claimed, apparently with good reason, that it had been "painted to deceive a friend who made the statement that a work of art is meritorious only as it may be mistaken for the original"; consequently Mr. Olney gave the picture the title *The Letter Revenge.*

— Alfred Frankenstein, quoted in M. L. d'Otrange Mastai, *Illusion in Art: Trompe l'Oeil, a History of Pictorial Illusionism* (New York: Abaris Books, 1975), p. 279.

VM: I have never been very good at organizing or classifying things, separating and filing them in specific places. On my bookshelves you will find Milton next to Little Lulu. I try to keep my mind and my environment as open as possible so that all kinds of unlikely alliances may form in a natural and organic way. Combining photography and drawing is no big deal because the two things were once the same and the need for a distinction came much later. My father once won an Encyclopaedia Britannica in a pool game. It was a very old edition and you could not tell if the illustrations were very good drawings or badly printed photographs. I remember, as a child, enjoying this fact. Some things never really change.

As for working method, I haven't worked long enough to develop one and I sincerely hope I never do. What I have is a repertoire of attitudes toward imagemaking that I explore aimlessly until I bump into something interesting. I try to leave the process as much as possible to intuition. If you work in an intuitive way, you generally discover afterward the reasons behind your decisions. My very first efforts in photography were a kind of transition between the object and the image. I wanted the image to be as light and penetrating as an idea. Again, I was reluctant to make images because of my previous experience in advertising. The work of advertising is to fabricate identities for everything from talcum powder to nations and their armies, to give form to the shapeless and a timeless image to the transitory.

This sounds very philosophical, I know, and I still think advertising is a very important part of our culture. But I wasn't interested in fabricating identities before I could find out for myself what identity is. How are we able to recognize objects in a picture, how are we able to recognize objects, period? Advertising made me aware of the dichotomy between an

---

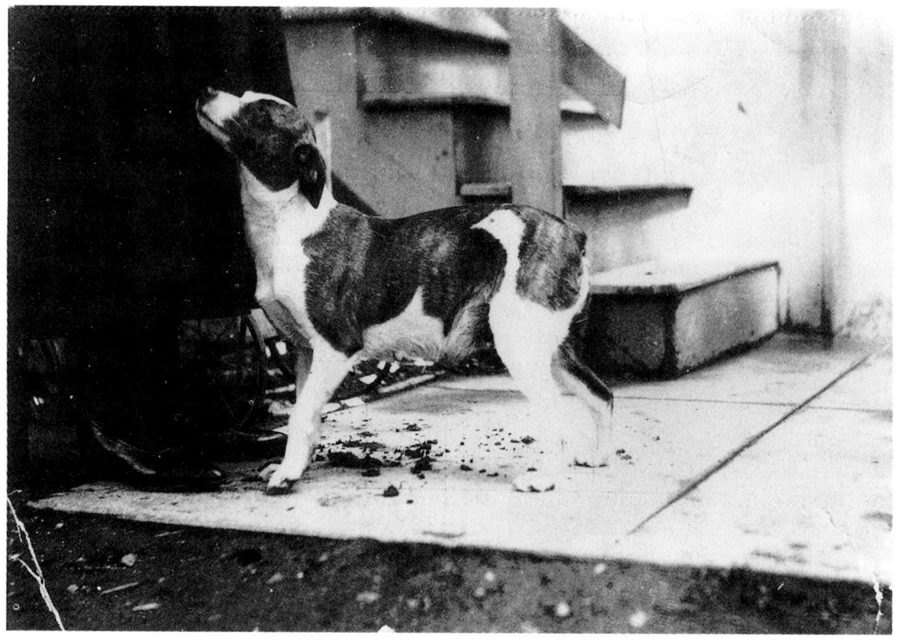

Dog with Duck on Hindquarters (photographer unknown).
© 1998 Ripley Entertainment Inc.

One of the most enduring legacies left by Robert Ripley is his insistence on the authenticity and verification of the facts presented in the cartoon. His chief of research, Norbert Pearlroth, worked six days a week for fifty-two years at the New York Public Library checking and double-checking the source materials for accuracy. The man who was frequently called the World's Biggest Liar was in fact a stickler for details. The hallmark of the Believe It or Not! phenomenon was that the basic outline of these outrageous claims was true, and that Ripley could invariably furnish some sort of proof, frequently in the form of an actual photograph of the oddity he described.

— From Mark Sloan et al., comps., *Dear Mr. Ripley: A Compendium of Curioddities from the Believe It or Not! Archives* (Boston: Bulfinch Press, 1993), p. 33.

object and its images. This sort of tension has consistently been part of my work. Today I look at older works such as *Two Nails*, *Tug of War*, and *Cogito Ergo Sum* and see clearly this dilemma unfolding in my mind. Reality or representation? As soon as I discovered how similar these two notions are once they become visual information, I began to feel more comfortable using this polarity to my advantage.

CS: After seeing the diversity of your work, I assume that you have a fascination with images embedded in objects or things, everything from topiary to silhouettes of ducks on the side of a dog to shapes in a cloud.

VM: A miracle is a phenomenon of interpretation. From Leonardo's stained walls to Mr. Ripley's horses to grafitti, we are bound to encounter "accidental representations" everywhere. It is as if meaning ricocheted throughout the elemental like oxygen atoms. That's somehow linked to the basic functions of perception, the stuff designed to keep us alive when we still were hunting the hairy mammoth. To really understand art, one must return to these simple things. There was probably a time when early man couldn't represent anything, but certainly found the shapes that were linked to his life in stone formations, cracks, tree trunks, and pebbles. We tend to think that art began with cave paintings, but I believe art started with the ability to recognize the form of one thing in something else. Some artists in nineteenth-century China did not produce any art of their own but simply looked for stones that conveyed a certain mood in their form. They were called dream stones

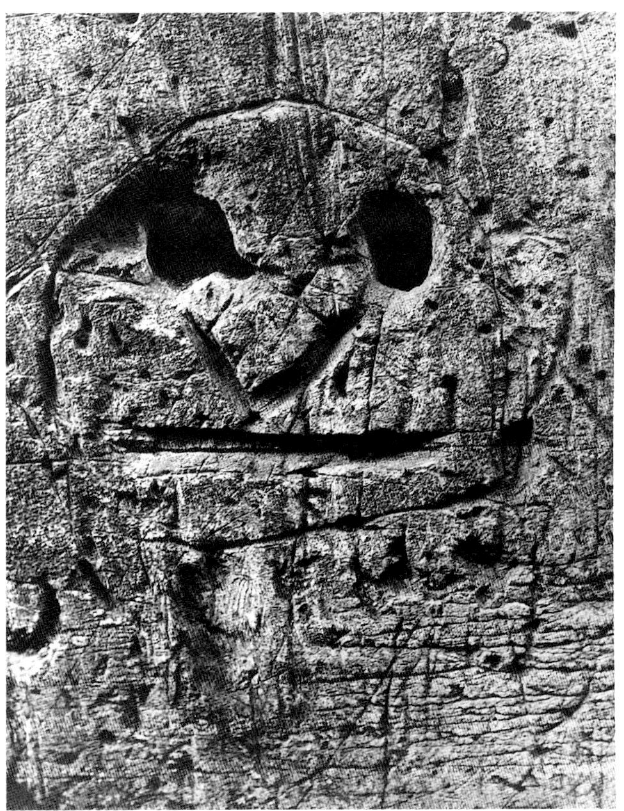

Brassaï (Gyula Halasz). *Graffiti*, n.d., gelatin silver print, 12 x 16 ½ inches. The Museum of Modern Art, New York. Gift of the photographer. Copy print © 1998 The Museum of Modern Art, New York.

and they predate the readymade by at least fifty years. What Duchamp made was an already-made.

I have always been intrigued with these things because they are the basic stuff of knowledge. The moment you recognize the similarities between two things, you have created a symbol, you have learned how to use language. When Noam Chomsky took on Piaget's theory and the nature-nurture controversy about language acquisition, he was onto something important about the nature of knowledge. The problem with the natural language theory is that it assigns an exclusively active role to our cognitive abilities. Cognition has its tidal movements. I believe that language is an innate thing, but its basic configuration is passive and contemplative and it was designed by evolution to function at the level of form recognition, a basic tool for survival. Some early man threw his spear at a bison only to discover that it wasn't a bison but a termite mound that carried an uncanny resemblance to a bison. He was "fooled" by nature. He went back to the tribe and told the other hunters about the bison. Soon they were throwing their spears at the termite mound while he crouched behind the bushes laughing. That man was the first artist.

> CS: For some individuals working with photographic imagery, the label "photographer" is less than desirable. They almost always prefer the label "artist." You, however, embrace the title of photographer and the photographic medium itself with great fervor, yet the work appears on first glance more closely aligned to our traditional notion of fine art. Do you see yourself as a photographic heretic or a shaman with a camera?

VM: I attended art school in São Paulo for a few years. None of the instructors there knew the work of Joseph Beuys or Bruce Nauman. We would sit for three hours at a time drawing and modeling geometric solids and nudes, and occasionally chat about Bernini or Tiepolo. The seeming mindlessness of those exercises taught me almost everything about artmaking that I use today. It taught me how to organize visual information in a hierarchical way, giving me a more detailed understanding of the mechanisms of representation. It also inspired in me a respect for craft and technique that I have many times tried to rid myself of, but obviously have failed. One can learn how to be a draftsman, a photographer, or a sculptor in school, but there is no way to teach someone how to become an artist. It would be like teaching someone to be sick or happy, or to be a good dice player. I am a photographer when I photograph, and a draftsman when I draw, but an artist is what I am always becoming.

Ovid begins his account of Genesis in *Metamorphoses* with this: "My mind is bent to tell of bodies changed into new forms." What a perfect way to start a work of art! A child picks up a piece of chalk and draws a circle on the sidewalk, then straight lines radiating from the circle. Any observer would immediately recognize in this doodle the image of the sun, an immense ball of fire 150 million kilometers from Earth. It takes less than a second for the meaning "sun" to embody that trace of chalk, while it takes eight minutes for the actual light of the sun to illuminate it. We have become so sophisticated in our visual habits that we often overlook the magic behind representation. It is said that when Renaissance artists started to employ three-point perspective in their paintings and frescoes, they were accused of witchcraft. Because we no longer experience fainting spells in front of a Giotto painting, all the perceptual impact of that work becomes history, but it is somehow satisfying to think of the confused viewers trying to figure out how those earthy pigments were organized so to produce a perfect likeness of tridimensional space. I try to focus my attention on this dynamic theater of visual forms, where powders and binders play the part of flying angels, charcoal traces act the role of Arcadian landscapes, and molten metal becomes the perfect likeness of animals. I try to pinpoint the moment where the change occurs, the moment a circle becomes the sun, and a triangle the tomb of a long-dead pharaoh. That is magic, in its most evocational, shamanic, and spiritual transformation that was once so distinct in art.

CS: I think that in most instances you do get that sense from your work. And that "moment" is what people find intriguing when viewing it. Nevertheless, you assume that even in today's fast-paced, hyperactive, gigabite, morphed, and

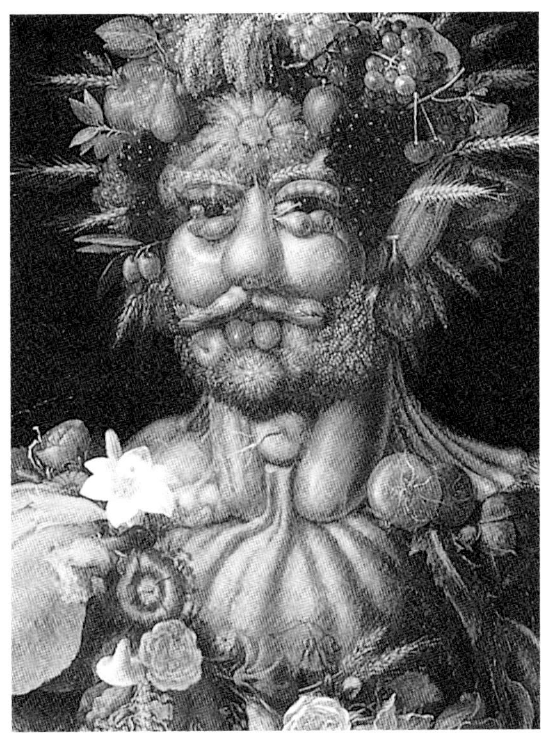

Giuseppe Arcimboldo (1530–1593), *Vertumnus*, a supposed portrait of Rudolf XIV, Prague, 1591.

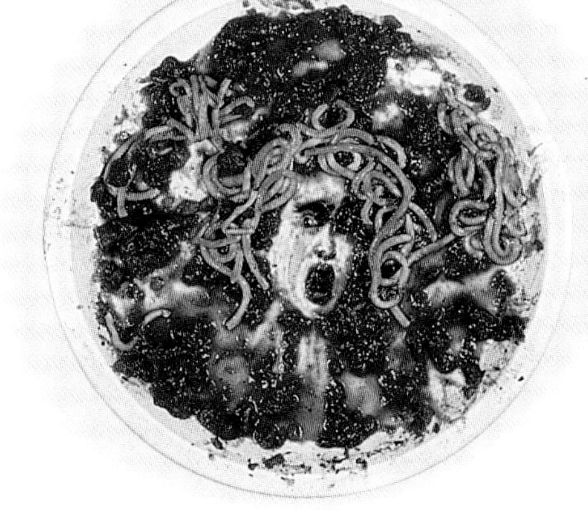

Vik Muniz, *Medusa Marinara*, 1998. Collection The Metropolitan Museum of Art, New York.

virtual world that the average man or woman on the street is aware of that "magic" associated with human creativity. Don't you think that all too often we lose sight of the wonder of human creativity and the ability of the eye, the hand, and the mind to produce amazing illusions?

VM: Images are produced at such staggering speed that we grow conditioned to retain only a fraction of what we see. The funny thing is that as we become more proficient in making images, we become increasingly unable to understand their form and semantic structure. The faster we can produce them, the less time we have to really see what they are. The power of an image lays precisely in its potential for being underestimated. In developing defenses against this noxious visual environment, one becomes numb to all kinds of images. Sometimes I try to imagine the world before anyone had a camera. A drawing of a rhinoceros like the one by Dürer must have been a wondrous thing for the sixteenth-century viewer. Today, not even a real rhinoceros will inspire that kind of awe. We need dinosaurs.

CS: But in a way, we have that kind of illusion — even dinosaurs — in many of today's high-tech/high-budget Hollywood movies. Don't these count?

VM: Isn't this a funny paradox, that the ultimate use of the latest technology is to make prehistoric creatures? I am usually more impressed by well-executed card tricks than by this computer stuff. After five minutes of *Jurassic Park*, the dinosaurs only scare you by sudden appearances: a hand puppet could appear suddenly on the screen and people would be just as shocked. Films by Ray Harryhausen, for example, are far scarier because they have very little to do with reality. They look more like nightmares.

CS: Like many artists of your generation, your work is informed by media — print and television — and popular culture. In *The Best of Life* series, was your intention to critique our mediated culture like so many other artists had done in the 1980s?

VM: If you come to consider what one generally does every day, almost everything that is novel and that adds to one's life comes in the form of mediated information. If you tally up everything you've learned through direct experience — in other words, by trying something yourself — it does not account for much compared to what you know by listening to other people, reading the newspaper, or watching television. The largest part of our memory, therefore, is allocated to events we were not directly part of. When it comes to photographic media, this phenomenon gets even more interesting: in all the photographs that have ever been taken, only the film was exposed to the recorded image, no human eye shares the precise moment and position of any photograph. That makes the history of photographed events the history of events removed from human experience. We can only share memories of images that in reality no one ever saw. If no one ever saw what everyone remembers, what exactly are these memories made of?

When I arrived in the United States in 1983, I spoke very little English and so initially did not make many new acquaintances. Reading the paper and watching TV were comforting because they were a way to participate in my new environment. I bought *The Best of Life* in a garage sale outside of Chicago. This book somehow made me feel safer. It made me feel more a part of the place where I was living. That "family of man" thing really works. I lost the book in the summer of '88 on a beach in Long Island and felt really sad. Immediately, it occurred to me that people do not keep picture books like *The Best of Life* solely for the written content. They also keep them to check their memory of events against the photographs, just as they would peruse a family album.

During that summer, I began to check how much I retained from the experience of those photographs. At first, it was a pastime. I would wake up and work on a few every day, and each day I would remember a bit more. When I could no longer remember anything, I began to call people (who didn't have the images in front of them either) and ask specific questions. I discovered that people store images in radically different ways: their descriptions had a completely different structure than mine. The visual world is like a crossword puzzle: we all have the same puzzle but each of us solves it differently. I had developed from memory a few of the images quite well when Stux Gallery offered to show them as drawings. Once I'd transformed the image-memories into drawings, I thought they should be returned to their photo state. So I photographed the drawings. When they were ready, I printed the photos with the same halftone screen the original pictures were printed on. People thought they were seeing bad reproductions of photographs of famous events, but in fact they were only looking at pictures of thoughts. They were convinced by the photographs because they have the same syntax as the real photos. It worked.

> CS: So your intention was to play with our collective visual syntax while testing the limitations of your own memory?

VM: Being aware of your memory limitations generally means being aware of your potential for underestimating what you see. We have been conditioned to formulate important opinions based on images we see, but the same mechanisms responsible for bringing us these images have also conditioned us not to ask many questions about the way they are produced. Photography, especially after World War II, has become increasingly transparent in this regard. If I describe to you a photograph consisting of a girl running naked on the street sprayed with napalm, you think of the girl and not the piece of paper where you originally saw the image. Documentary photography before the war – the Farm Security Administration pictures, for example – is a lot more sophisticated in terms of light and composition. Consequently, you imagine the relationship between the artist and the subject, and formulate opinions based on this negotiation. What I did with *The Best of Life* series was to make these very subjective, transparent images more objective and opaque by adding more interpretive layers. At that point, I had started to make objects that were very thin, so I decided to make photographs that were very thick. I guess that's been my working principle in photography ever since. When these images are reinserted in the media world, they act like a vaccine, creating more antibodies against similar images. These are suspect images that make all other images look suspicious.

> CS: I want to shift gears and ask a direct question about a specific image in *The Best of Life* series, the one of the student in Tiananmen Square. Interestingly, seeing the real – or should I say, the original – image/photograph next to yours, one is most immediately struck by the limitations of visual memory. I wonder if this photo presented special issues in that, unlike the others, it has not attained the longevity within our collective memory and therefore might be more difficult to remember and render.

VM: When it comes to photojournalism, there is a certain law of compensation that maintains the intensity of images, new or old, always at a similar level. A relatively recent image is remembered because it was seen not so long ago, an old image is remembered because

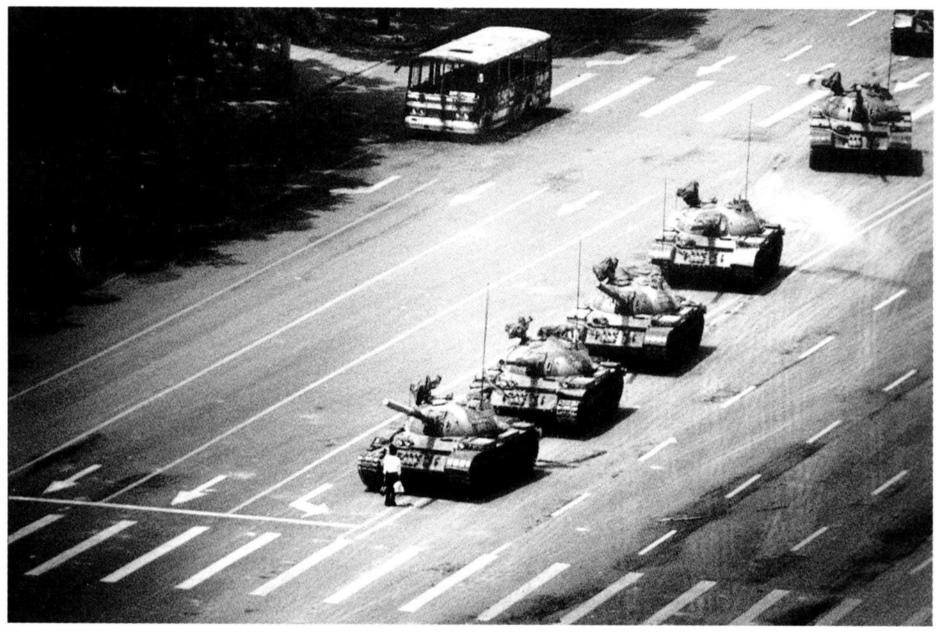

Stuart Franklin, *Beijing, China, 1989: A solitary protester blocks T59 tanks coming from Tiananmen Square*. Courtesy Magnum Photos, Inc. © 1989 Stuart Franklin.

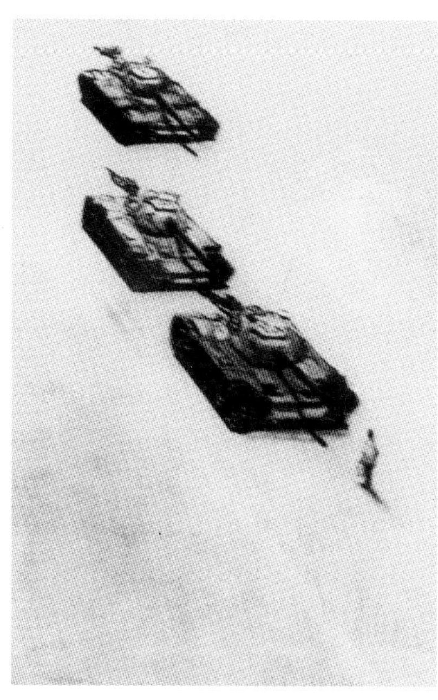

Vik Muniz, *The Best of Life: Memory Rendering of Man Stopping Tank in Beijing*, 1989, gelatin silver print, 11 x 14 inches.

it's been seen multiple times. To my surprise, the difficulties that I encountered in rendering these images had more to do with form than time. Facial expressions, for example, were very hard to draw from memory because the huge repertoire of templates for facial expressions that we have stored in our brain is designed to work by deduction but is fairly inept when it comes to performing inductive operations. Specific details of clothing and architecture are also easier to remember than correct body positions. One thing that in almost all pictures (except the Tiananmen Square photo) remained consistent with the original photograph was the point of view from which the photograph was originally taken. This seemed to be the most remembered aspect.

> CS: You mentioned technology earlier in reference to illusion and our conflicting notions of photographic veracity. Since you play with the issue of a photograph's believability in your work, I wonder why you don't use computers to help you generate the illusions.

VM: As I said before, illusion *informs* my work, making illusions is not what my work aims to achieve. The kind of illusion produced by a computer will reveal a lot about the competence of the person who produces the illusion. I am more interested in making the viewer confront his own incompetence in resisting an illusion by making them without the use of such effects. Illusions have developed in sync with basic evolutionary patterns of perception. In other words, it is natural that you believe certain images because whatever makes you fall for certain tricks also helps you to survive others. Perceptual short-circuits will ultimately inform you in a very effective way of the manner in which you perceive things, and that can be something very personal as well.

> CS: Earlier you discussed the importance of photography and made a comment about the photograph of sandpaper looking coarse. This made me think of the image of Meret Oppenheim's fur-covered cup and saucer that I had seen in art textbooks. When I finally saw the object itself at an exhibition, I can't say I was impressed, but I do remember thinking that I liked the photograph better. Which do you prefer: fiction or reality?

VM: Reality is hard to like because it does not have a definite form, size, or color. We tend to like things with certain formal or narrative distinctions, things that convey specific meanings. The origin of fiction is closely connected to the origin of language itself. Exaggeration, emphasis, all modal elements of language, seem to be always secretly conspiring against reality. Ernst Cassirer brilliantly illustrated the effects of nonrational thought in the makeup of our culture. Photographs of objects, especially Surrealistic ones, place the object into the context of their own time, while the display of the object itself is bound to be out of context. I don't see a need to walk around sculptures: if an object is made to be looked at, there is always a best side from which you can do it. A photograph is just simplifying this process. It is telling you a story about the object (perhaps a lie), subtracting one particular view of the object from the infinite number of views that one can have by simply positioning one's head in front of something. This ultimately effects the object's causality: the object in the photo will not fade or rust, it will always remain the same, only the photograph will change. To ask me if I prefer reality to fiction is the same as asking if I prefer the ocean to swimming.

> CS: Sure, then I would have to ask if you can swim, or do you wear a bathing suit just for the sake of appearance?

VM: The ocean of reality is pretty much of a diluvial scale and doesn't leave you much choice between swimming or not. You either stay afloat in whatever style you can or you sink. There is nothing to hold on to. I am not much of a swimmer anyway. I prefer wading.

> CS: Here comes a $100 question. Would you say that your *Individuals* series fits into a Dadaist or Fluxus notion of art production that rebels against the so-called bourgeois treatment of art objects as commodities?

VM: Funny you should mention that amount of money. When I made the *Individuals* series, I had just come back from Europe with about $100 to my name. I had a piece of plasticene,

---

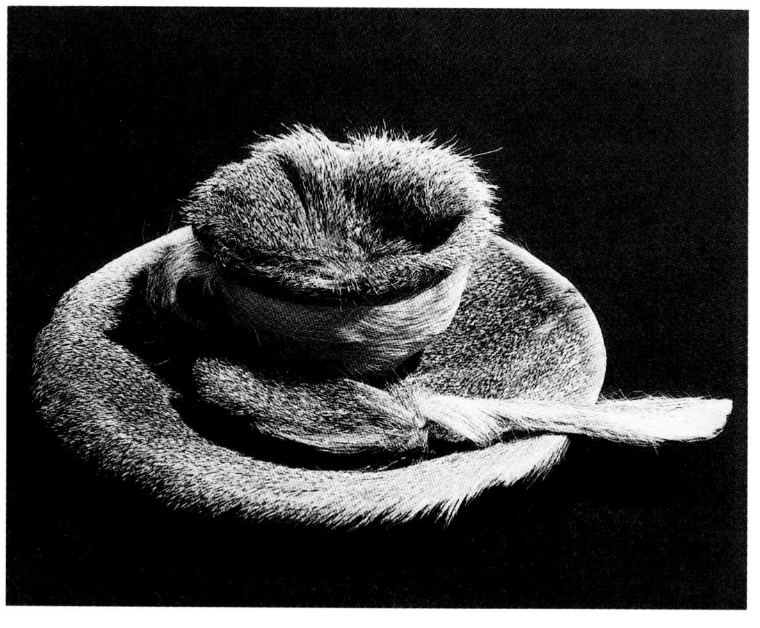

Meret Oppenheim, *Object (Le Déjeuner en fourrure)*, 1936, fur-covered cup, saucer, and spoon. The Museum of Modern Art, New York, Purchase. Photograph © 1998 The Museum of Modern Art, New York.

In connection with Déjeuner en fourrure, 1936, the all-too-narrow basis of her international fame, Meret Oppenheim would obstinately tell anyone who wanted to listen a superficially banal story about its genesis. In 1936, sitting at the Café Flore one day with her friends, Dora Maar and Pablo Picasso, she happened to be wearing one of the bracelets she had been making for Schiaparelli out of lengths of fur-lined, polished metal tubing. Talking and joking about the bracelet, Picasso quipped that one could actually cover anything with fur, to which Meret replied, "Even this cup and saucer ..." Shortly afterwards, when André Breton invited her to contribute to the exhibition of Surrealist objects at the Galerie Charles Ratton, she recalled the conversation and, without further ado, bought a large cup and saucer with spoon at the Parisian department store.

— From *Meret Oppenheim* (New York: Parkett Publishers, 1989), p. 39.

a camera, and some film — and no other materials for making art. I made a sculpture and liked it, in a kind of "art therapy" style, but I used all the plasticene and couldn't buy anymore. So I took a picture of the sculpture, destroyed it, and made another. Pretty soon I had sixty pictures of the same lump of plasticene conveying completely different moods. Kim Caputo, a friend, offered to print them for me so I could jump-start my career, and we printed all sixty of them slightly diffused (like pictures of Barbara Streisand). I then exhibited them with pedestals of different sizes on the floor. People told me the photos evoked death, memory, and loss. I thought about my mood swings and how many crazy things the same lump of plasticene can become.

Now, to answer your question, Fluxus and Dada are a constant intellectual source for my work, and yes, Man Ray and Max Ernst are like gods to me. But when I made the *Individuals*, I was too poor to think about the bourgeoisie and the commodification of objects. Although they are ambiguous enough to contain a lot of ideas, that series is more personal than it might appear: I was dealing with a separation from my son and trying to survive as an artist. Well ... do I still get the hundred dollars?

> CS: Intuition seems to play a significant role in your work. Would you talk specifically about the moment you realized that drawing or painting and representations of the three-dimensional world did not have to be rendered solely by the pencil or the paintbrush. Were the *Cord* pieces, for instance, *Cogito Ergo Sum*, your first venture into the land of limitless materials for mark making?

VM: If I make an exceptionally good pencil drawing of you, a viewer will look for veracity, expression, fluidity, etc., but the basic fact that a trace of carbon becomes processed as not only the form and texture of your face but also your personality at this very moment rarely occurs to someone looking at a drawing. Now, if I make the same drawing with molasses and have a trail of ants walking on it, people will find it "miraculous" — or at least strange. When I visited Florence, I saw Lorenzo Ghiberti's Baptistery gates, and no work of Renaissance art has had a more profound impact on me. Here you have an exquisite mastery of perspective which is basically intellectual and illusionistic, combined with detailed relief work which is highly physical and realistic. The two forms of rendering combined seemed to be simultaneously enhancing and cancelling each other. The haute relief combined with three-point

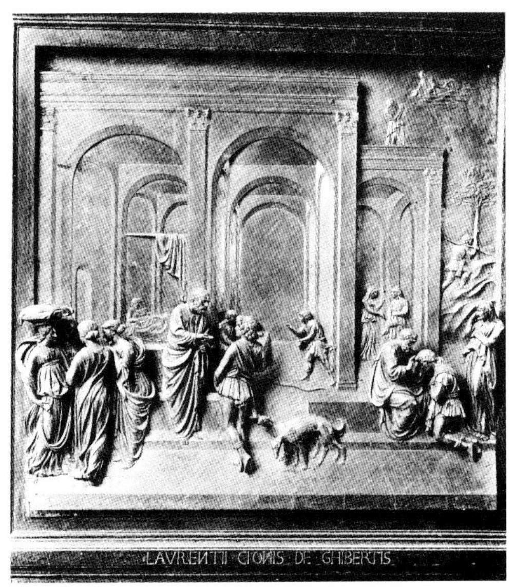

Lorenzo Ghiberti, *The Gates of Paradise* (east door of the Baptistery), detail: *Isaac*, Florence, 1424.

perspective was definitely overkill, but it made my mind go beyond what I was looking at. It made me think about vision as a process and not as a result. All of a sudden, I became aware of this incredible dichotomy, of real things and things that are images of things. That was when I started to play with ideas of reality and representation within a single narrative. *Cogito Ergo Sum*, *Historical Photo*, and *Cozy Couple* are pieces from this time.

> CS: In thinking about the subversive nature of some of your images, it's curious to remember that you worked in advertising, a business known for such tactics as hiding suggestive or seductive images. Did your advertising experience influence any particular series or ideas about images?

VM: I think my own ideas about images had more to do with my decision to study advertising than advertising influenced the development of these ideas. Advertising helped me organize these ideas a little better though. When I was a kid, I would follow the progress of a humidity stain on the ceiling above my bed by drawing it and writing reports about it. It started as a swan, then turned into a gorilla, then an old car named Gordini. As far back as I can remember, I liked to give forms to things. I would make sequential drawings trying to find the exact moment when a monkey turned into a helicopter. The idea that I could airbrush people frolicking inside ice cubes to sell more whiskey definitely had an effect on my decision to study media. But I wanted to sell ice cubes more than I wanted to sell whiskey, so I gave it up.

> CS: In working with various drawing media—dirt, Bosco, sugar, pinholes, whatever—how much significance do you attach to the thing rendered—binoculars, eggs, Freud—and the material used to create the image? Is there a material or substance that's offlimits? I'm thinking of Serrano here, as well as Warhol's *Oxidation* paintings.

VM: Jean-Luc Godard once famously quipped, "C'est ne pas du sang, c'est du rouge," which means, "It's not blood, it's red." That demonstrates a lot of lucidity about the stuff of representation. Serrano's photographs were not piss, they were yellow. Conservative Republicans are the ones who get pissed when they see yellow. Warhol, on the other hand, showed the real thing and made an abstraction out of it. I always thought it was great that he chose to call them *Oxidation* paintings. In my work, I am not that interested in the nature of the material that I photograph as much as in the way the viewer recognizes the material in the photograph. Serrano's work relies on the viewer's awareness of information about the subject; Warhol, on information about the process. I want to work with both notions simultaneously without relying too much on outside explanations. The choice of subject is often very intuitive and it often comes after the choice of the process. They are linked in a strange way that I am not sure I can explain, but I think it is exactly this doubt that gives me satisfaction when I make things.

CS: You've described your photographs as "low-tech" illusions. Yet like certain conceptual artists – for instance, Jan Dibbets and John Pfahl, or more mainstream artists such as M. C. Escher – your photographs do toy with a viewer's perception in a way that merges high-art concepts. Can you explain how your "illusions" fit into the larger picture of art and perception?

VM: I remember realism being a dirty word in New York for a long time. I often visited a photorealist gallery in Soho and I am almost ashamed to admit that I got more inspiration from that place than most of the other idea factories I visited. Some mysterious iconoclastic conspiracy has forced people to separate illusion from serious art. But I can't help myself – I have always been a sucker for figurative art. During my first visit to New York, the only thing that remained in my head was a huge Chuck Close portrait in the Whitney. I guess I am old enough now to become shameless and confess that I always liked Salvador Dali and grew up collecting Frank Frazetta and Roger Dean posters. I am definitely over my airbrush envy complex, but still I can't help but respect anyone who has tried to make a faithful representation of something, even if just to learn that it's hard and invariably enlightening. In the 1960s and '70s, a few artists started to get back at it via Neo-Platonism. Dibbets and Pfahl got away with what they were doing because their work was inserted into the

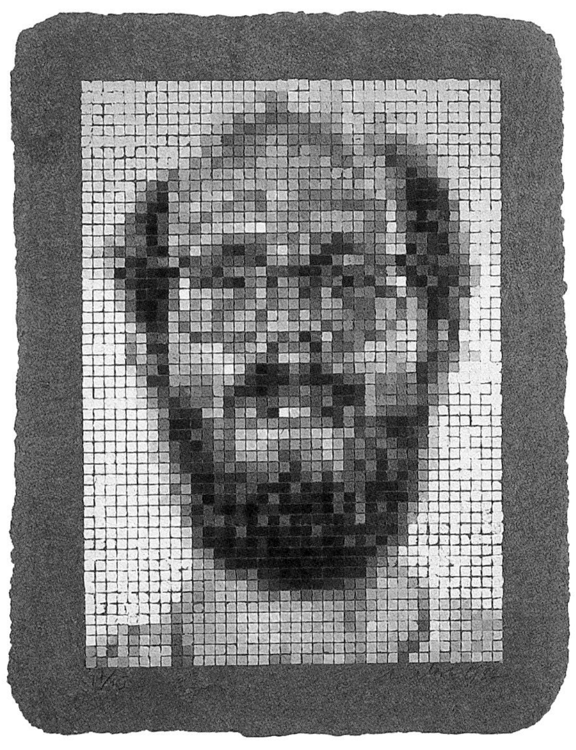

Chuck Close, *Self-Portrait (Rigid)*, 1982, handmade paper, edition of 15, 38 ½ x 28 ½ inches. Published by Pace Editions, Inc.

discourses of minimalism that were predominant at that time. But even those with no understanding of minimalism would find their work interesting.

Come to think of it, in a very unconscious way I am always trying to do the wrong thing. I have always felt that fear of illusion and wonder was making the art world a place for cultured hypocrisy where the sole pleasure of the viewer was to share this deprivation honorably. I had a funny dream about that once: I was with Barnet Newman at his deathbed. Unable to talk, he gestured for a pencil and paper, then nervously scribbled something and died almost immediately after with a smile on his face. It was a drawing of Mickey Mouse.

CS: I wonder what Freud would say about that. What if Mickey Mouse were on his deathbed and he drew a Barnet Newman painting? Would he die laughing?

VM: With his academic sense of humor, Freud would probably fail to see that a vertical line crossing a piece of paper is a good thing for a moribund cartoon character to do before he dies. I bet if Mickey Mouse made any art, it would definitely be monochromatic painting. But don't get me wrong. I love abstract art. A lot of what happened in both abstract and representational art in the second half of this century was too hung up on the dualism between the two. What created the chasm between abstract and representational art is that people began to assign too much importance to the way art is produced and not enough to the way it gets interpreted. Again, I am not fit to work on the extremities, I try to squeeze myself between the two, trying to find out what makes something an abstraction and something else an octopus. I love people like de Kooning and Arshile Gorky because they operate between language and

---

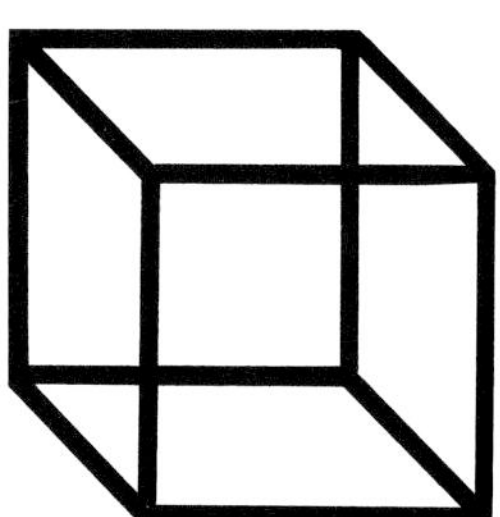

The Necker cube, named for L. A. Necker, a German professor of mineralogy.

> In the case of the object to which I would like to draw your attention, we are dealing with a perceptual phenomenon in the field of optics, a phenomenon which I have observed many times when studying pictures of crystalline shapes. I am referring here to a sudden and involuntary change in the apparent position of a crystal or other three-dimensional body reproduced on a two-dimensional surface. What I mean can be more simply explained with the help of the attached illustrations. The rhombus AX is drawn in such a way that A is nearest to the viewer and X furthest away. ACBD thus represents the frontal plane, with XDC a lateral plane behind it. If you study this figure for a while, however, you will observe that the apparent position of the rhombus sometimes changes, whereby X appears to be nearest and A furthest away and plane ACBD moves behind plane XDC, giving the whole body an entirely different orientation. ... You will no doubt be able to draw many conclusions from the observations described here which I, in my ignorance, am unable to predict. You may use these observations according to your own discretion.
>
> — Excerpt of a letter from L. A. Necker to Sir David Brewster, May 24, 1832, quoted in Bruno Ernst, *The Eye Beguiled: Optical Illusions*, trans. Karen Thomson (Cologne: Benedikt, 1992), pp. 23–24.

perception without ignoring facts pertinent to one or another. I also feel very close to minimalism because it brought simple perceptual ideas back to art in a dynamic way. Artists like Serra, LeWitt, and Robert Morris are very important to me.

CS: Because of the minimal aspect of your work, or because Serra, LeWitt, and Morris broke with conventions of representational art?

VM: I think because their work was a disguised comeback of formal and structural ideas.

CS: How much exposure to contemporary art did you have prior to coming to the United States in 1983? Did any particular artists/artworks stand out?

VM: In the 1970s, because of the military government in Brazil, intellectuals lived in constant fear of being persecuted. Most of the music and art of that time is either camouflaged activism or corrupted by patriotism. There was always this lingering climate of a semiotic black market where hidden messages seemed encoded in every phrase: everything meant something else. People who carried books in their bags were considered a different kind of criminal by the semiliterate authoritarian police state, so reading books and hanging out with intellectuals was a way of being rebellious. That atmosphere gave me a chronic allergy to slogans and a clear vision of how information can be manipulated to serve certain ends. For obvious reasons, in those days I thought political art to be a government thing and

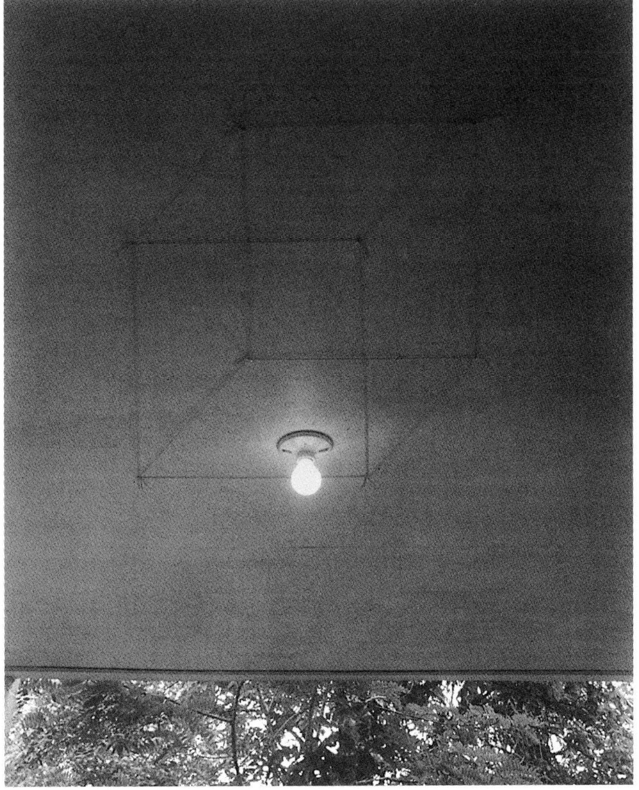

John Pfahl, *Necker Cube, Penland, North Carolina*, 1975, color photograph. Courtesy the artist and Janet Borden Gallery, New York.

abstract art to be for people who never walked the streets. I liked drawing the old paintings at the museum and didn't give much thought to contemporary art. The first contemporary artist I met was Leonilson. In 1979 we were both helping the experimental theater group Asdrubal Trouxe o Trombone during their stint in São Paulo. I worked with him designing a poster and I told him that the boat he drew was crooked. He told me that the boat was crooked because that boat was his own. Leonilson made things that were infused with fragility and ambiguity, one of the very first Brazilian artists to show that side of an art object. He was an extraordinary artist and a great person. I miss him a lot.

CS: Would you say that in some way your works pay homage to artists of the late '60s or early '70s like William Wegman, Robert Cumming, even Douglas Huebler? I'm thinking in particular of the dry, often banal humor and the low-tech illusions associated with much of their conceptually based photo works.

VM: There is something about the art of the '70s that I can't seem to escape. Maybe it's a generational thing. There is a certain homemade feeling behind the works of these artists that makes me think of itinerant circus troupes and high school science fairs. I have always liked Dada and Fluxus, which probably influenced their work, and tried to cultivate that attitude toward artmaking. It's like conceptual art without a frown.

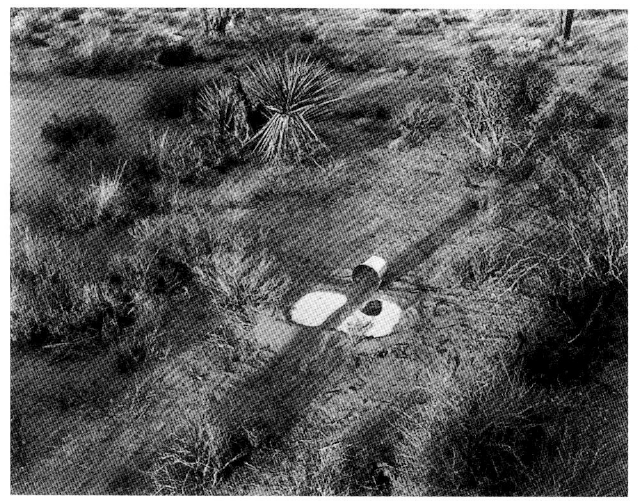

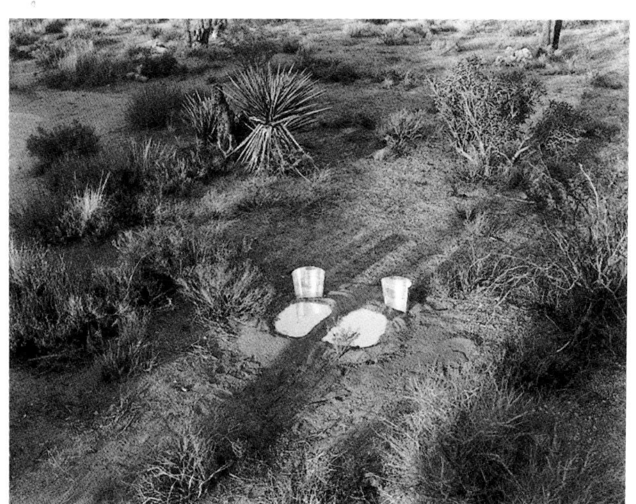

Robert Cumming, *Two Explanations for a Small Split Pond*, 1974, gelatin silver print, 19.5 x 24.5 cm. Gift of Temmie and Arnold Gilbert, 1983.818. Photograph © 1998 The Art Institute of Chicago. All rights reserved.

CS: Do you consider yourself a conceptual artist? Loosely defined, of course, since we know that the true conceptual artist never really produces anything.

VM: It is hard not to be conceptual. The term "conceptual art" always bothered me because it's impossible for me to imagine an art form without a concept. I think art becomes "political," "conceptual," or "spiritual" only by subtraction. Basically what the so-called conceptual artist is saying is that he does not dance, sing, carve wood, draw nudes, or practice easel painting: he thinks ideas without form. If you find an idea without form, please let me know because I would love to take a picture of it. "Conceptual art" only emphasizes the concept of an art object by the systematic impoverishing of its aesthetic value. I am an artist, and I think a real artist could not stand the sacrifice of beauty for the sake of smartness. You don't have to do that! Take people like Courbet or Manet, for example. You can't get more conceptual than that. You don't need a neon sign to proclaim your intellectual intentions, all you need is a good story to give them form. Leonardo is always quoted for saying that art is a mental thing. I think what he really meant is that art is mental without exception. Marcel Broodthaers is a conceptual artist. So is Grandma Moses. On this subject, de Kooning had the final word when he said that in art, one idea is just as good as another.

CS: Chuck Close was quoted as saying to de Kooning that "he was glad to meet someone that had painted more de Koonings than he had." Close was referring to his own early work, which was quite derivative of de Kooning. Is there a de Kooning out there for you?

VM: If I met the guy who photographs Chuck's paintings for documentation, I would probably say, "I am glad to meet someone who has photographed more Chuck Close paintings than I have."

CS: Have you ever considered doing theater or performance art? I have to say that it would suit your personality. Are you always "on"?

VM: I worked in theater in Brazil, basically experimental amateur groups. One of my thoughts behind moving to New York was to study theater. I like reading plays, but now I rarely go see one. Theater is perhaps the most important component of my work today. For example, if I see a performance of *King Lear*, say, with Anthony Hopkins in the main role, the excellent actor with his body and voice alone will be able to temporarily convince you that he is indeed a king. It is a great illusion that you only learn to appreciate when you get a chance to watch the same piece performed by a bad actor. Now, here is the beauty of the whole thing: the good actor, Sir Anthony Hopkins, seems to disappear as himself once he embodies the old king. You forget about him and you only see what he represents. The bad actor, on the other hand, keeps shifting back and forth from his royal character to his incompetent self. The good actor lets you experience the play while the bad actor allows you to experience theater itself. I think of my photographs as very short plays, sometimes a fraction of a second long, in which a bad actor, say, soil, thread, or chocolate, performs the role of an object, a person, or a landscape only for the lens of the camera. I cast bad actors in my pieces because I don't want people to simply see a representation of something. I want them to feel how it happens. The moment of that embodiment is what I consider a spiritual experience.

CS: You seem to draw many of your ideas, or at least your inspiration, from art history, in particular those artists and works that have seemingly been of little significance, or at least overlooked by much of the contemporary art world. Where would you place your work in today's art world, an arena that puts such a huge premium on theoretical discourse?

VM: I'd rather say that I sometimes make work based on "old pictures" than on art history, which in general implies that there are some things to be considered before a certain work is perceived by the eye. I am more inclined to work with anonymous pieces because they are less polluted by historical information than masterworks. I've never taken a class in art history and sometimes think I'm very fortunate to have learned art by responding to

Giacomo Brogi (1822–1881), Refectory of the Church of Santa Maria delle Grazie, Milan, c. 1870s. Private collection.

Leonardo conceived the painting's setting as a trompe l'oeil extension of the end wall of the actual dining hall, with Jesus and the apostles understood as being at the head table, in the traditional Tuscan manner. ... There has been much written about the narrative and theological nuances of the interpretation, but the basic point could not be more clear: Jesus has announced that one of the gathered company will betray him, and waves of emotion roll through his apostles.

— A. Richard Turner, *Inventing Leonardo* (New York: Knopf, 1993), p. 38.

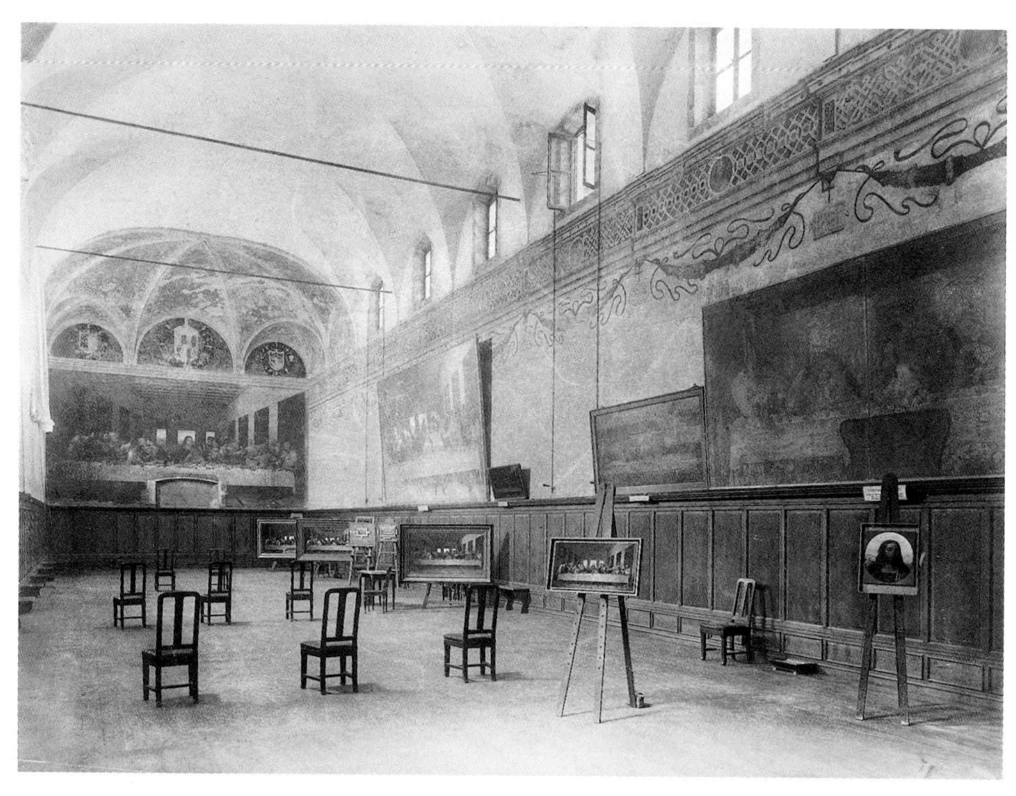

pictures at a very personal level. The work of art that changed my life and prompted me to become an artist was a painting of a slightly cross-eyed girl whose facial asymmetry made the painting look alive. Her name was Clara Serena and it was just a coincidence that her father, the painter who executed the portrait, was Peter Paul Rubens.

I tend to like works from periods when new media emerge, forcing the existing ones to change. Early nineteenth-century painting, sculpture, and photography; Impressionism; photography and painting between the wars – these are works that I am always scrutinizing. One day I was looking at a book by Sister Wendy and saw this very sweet portrait of Saint John the Baptist and a lamb done by Murillo. I have no idea why, but the silly little picture brought tears to my eyes. If I had studied art history and learned how corny Murillo was, I would have been deprived of that poignant experience. I have done some pictures after better known works, but tried to play down their iconographic value by emphasizing their perceptual output. I did Leonardo's *Last Supper*, for example, but I wasn't thinking of Leonardo. I was thinking of perspective and the idea of the Eucharist as an early form of broadcasting.

As for theory, I think that the only bad thing about art criticism is that it makes possible art *about* criticism. I like reading philosophy and history books. I even have an interest in neurology, psychology, and physics. But when I want to read something that will ultimately influence my work, I pick up a novel or book of poetry.

CS: Do you ever write poetry or fiction yourself?

VM: Yes, but most of it is still garbage. I say this because I just saw the *Drawings of Victor Hugo* at the Drawing Center. These drawings are the most incredible things I've ever seen, and they were done by a writer. I can't even *draw* like Victor Hugo, much less expect to be a writer.

CS: Could you talk a little about the actual process of making an image, one of the *Thread* pieces, for example.

VM: These developed out of my inability to do a landscape with wire. I tried but they were really sad. I wanted to try different subjects, but I discovered by changing the material in which I was drawing that each material could only render certain things well. I needed something more fluid, so I began to work with sewing thread. The process is very similar to the wire objects except that it allows me to build up the material and create volume. In one hand you have a drawing and in the other you have the photograph of the "actor" responsible for the enacting of that landscape. When you perceive one, you loose the other. It works like a visual puzzle, like the Necker cube or the Rubin vase.

CS: Did you intend to mock the pompous seriousness of Alfred Stieglitz's cloud images, *Equivalents*, when you made your cloud pictures?

VM: No. Stieglitz may not have been America's greatest artist, but he was definitely its most influential one. He spread himself thin but covered a lot of territory. He worked on many fronts and used many devices to help shape the artistic milieu of his time. He single-handedly introduced modern art to the American public. I usually use images from people I admire or find important in the context of general culture. I wouldn't want to mock anyone, especially someone with Stieglitz's mind and reputation. If you look at one of his *Equivalents*, you will get a glimpse of the ungraspable nature of sensations and the artificial ways in which meaning is fabricated. If you look at one of my *Equivalents*, you will see—depending on the way you choose to interpret it—either a cloud, a lump of cotton, or Dürer's *Praying Hands*. The title "equivalents" was chosen because these "clouds" had something to do with what Stieglitz was trying to say: that the objective of a photograph is not merely portrayal of a subject but the range of symbolic and emotional associations the formal treatment of a subject will bring to the viewer. He treated the question by pushing it toward ambiguity. I decided to push it toward specificity.

CS: Thinking about the need to solve the riddle, I imagine that you might be interested in mysteries: murder mysteries. Yes? Have you ever had an opportunity to closely examine crime scene photographs?

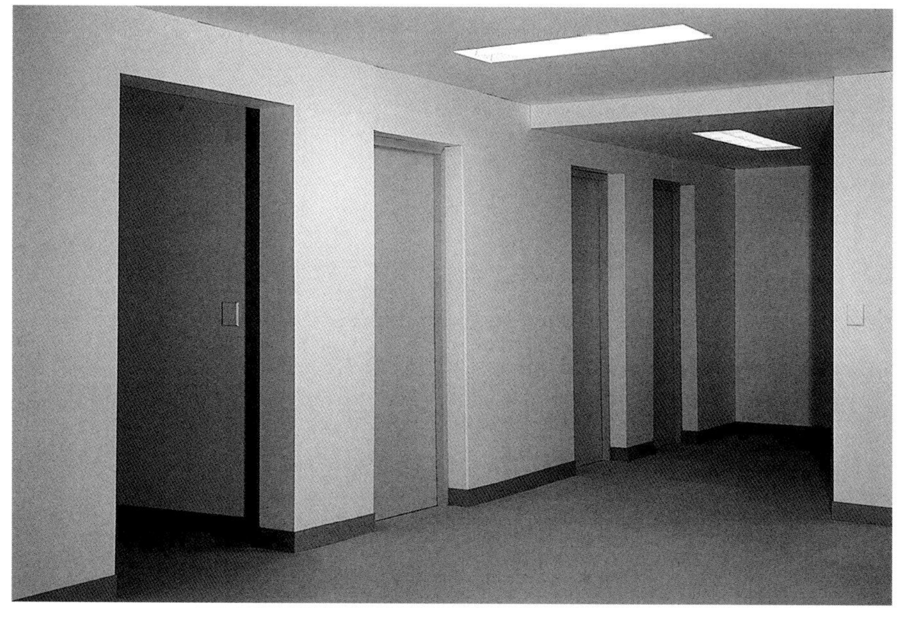

Thomas Demand, *Flur (Couloir/Corridor)*, 1995, color photograph, 183 x 270 cm. Courtesy the artist, 303 Gallery, New York, and Victoria Miro Gallery, London.

Rene Ammann: Of course, but Thomas thinks obviously that mentioning [the background] reduces the possibilities of interpretation.

John Waters: I understand this. It doesn't concern me, but I know what he means. It becomes too simple. People say, well that's it and don't think any further about it. I liked his work before I knew what's behind it. I looked at those images and I suspected: there's something wrong. Besides the "Archive" I had seen the "Corridor," which leads to the apartment of Jeffrey Dahmer. But to know about the content of the work is making the work only better! When you looked at the "Corridor," you knew something about it is awful, weird, [even though] the work itself doesn't carry anything shocking about it ...

— John Waters interviewed by Rene Ammann, *Kunstbulletin* (April 1998), pp. 19–20.

VM: The problem with mysteries is that in the end they cease to be a mystery. There is a great murder-mystery writer in France named Daniel Pennac. His main character, Benjamin Malaussene, is a guy who takes care of eleven siblings and gets blamed for every single death in the city. The book always starts with his mother returning home with another baby and ends with her leaving with another man. The killer is always an old lady. There is very little mystery, and as I have said, I don't care for the mystery itself, but the way he constructs the plot and illustrates the scenes is absolutely brilliant. It's like Bulgakov meets Conan Doyle. I like the Columbo films too because you know the identity of the killer from the beginning, and you spend the rest of the film trying to understand how that half-witted cop is going to solve it. That's the real mystery. Well, there is certainly something about crime and medical photography that gets to you. I have seen a lot of police pictures, but they don't do much for me. I guess I have seen too many police movies where those scenes are abundant and the only difference between the real and the fake ones is a caption, something outside the photo. I think medical photography has a more potent effect on me.

CS: In many of your works, text, language, or the caption are integral aspects of the viewer's understanding of the work. In a way, your captions — especially with the *Displacements* series, where there are no images — totally subvert the notion of photographic veracity and toy with the notion that we should believe everything we read. Do these little white lies ever get you into trouble?

Sashimi Tempura Combination

Plate 268, Vincent Van Gogh.
Still Life: Vase with Fifteen Sunflowers.
Arles, August 1888. 92.1x73cm.
National Gallery London

Vik Muniz, *Displacements*, details, 1996, cibachrome prints.

VM: The newspaper clippings that I make up are partly inspired by the wacky abstract pictures I find in the science section of the *New York Times* every Tuesday. There, what looks like a wine stain is identified in a caption as a field of antimatter in the middle of a galaxy several light years away. I made a bunch of drawings that look like wine stains while talking on the phone and decided to start writing little stories for them. Like the one about a virus that makes people unable to read, or the photographer from *National Geographic* who was indicted for photographing his girlfriend's underwear in such a way that it looked like a rare mushroom. I wrote a silly story about the guards at Yosemite not letting people take pictures with small-format cameras and faxed it to a friend, who faxed it to a friend, who faxed it to a million other people. When I showed these images to a group of people in San Francisco, an old lady approached me and said that I was lying about having fabricated these stories because that particular story was true – she had heard it on the radio. There I was being called a liar by claiming authorship of a lie that had become a truth by convention. It's hard to own a lie when everybody owns the truth. The *Displacements* series also comes straight from the stuff I did while working with the *Life* magazine images. I was trying to gauge the power of a caption over the image.

CS: You've moved away from the three-dimensional aspect of your earlier work, but do you have any interest in going back to sculpture or even installations?

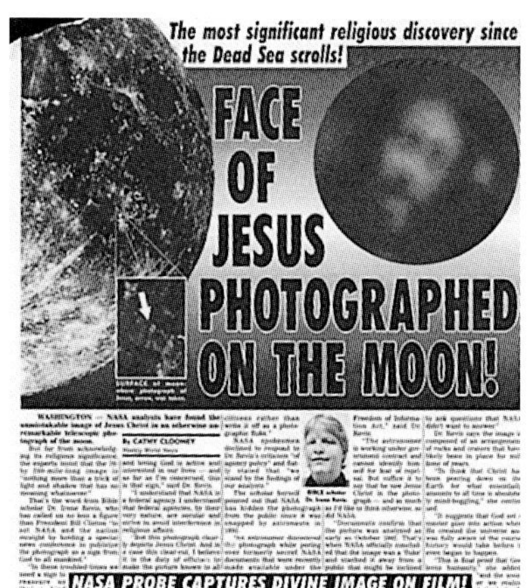

The most significant religious discovery since the Dead Sea scrolls!

FACE OF JESUS PHOTOGRAPHED ON THE MOON!

NASA PROBE CAPTURES DIVINE IMAGE ON FILM!

"Face of Jesus Photographed on the Moon," *Weekly World News*, December 5, 1995. Reprinted with permission of Weekly World News.

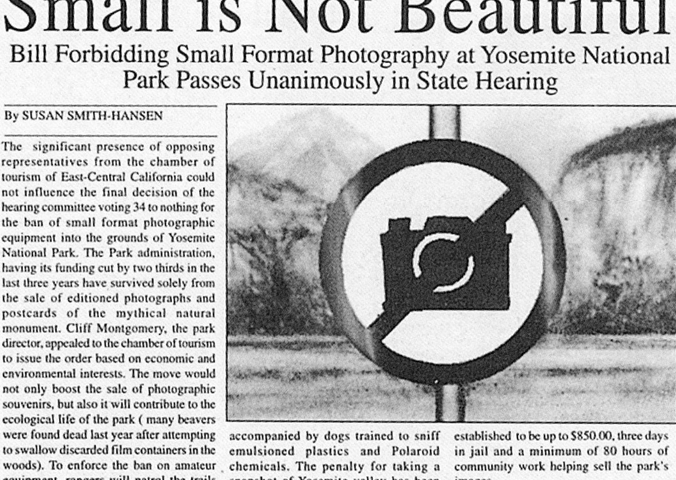

Small is Not Beautiful

Bill Forbidding Small Format Photography at Yosemite National Park Passes Unanimously in State Hearing

By SUSAN SMITH-HANSEN

The significant presence of opposing representatives from the chamber of tourism of East-Central California could not influence the final decision of the hearing committee voting 34 to nothing for the ban of small format photographic equipment into the grounds of Yosemite National Park. The Park administration, having its funding cut by two thirds in the last three years have survived solely from the sale of editioned photographs and postcards of the mythical natural monument. Cliff Montgomery, the park director, appealed to the chamber of tourism to issue the order based on economic and environmental interests. The move would not only boost the sale of photographic souvenirs, but also it will contribute to the ecological life of the park (many beavers were found dead last year after attempting to swallow discarded film containers in the woods). To enforce the ban on amateur equipment, rangers will patrol the trails accompanied by dogs trained to sniff emulsioned plastics and Polaroid chemicals. The penalty for taking a snapshot of Yosemite valley has been established to be up to $850.00, three days in jail and a minimum of 80 hours of community work helping sell the park's images

Vik Muniz, *Personal Articles: Small is Not Beautiful*, 1996, newsprint.

They mean absolutely nothing, but in the context of this fictional apparatus that surrounds them, they become meaningful, and all of a sudden you read a story, and you don't even care if they're drawings or not. I just wanted to make them barely convincing, but when you have these elements—you see the paper, you see the coherent blocks of text—you believe in it. I didn't proofread the text, so it's filled with typos and my own version of English. It reads like a newspaper but it has all this bad English. ... The texts are funny, if you take the time to read them.

— Vik Muniz, from interview with Vincent Katz, *On Paper* 1, no. 4 (March–April 1997).

VM: It's hard to forecast what I will do next. I don't have much of a plan and neither am I bound to a specific style or technique. Photography has allowed me to pack drawing, sculpture, painting, and theater into one tight bundle. I have been developing series of drawings and sculpture for years; it just happens that the photographic work has matured at a faster pace. I am also working with film now, but so far have created very short loops with not much going on - they look more like a photograph than a film. As for installation, I've never felt the need to walk around sculpture and I don't see a point to being inside one. I am very claustrophobic.

CS: Is there a way of making marks that you've always wanted to do, but could never get it to work?

VM: The things that work are few compared to the ones that don't. Once I thought I could duplicate the dot pattern of a billboard with M&Ms. I almost died of nervous exhaustion. Live ants, rubber bands, black beans, chains, electric sparks, magnets, oil and milk—you name it, I've tried a lot of things but only succeed with a few.

CS: One might say that the *Soil* pieces are small-scale earthworks. Have you ever thought of doing something larger like a real earthwork or the ancient land drawings photographed by Marilyn Bridges?

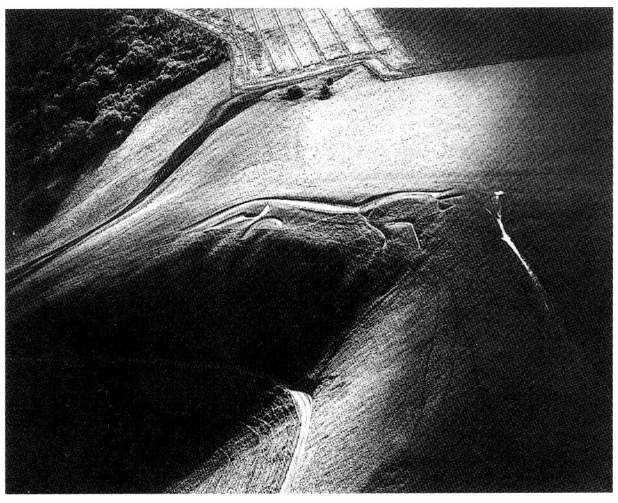

Marilyn Bridges, *Uffington Horse, Oxfordshire (England)*, 1985.
© Marilyn Bridges 1985. Courtesy the artist and Felicia Murray.

It is to ancient times and ancient beliefs that the origin of the oldest of the equine chalk figures belongs. Nearly 2,000 years ago, Celtic tribesmen tore away the turf covering a rolling slope of Berkshire Downs, revealing the white chalk beneath the surface in order to create the image of a magnificent galloping white horse on the landscape. Known today as the Uffington Horse, the 360-foot creature was not designed at the whim of a passionate artist. It was a ceremonial icon, and perhaps a territorial claim, of a people known as the Belgae.

Although the actual date of its creation is unknown, the period 100 BC to AD 100 is suggested, making it the oldest of Britain's hill figures. The figure was attended to over the centuries by a ritual scouring which took place every seven years during Whitsuntide when celebrations were held within the nearby Iron Age hill fort of Uffington Castle, the ramparts of which enclose eight acres. During the festivities there were horse races, wrestling, cudgeling, and cheese-rolling, a curious event in which round cheeses were rolled downhill into the combe below the white horse, which is known as the Manger. The festivities were abandoned in 1857, and for a long time the horse was neglected. The horse is now maintained by the Department of Environment.

VM: Yes, I would love to make land drawings, but they would be portraits of TV personalities, old cars, or marsupials. I would use half of Patagonia to draw the RCA dog, and the gramophone would have lines as large as the Suez Canal. However, the final result of this work would be a 4x5 platinum print.

CS: What is particularly intriguing is that your illusions are becoming more and more about flatness. The *Soil* and *Sugar Children* series seem to have a similar methodology. Were they done at around the same time?

VM: The early pieces took ideas from drawing. I was replacing the drawn line with physical things like thread or wire. The sugar and soil pieces have a lot more to do with photography itself: the idea that the image is composed by a certain logical arrangement of tiny dots that we can't really perceive individually. Well, I just made the dots bigger and gave them identity.

The Sugar Children also developed out of a very personal circumstance. Marion and I spent a few days in St. Kitts and swam every day with a group of local children who were very sweet and unspoiled by Nike commercials. We got to know their names and a few things about them. They were very happy kids. Later on we had a chance to visit the place where most of their parents worked on the sugar plantations. The hard labor in the scorching sun had certainly taken a toll on their outlook. They were very sad and bitter. I took photographs of the children and brought them back to New York, and one morning as I was drinking my coffee and looking at the pictures, I remembered this poem by the Brazilian poet Ferreira Gullar in which he is drinking coffee and begins to wonder about the origin of the sugar. He ends with a seminal phrase: "It is with the bitter lives of bitter people that I sweeten my coffee on this beautiful morning in Ipanema." The radiant childhood of those children will inevitably be transformed by sugar. Children who become sugar. It hit me like a brick. I went to Canal Street and bought black paper and tried to copy the snapshots by sprinkling sugar over its surface. I was very surprised when it worked.

The *Soil* pieces are the opposite of *The Sugar Children*. The potting soil is dispersed over a lightbox and then systematically cleaned with the aid of miniature vacuum cleaners, straws, moistened Q-tips, and other improvised tools.

CS: One of my least favorite bodies of work is the *X-ray* series, I assume because they seem too easy. They don't have the rigor – intellectual or otherwise – of the other series. Now, I guess I'll have to pay you that $100 after saying that?

VM: The *X-rays* are very hard to do because you can try only so many times. They are about those theater ideas that I mentioned earlier. I was talking to a friend about mimes and how we hated them. I think that has something to do with the *X-rays*, but I am not sure what. I was trying to photograph shadows and have them X-rayed. I was also frustrated trying to make photograms of hand shadows. Well, all of these things came together at one point. I thought it would be funny to provide an illusion and the wrong explanation for it at the same time.

CS: In the *Pictures of Chocolate* series, you use chocolate syrup. Maybe I'm stretching the point, but in photography and film chocolate syrup is often associated with death. In old black-and-white B-movies, chocolate syrup is substituted for blood. And to take one example from photography, Les Krims used chocolate syrup for a series of photographs in the early '70s entitled *The Incredible Case of the Stack-o-Wheats Murders.*

VM: Alfred Hitchcock used Bosco for the famous shower scene in *Psycho*. Apparently, real blood does not look bloody enough on screen. There is a major difference between the "real" and the "realistic," and sometimes the real thing does not make a persuasive representation of itself. I chose to work with chocolate because it had something to do with the feeling of painting. Chocolate inspires a multitude of psychological phenomena: it has to do with scatology, desire, sex, addiction, luxury, romance, etc. I have never met anyone who doesn't like chocolate. Freud could probably explain why everybody loves chocolate. That's why he was my first subject. I also wanted to make a drawing that challenged me in time. It usually takes an hour before the chocolate starts to dry and only a few minutes for it to melt under the hot lamps. I have to run a lot and the studio can get messy at times.

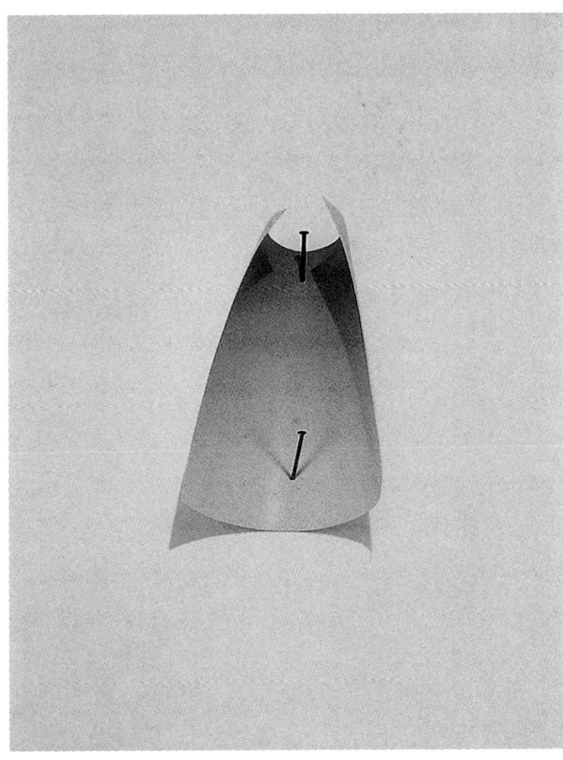

Vik Muniz, *Two Nails*, 1987, gelatin silver print and nail, 8 x 10 inches. Collection Not Vital, New York.

CS: Besides cleaning up all the messes you make, you also teach. Photography? Drawing and painting? It must be a great class and I would love to see the supply list you pass out at the beginning of the year.

VM: One of my greatest heroes is John Dewey, who always spoke of the individual's responsibility to pass on one's experience in the form of education. I teach photography, and drawing for photographers. (I do that more often than I clean up after myself.) Teaching, like writing and editing, is another way to pass on to others things that I consider important for everybody. I am always thinking of the responsibility – which we all have – to leave something for others. Recently, I began some research in the field of education concerning the development of programs for teaching visual literacy to children. There is very little being done in that area. It is important to teach kids the visual grammar behind the images they so readily consume. As images become increasingly more eloquent than the text that accompanies them, visual literacy becomes as important as reading itself.

My classes have nothing to do with what I make. I don't tell them to bring mustard, gunpowder, and maple syrup to class (although they do anyway). The school is where I vent those formless ideas and go wild about the immateriality of things. It saves me the trouble of having to cover that in my work. It also keeps me from making art that is didactic. I want these things to be beautiful, and I want this beauty to conceal the rhetoric behind them.

[PLATES]

THE BEST OF LIFE

1988–90

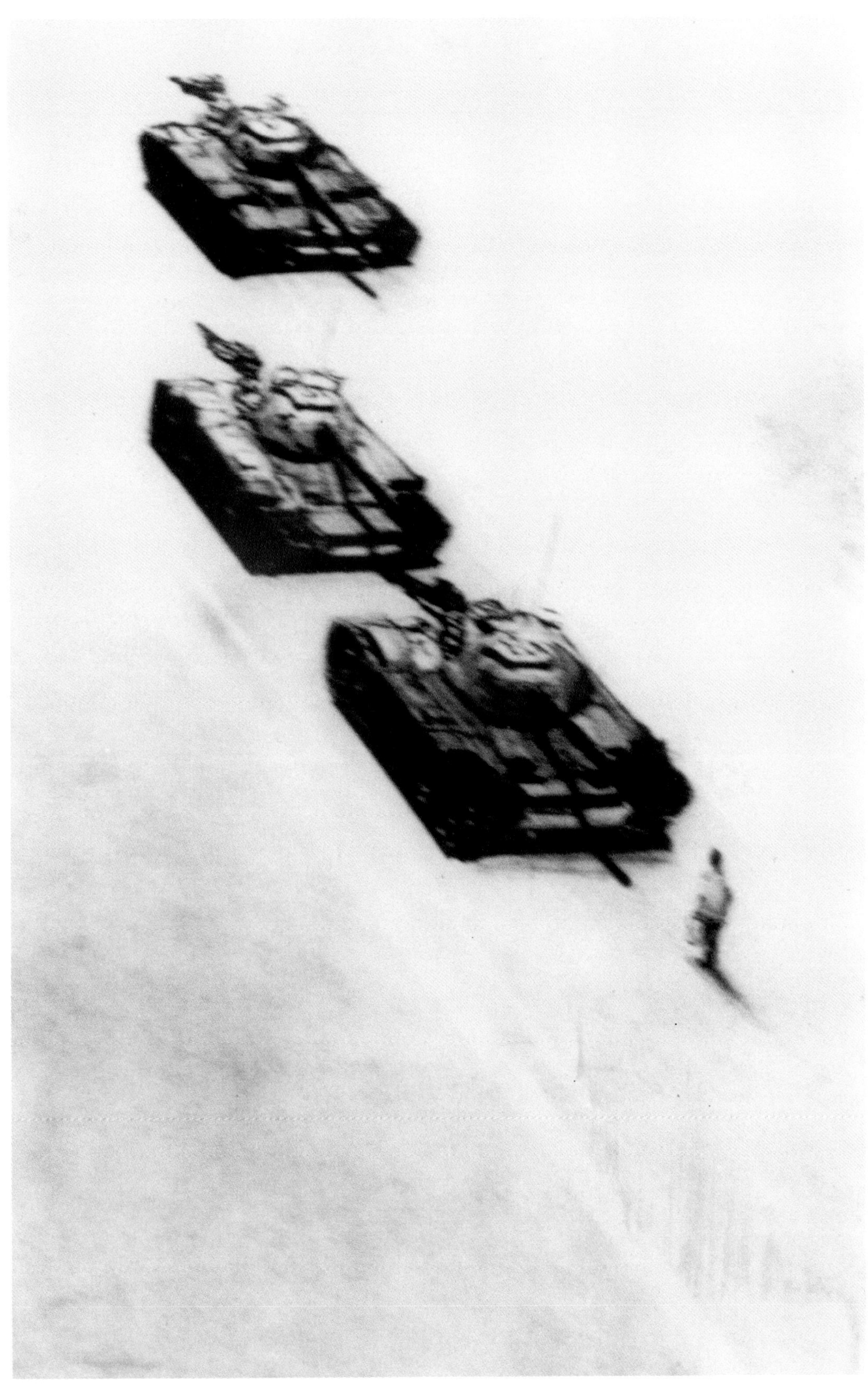

Memory Rendering of Man Stopping Tank in Beijing

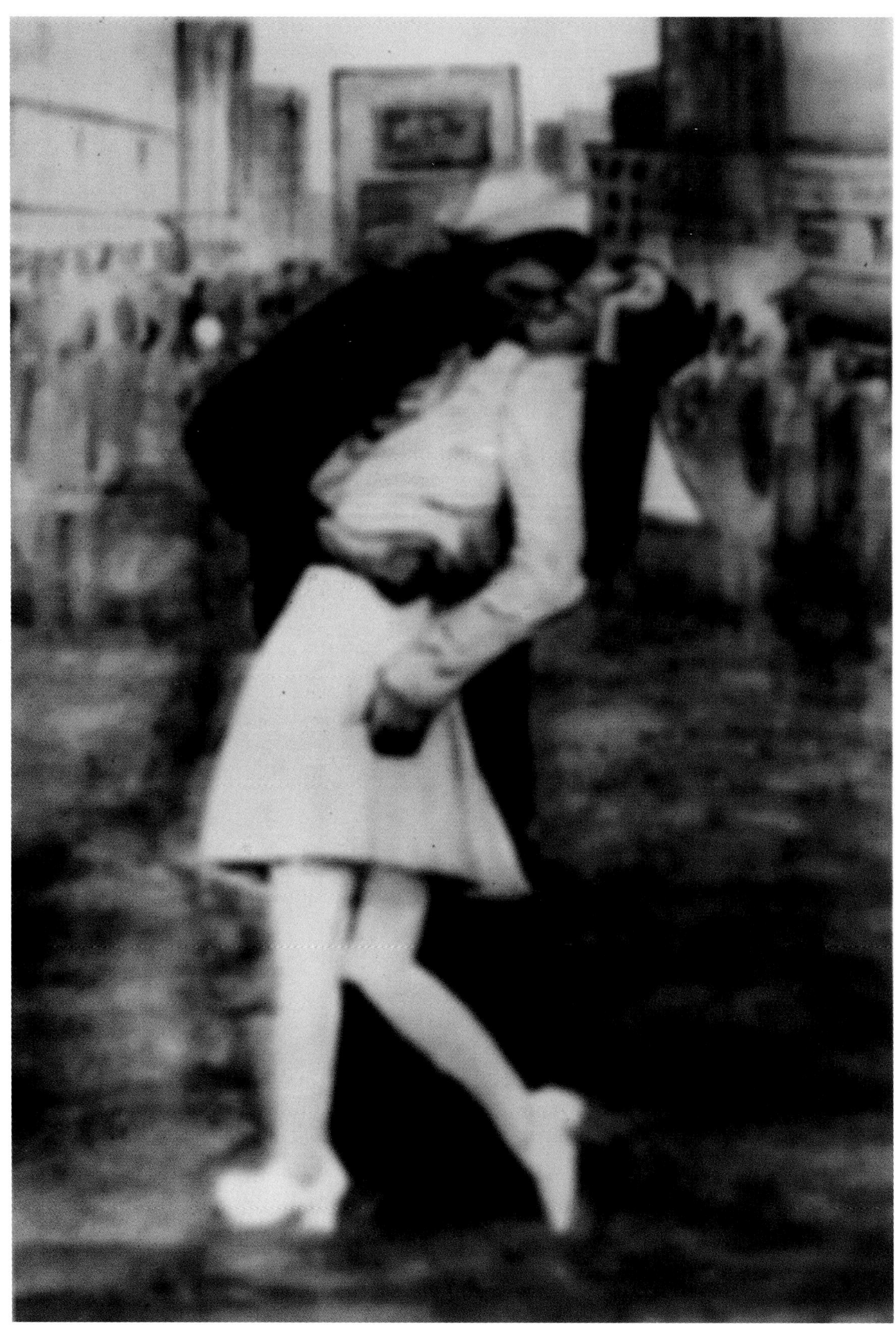

Memory Rendering of Kiss at Times Square

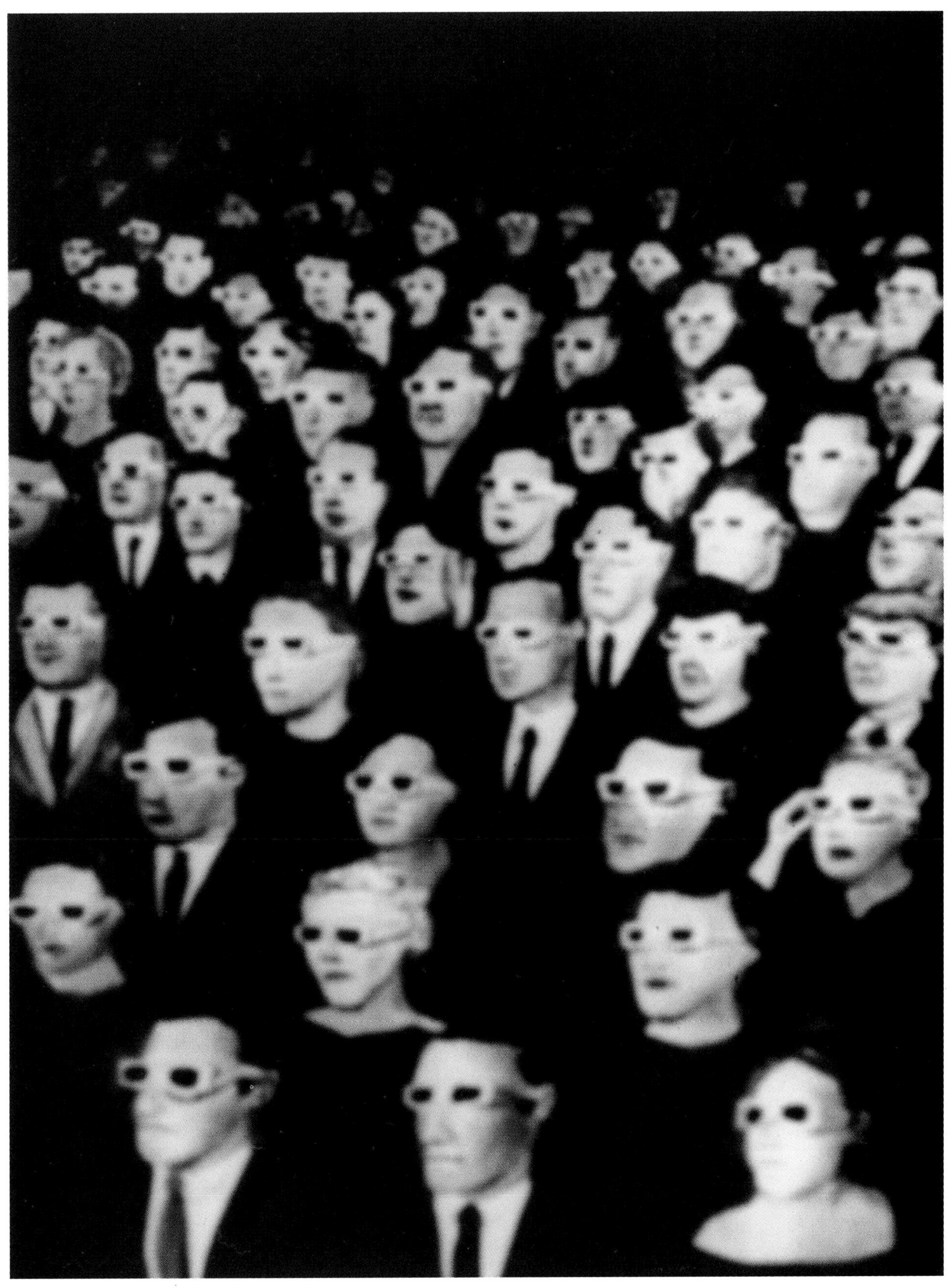

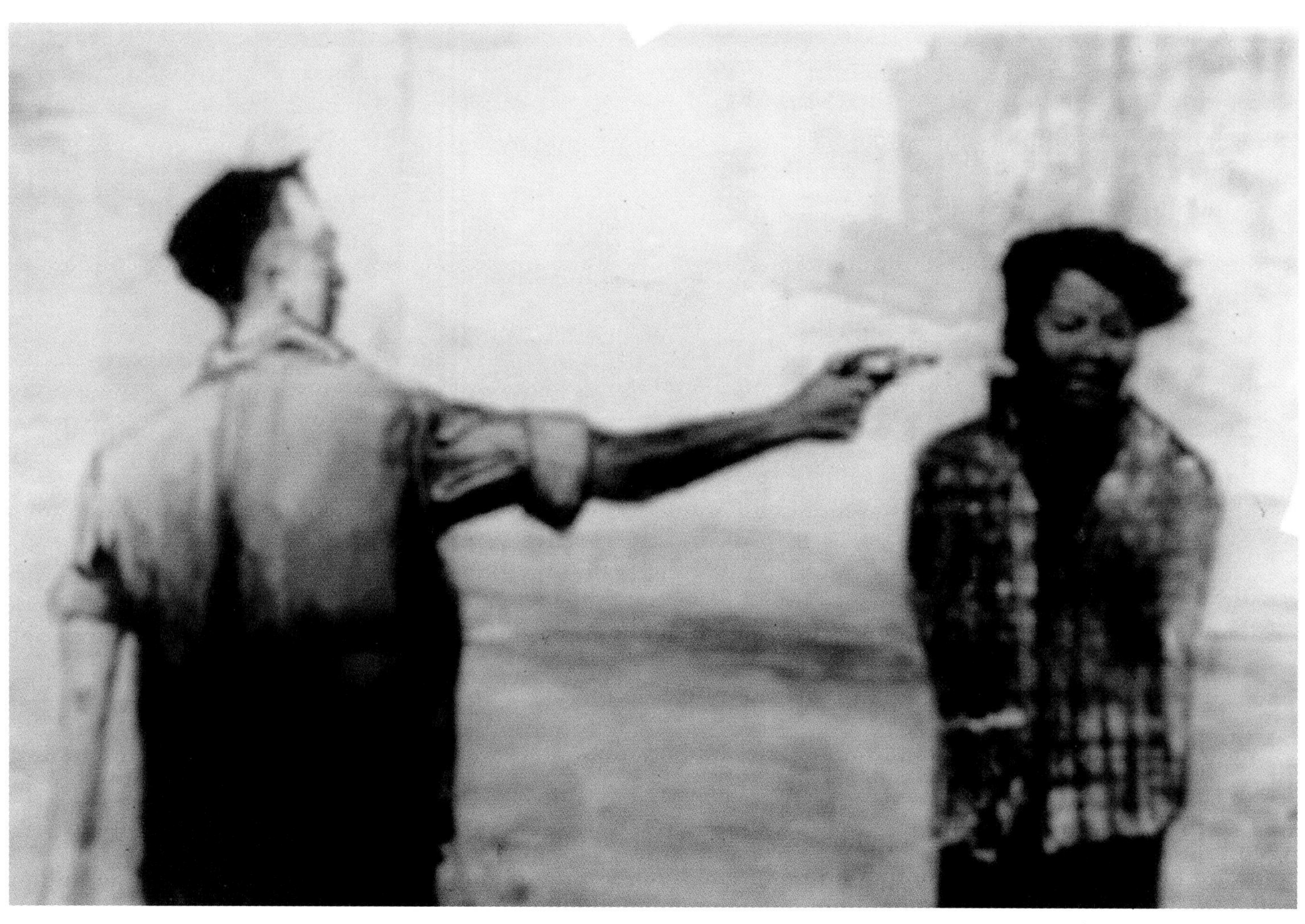

Memory Rendering of Saigon Execution of Vietcong Suspect

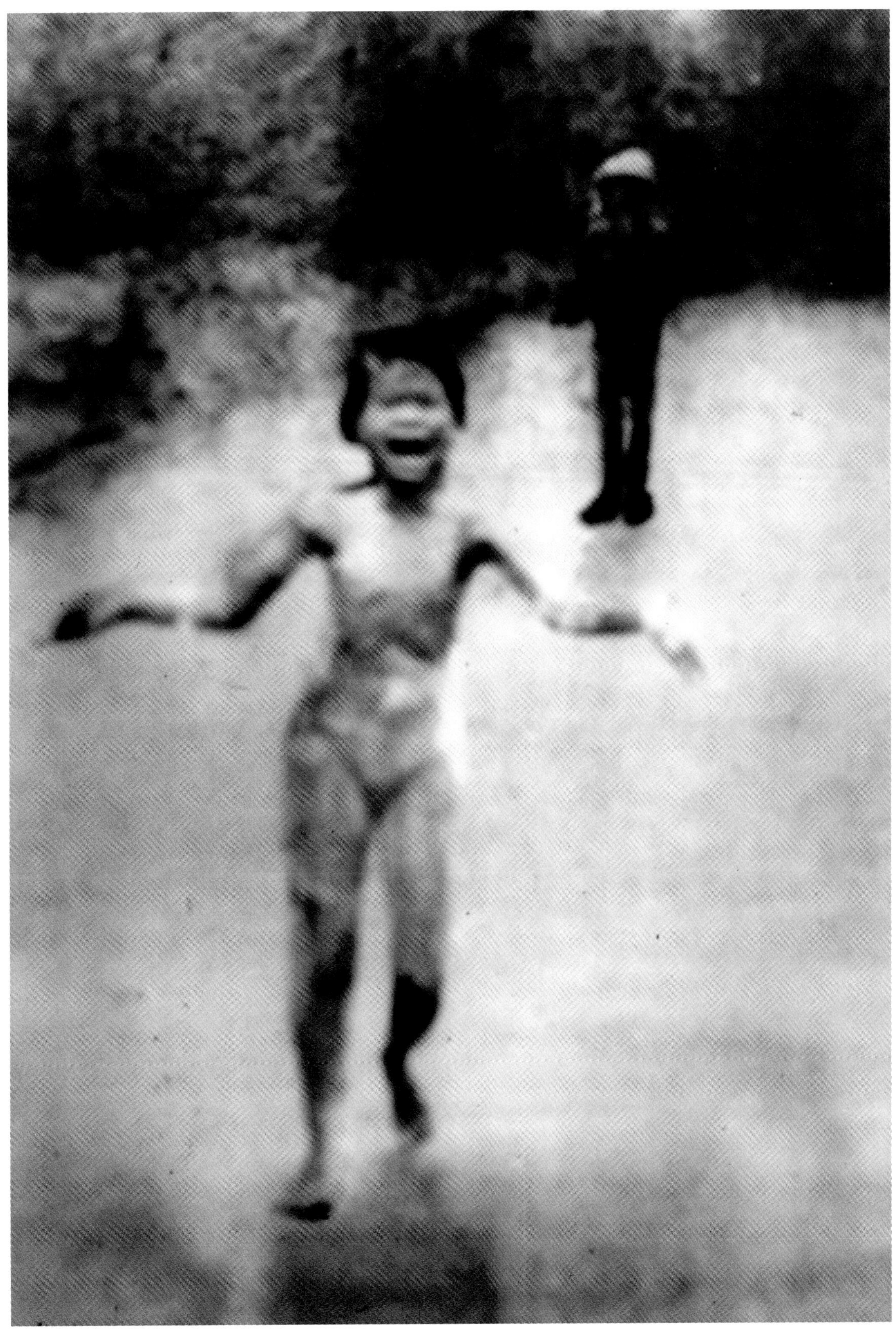

Memory Rendering of Tranbang Child

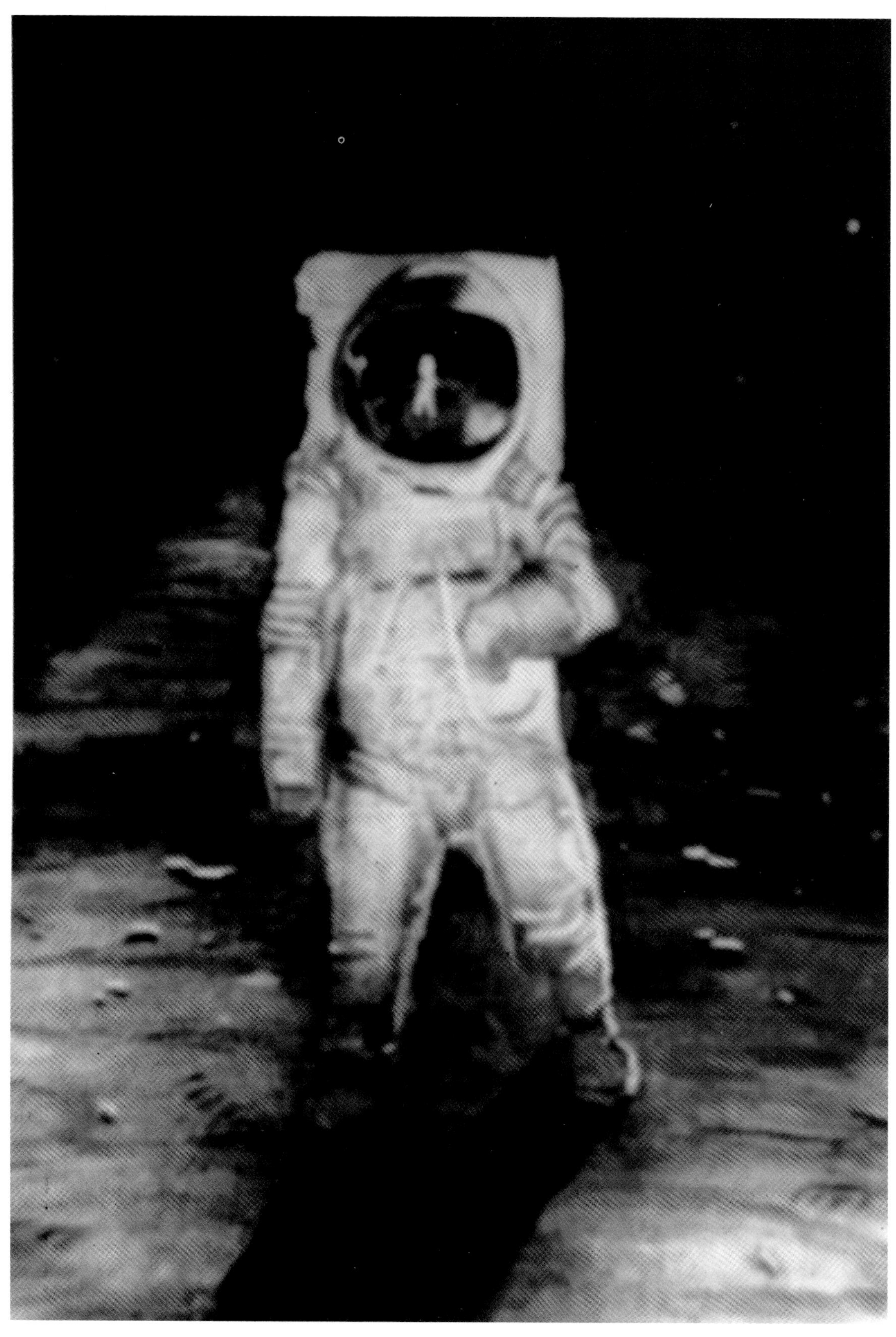

Memory Rendering of the Man on the Moon

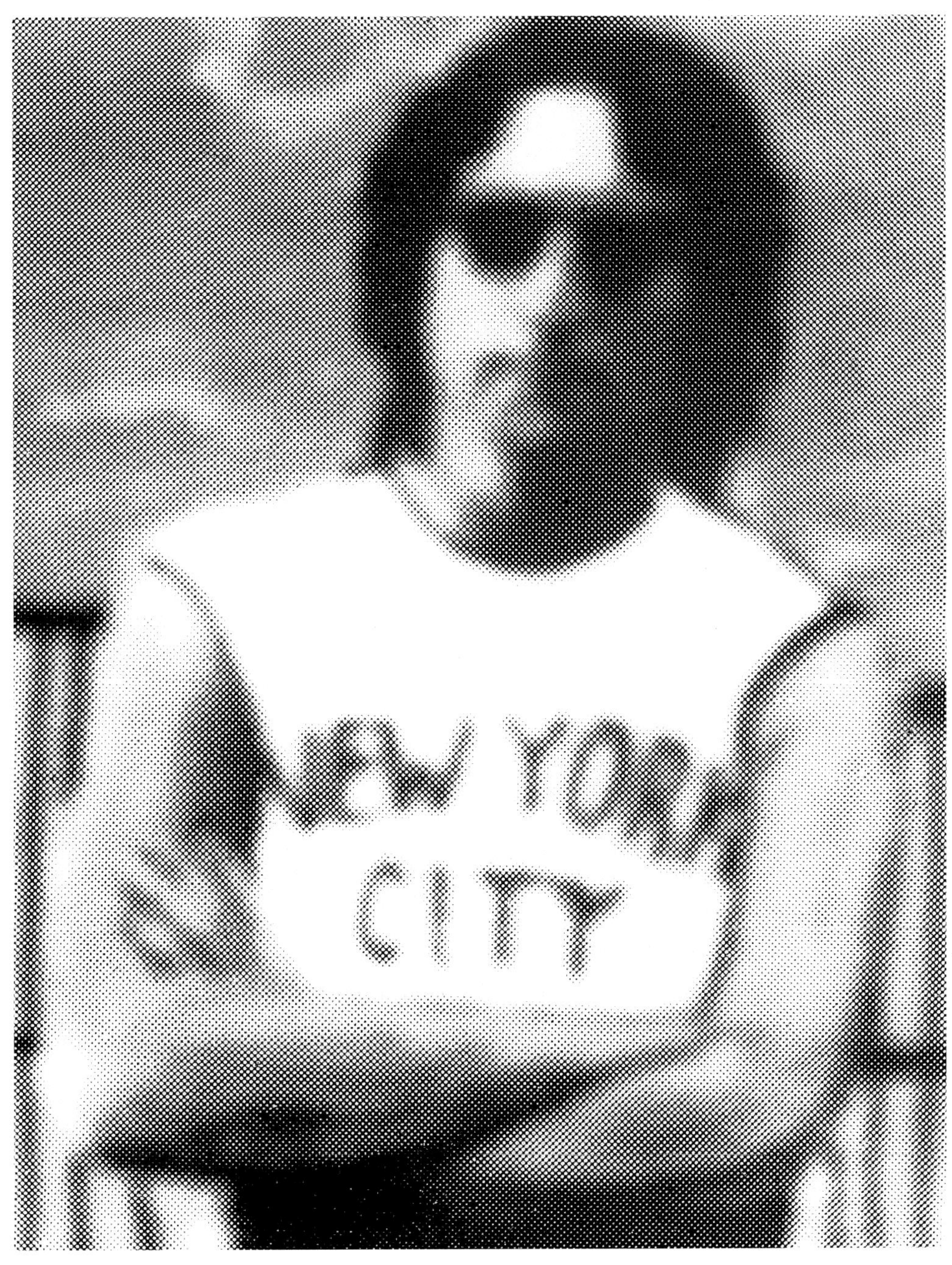

Memory Rendering of John Lennon in Manhattan

INDIVIDUALS

1992-93

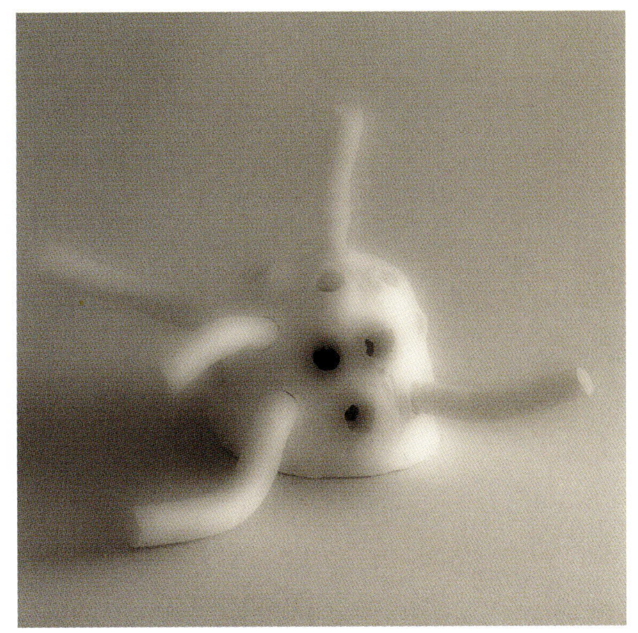

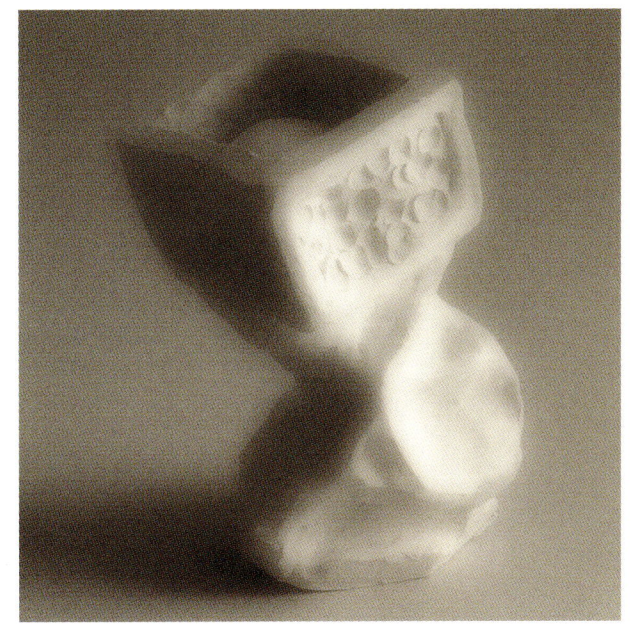

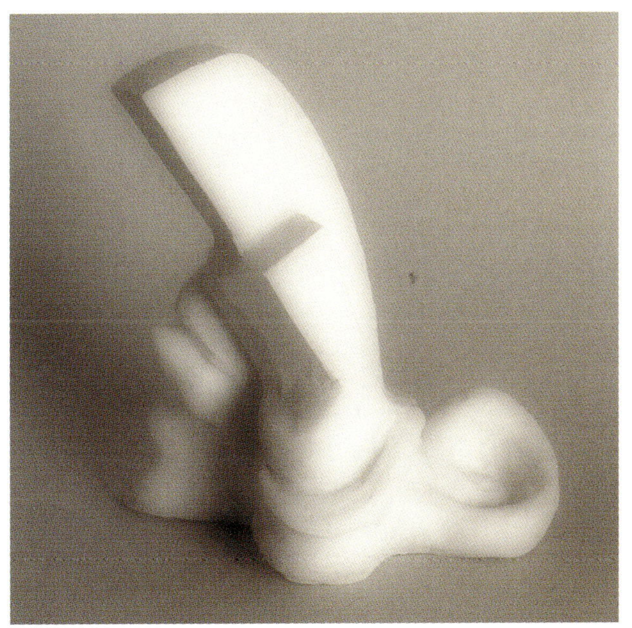

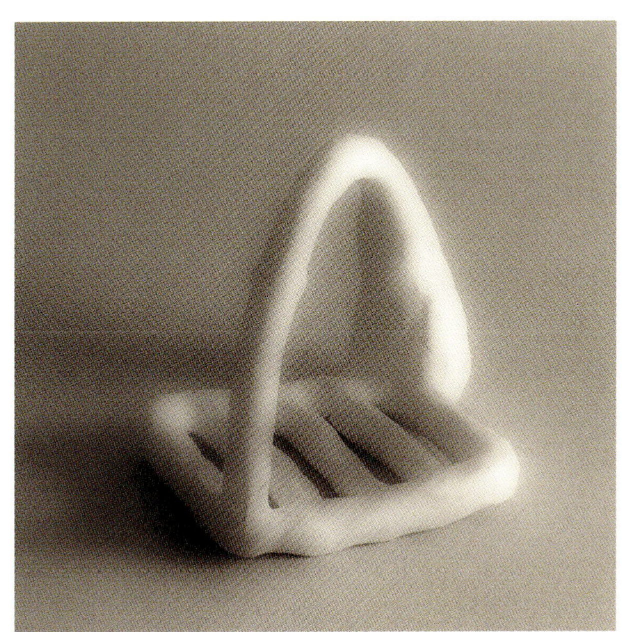

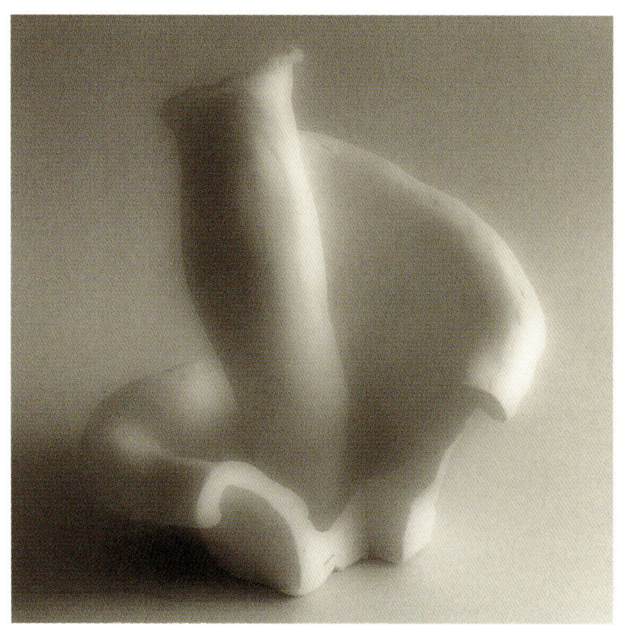
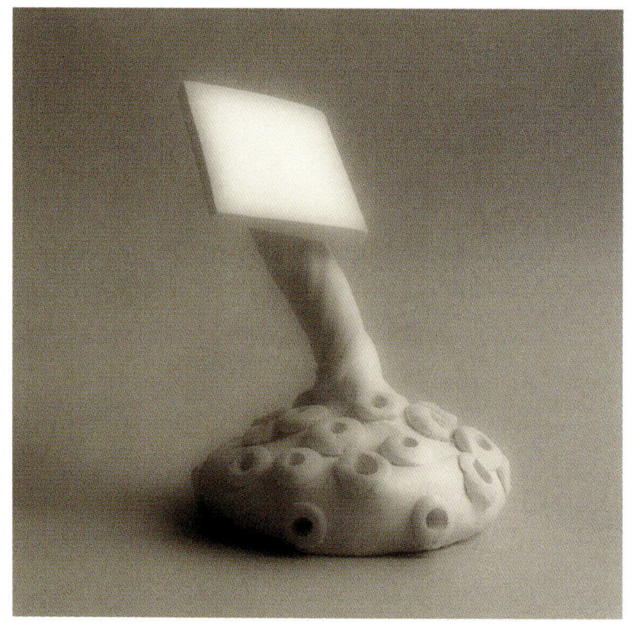
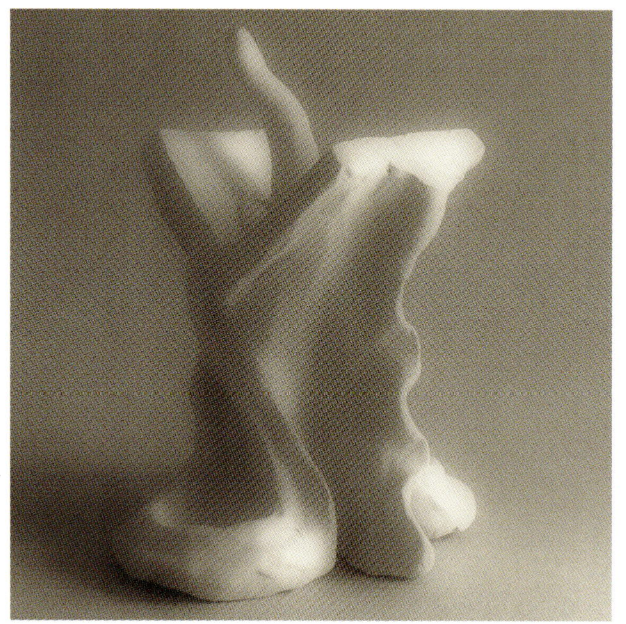
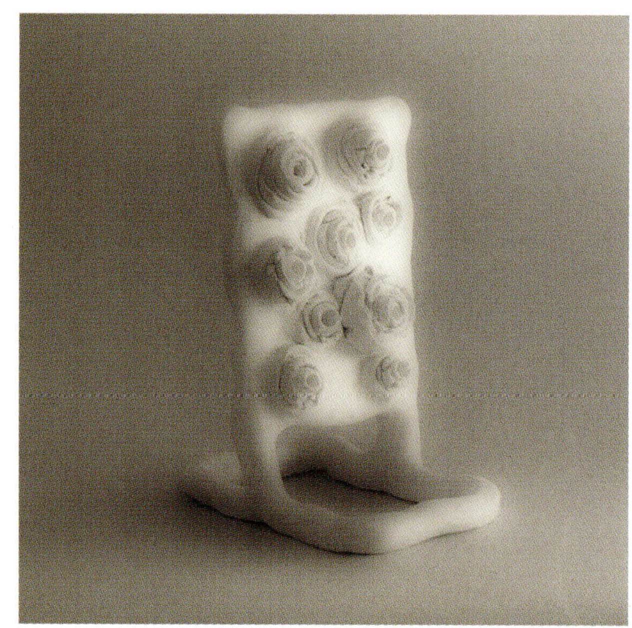

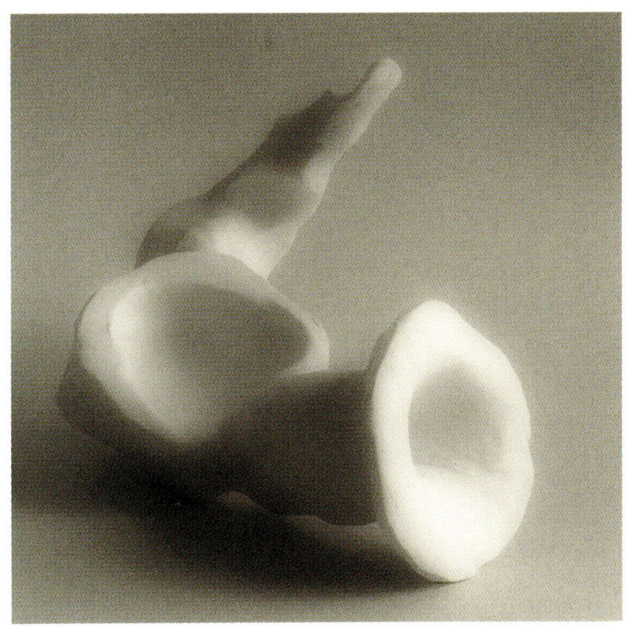
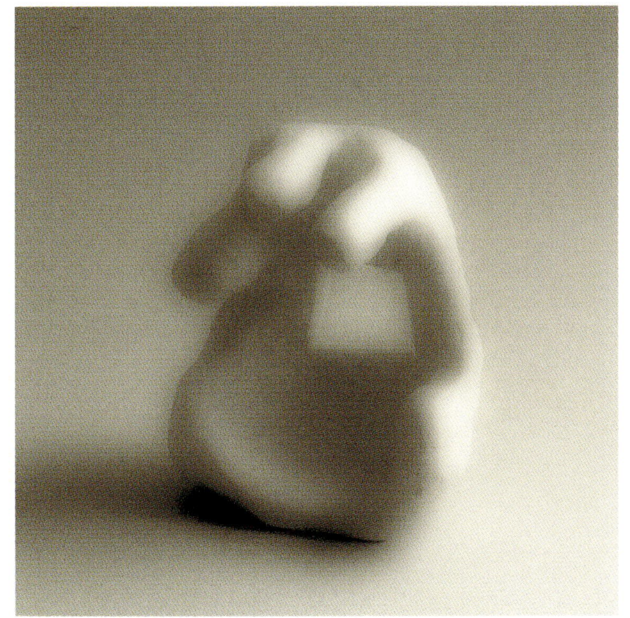
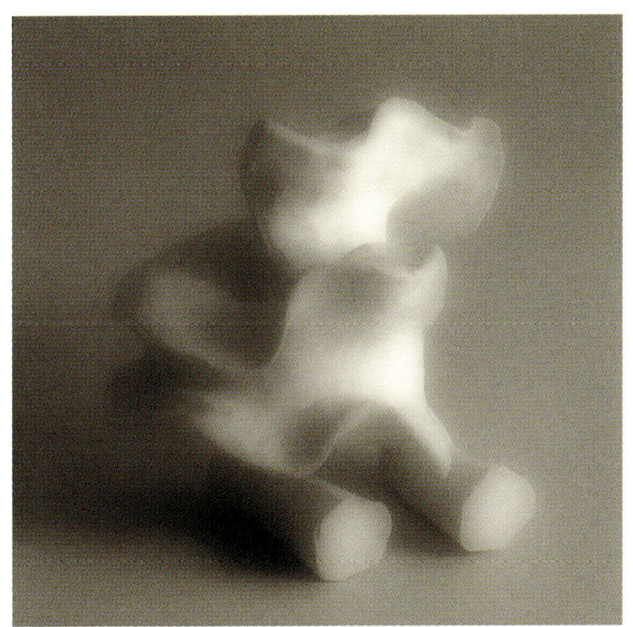
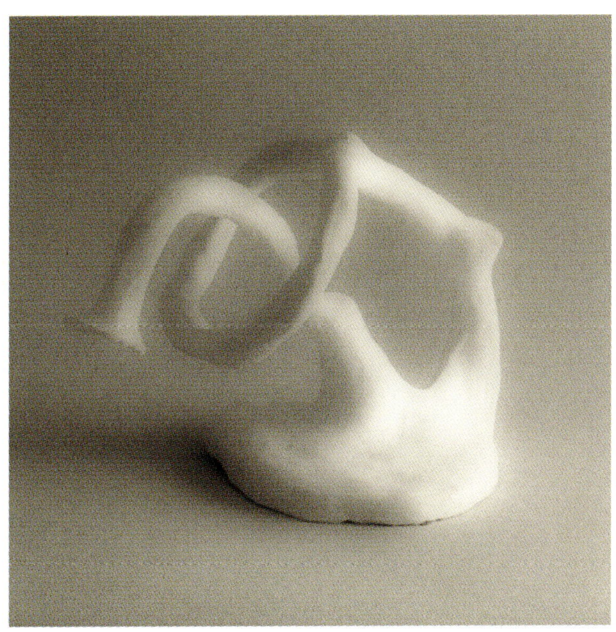

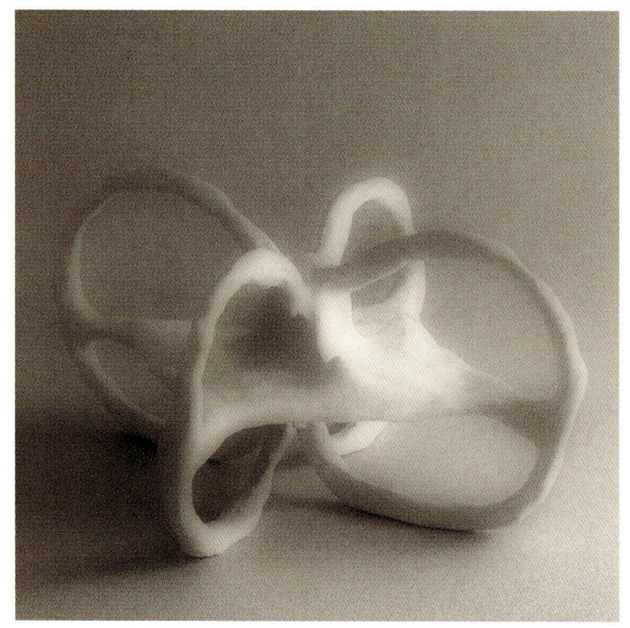
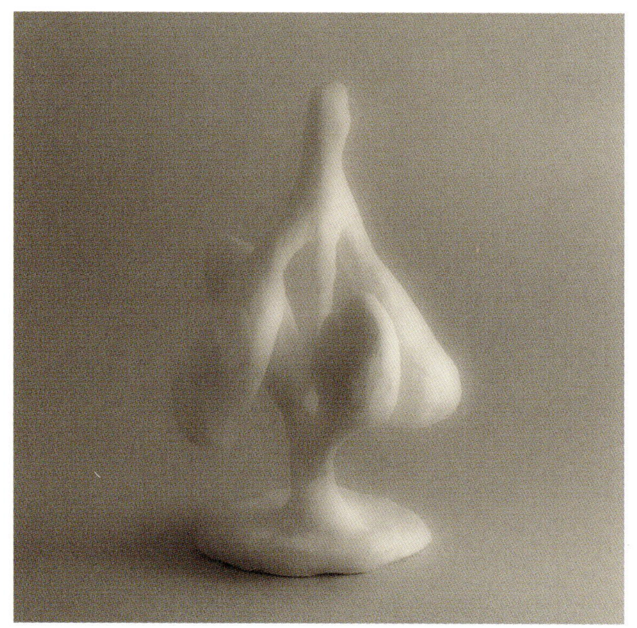
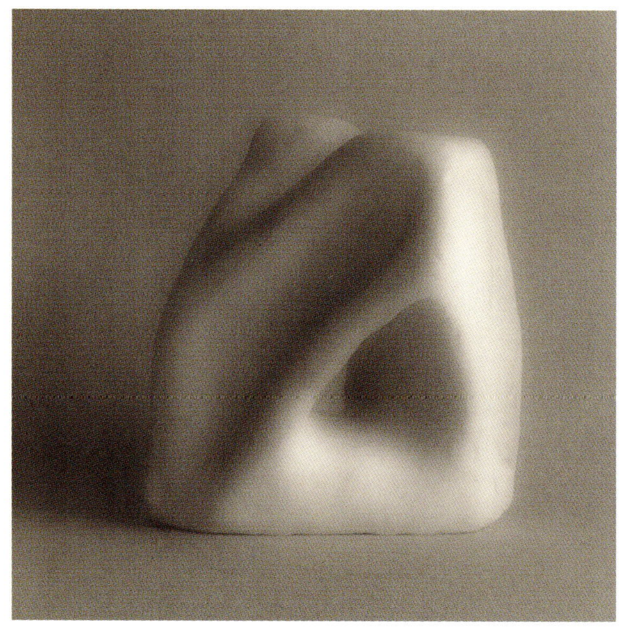
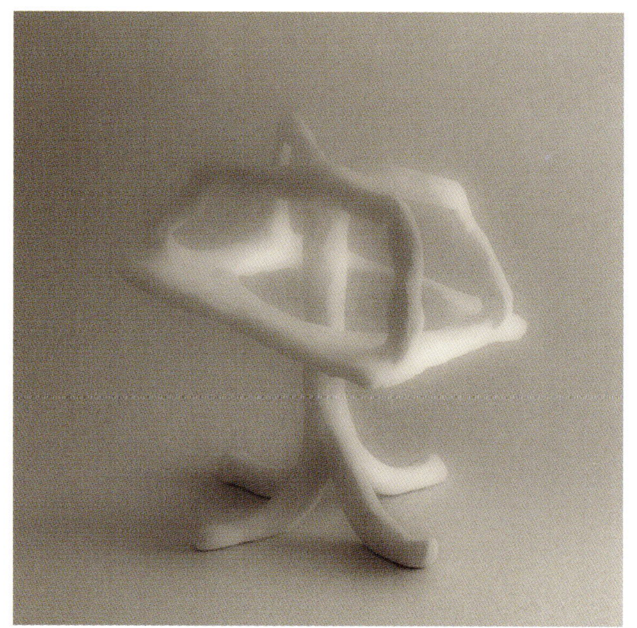

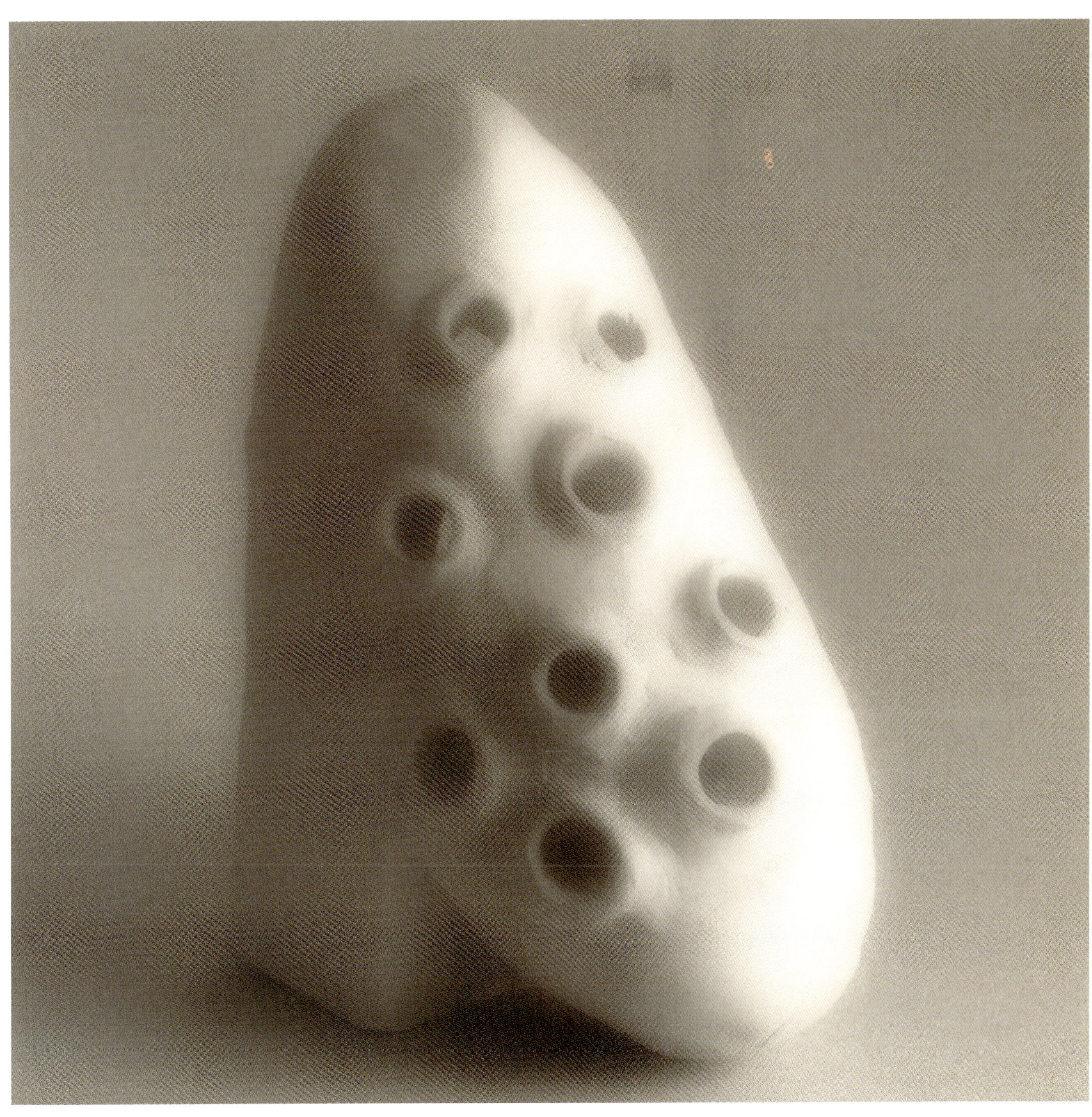

EQUIVALENTS

1993

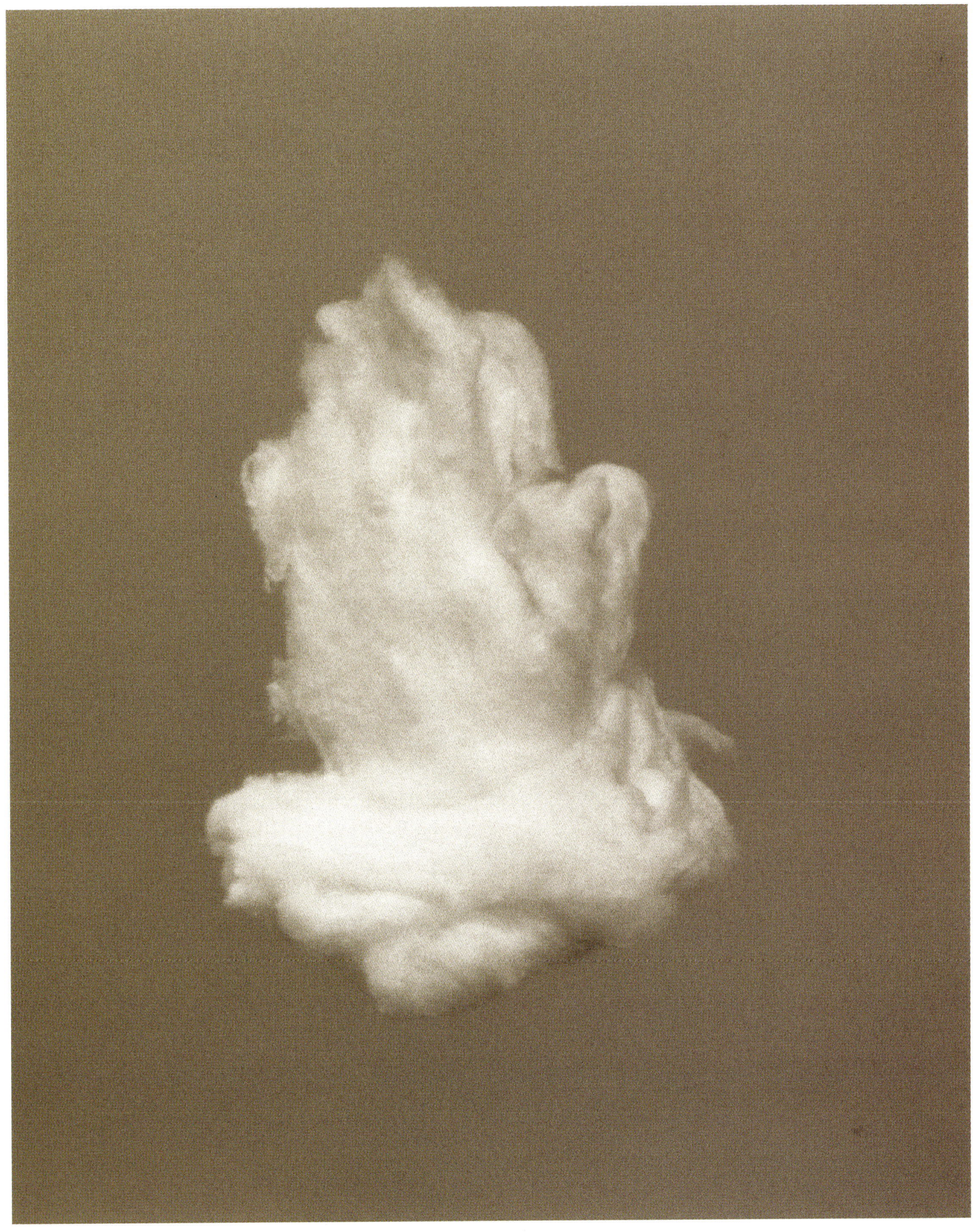

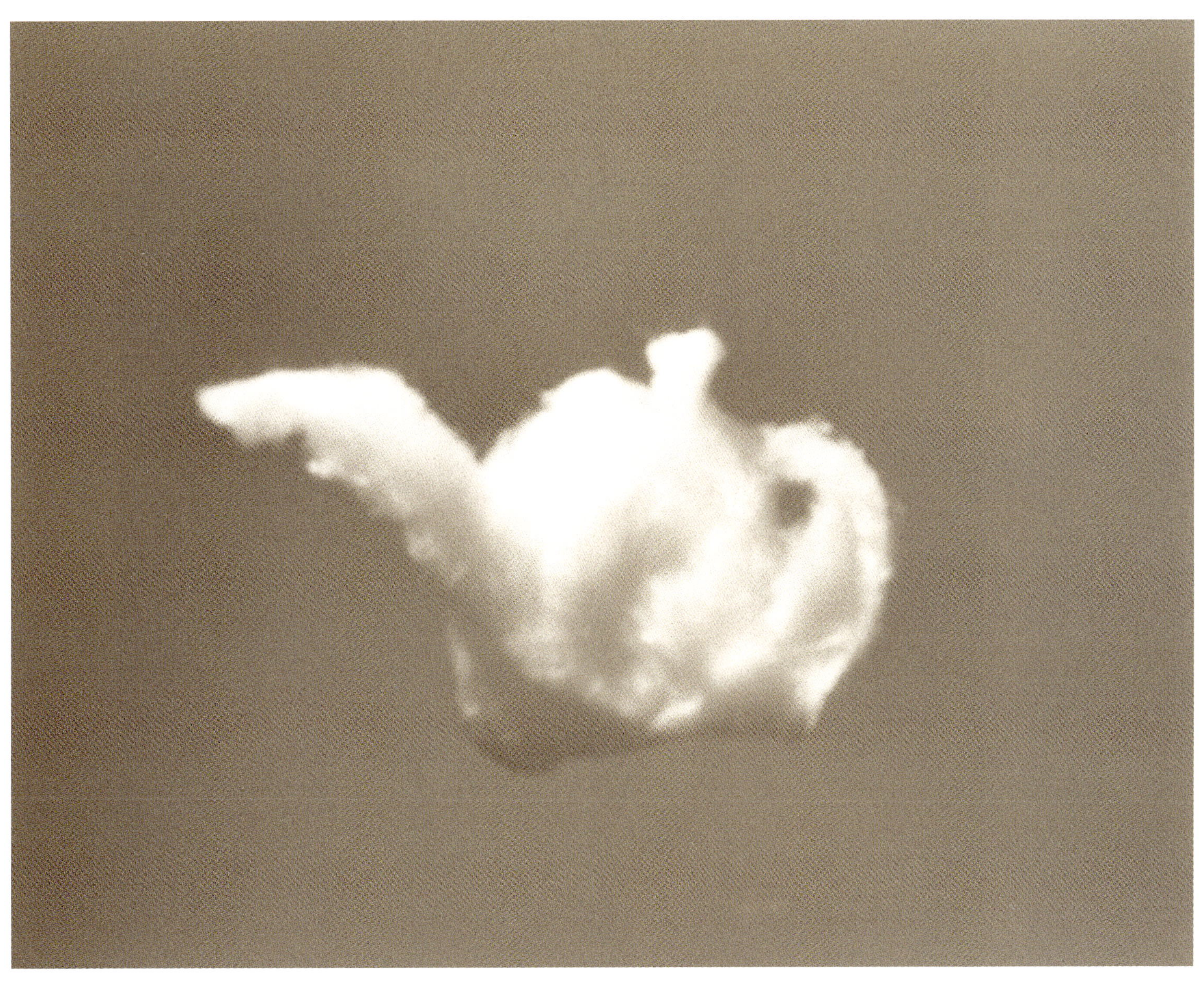

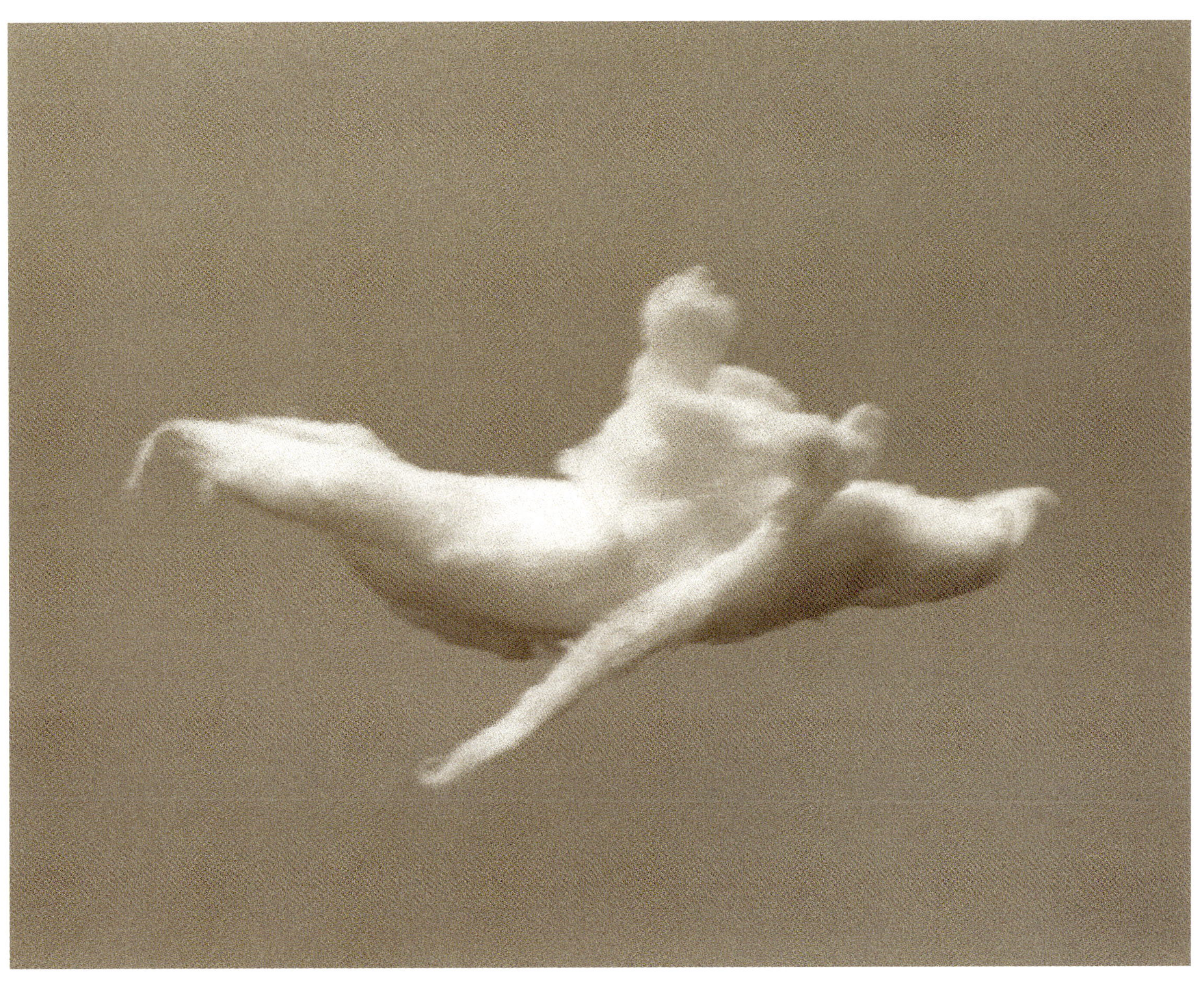

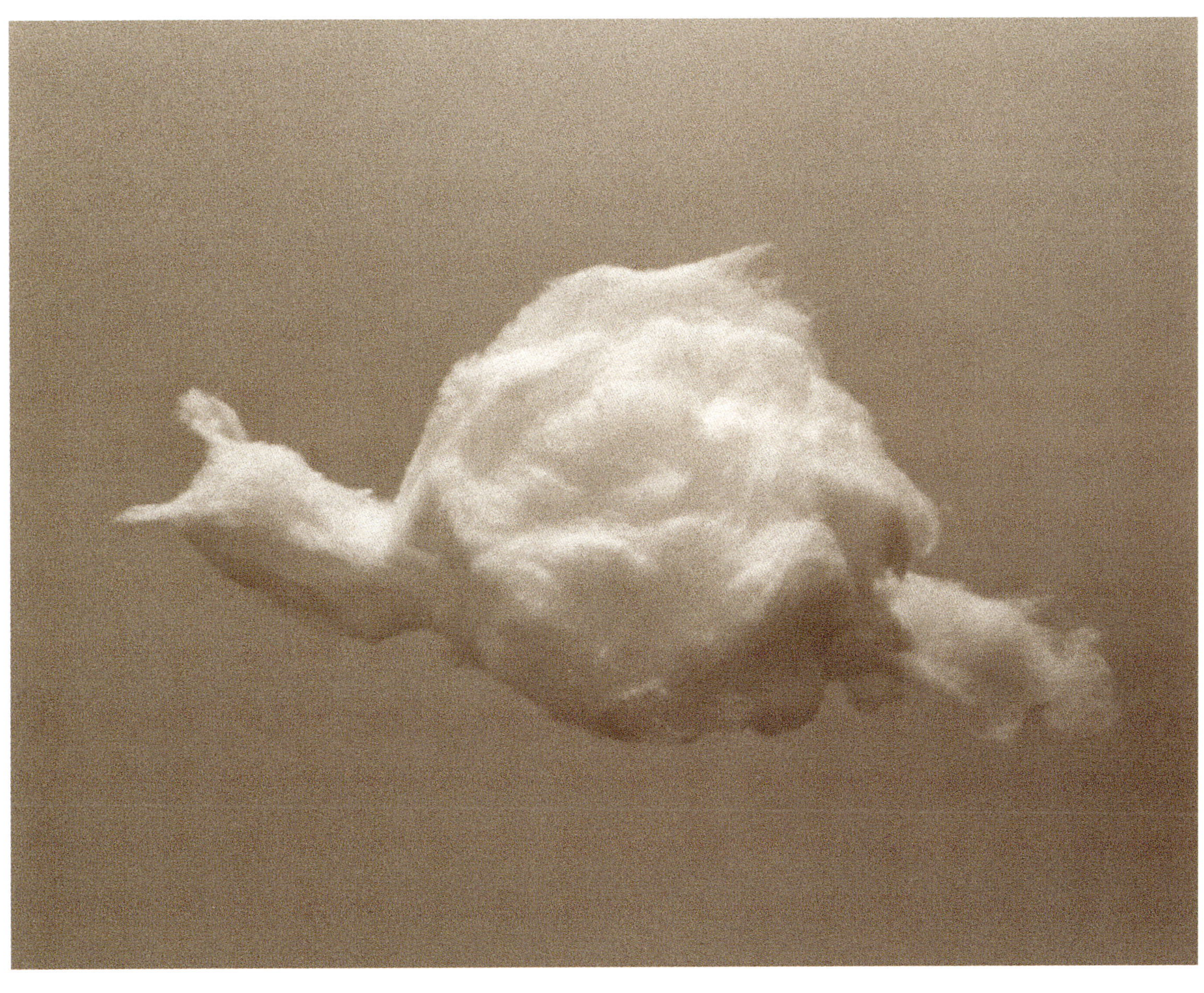

The Snail

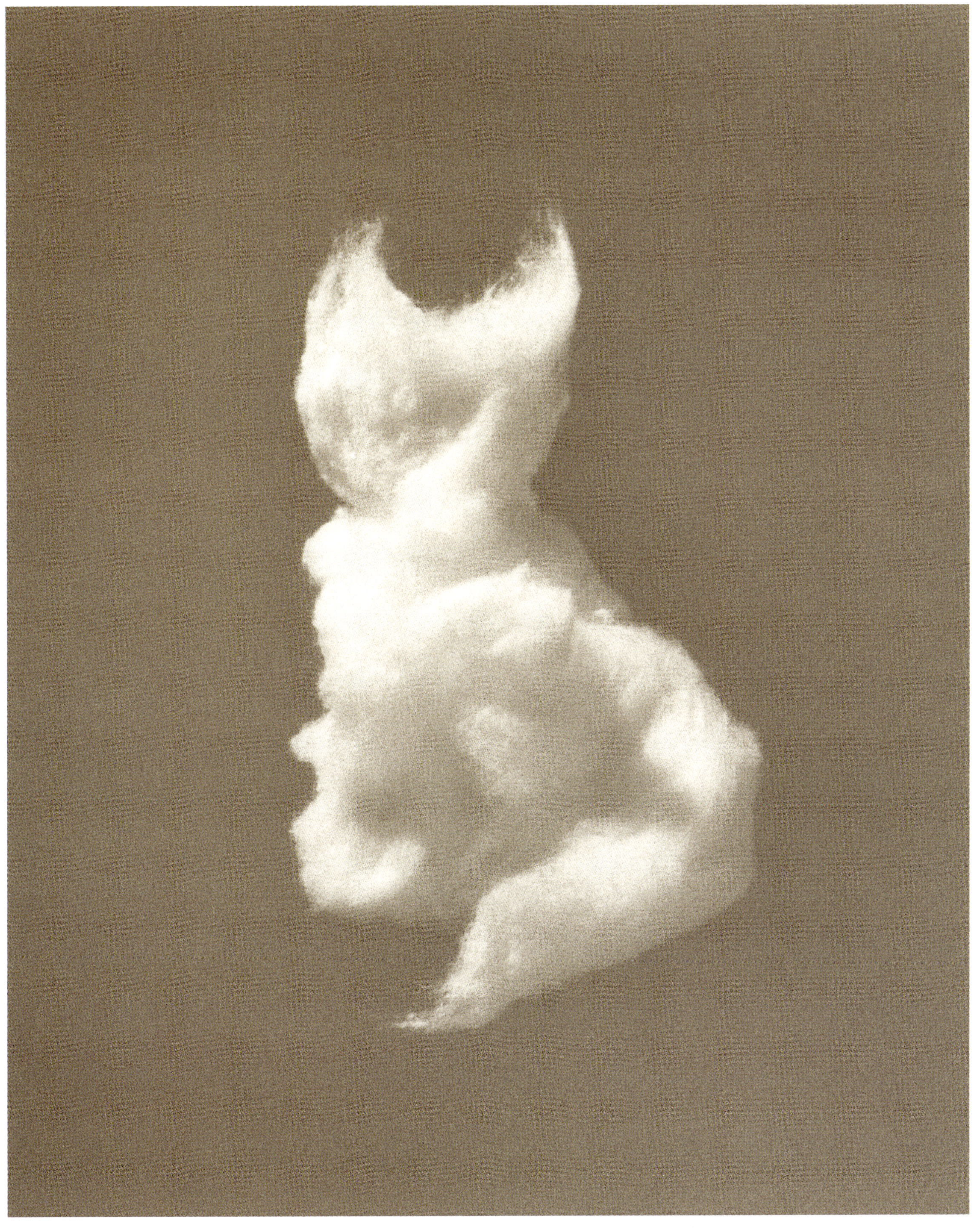

Kitty Cloud

PICTURES OF WIRE

1993–97

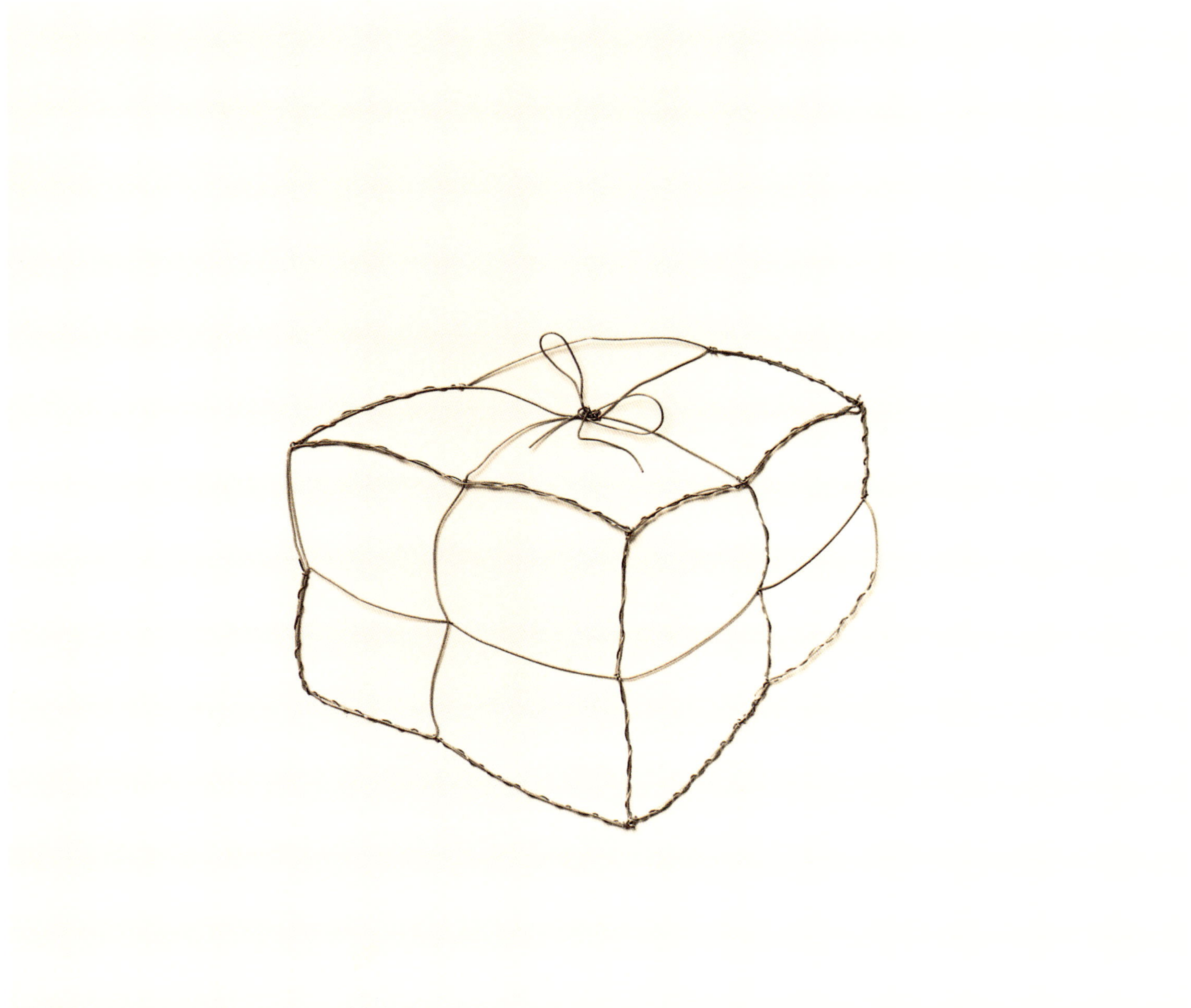

Parcel

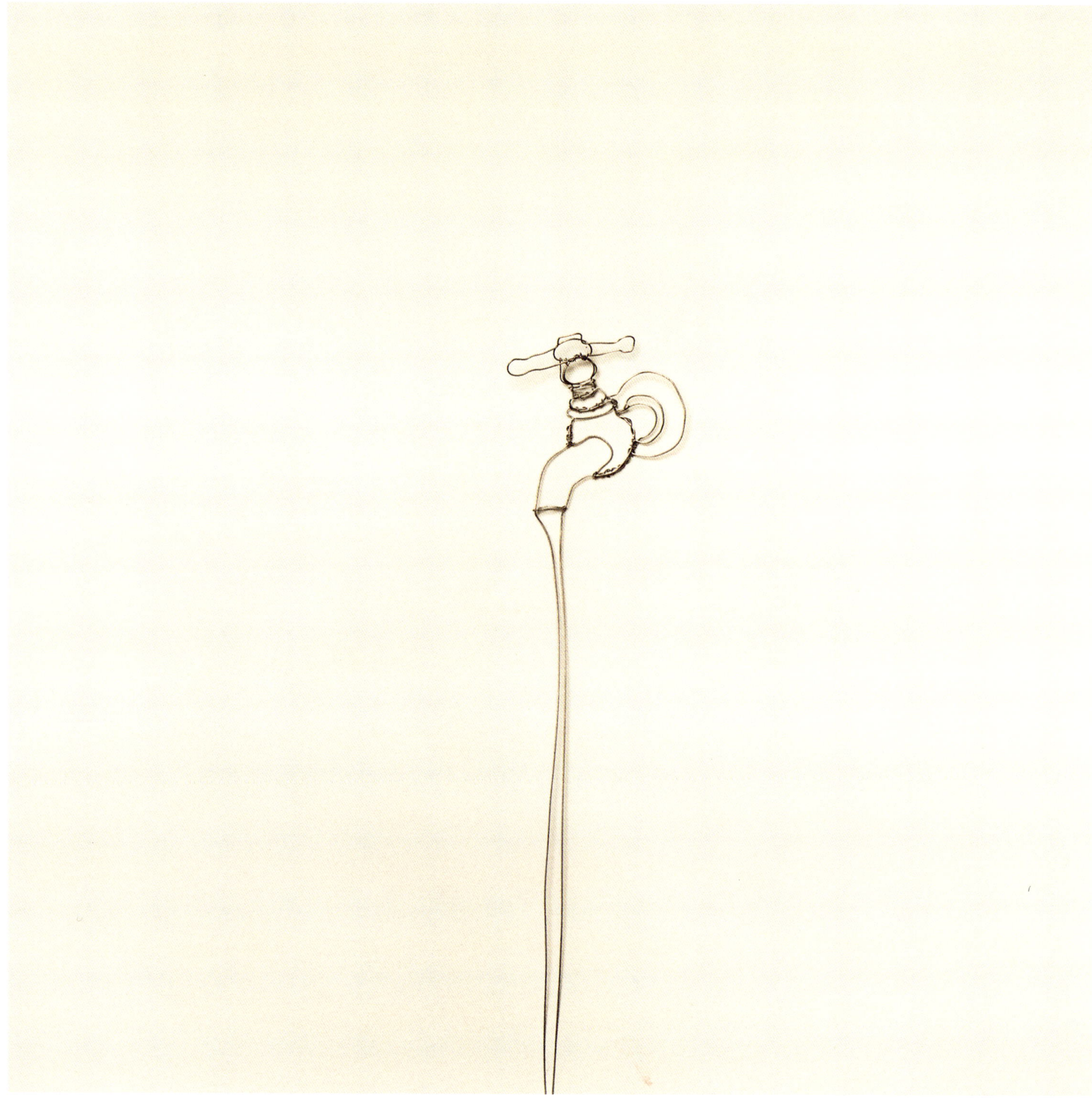

Faucet

Fiat Lux (Lightbulb)

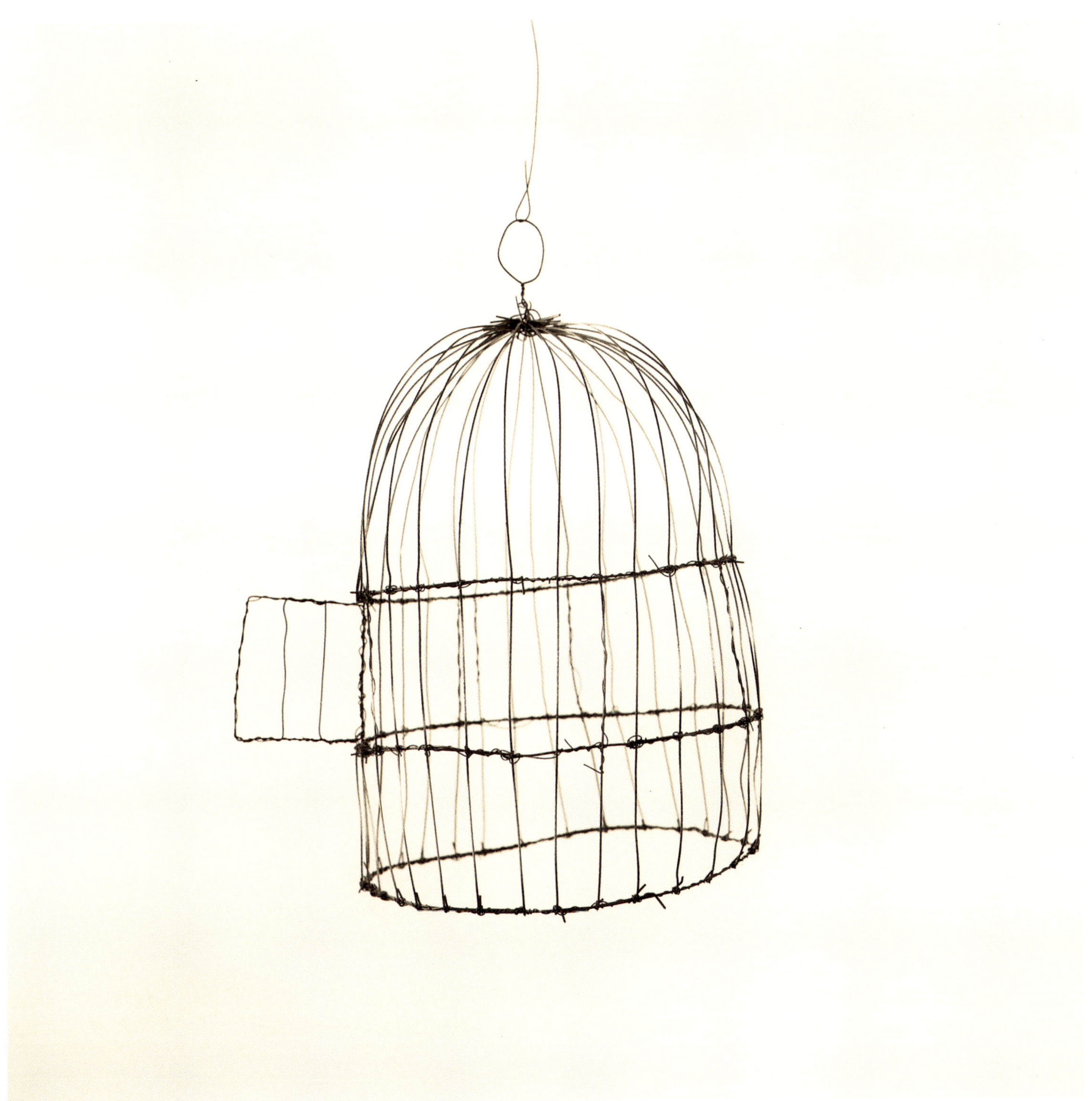

Cage

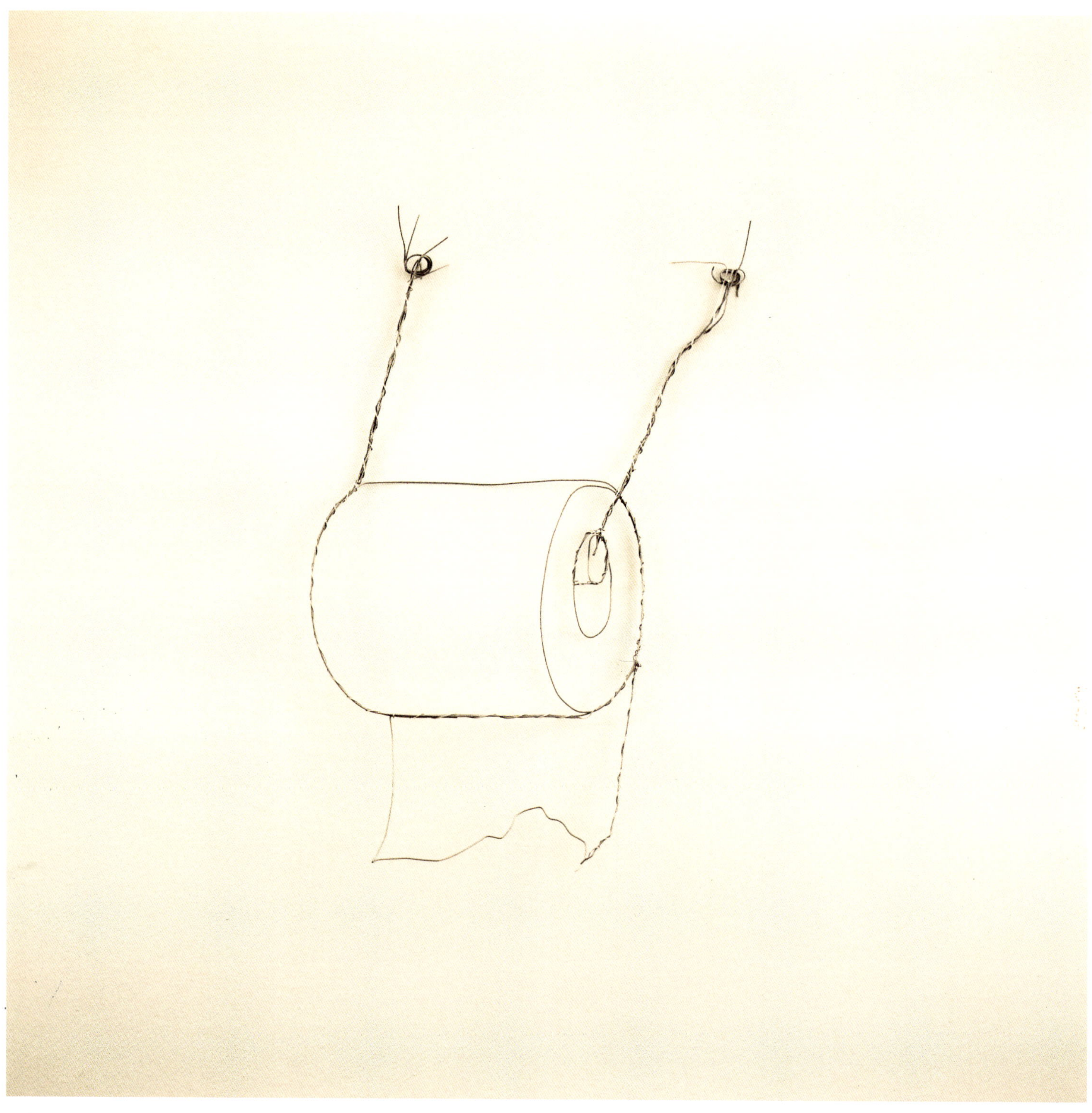

Paper and Wire 1

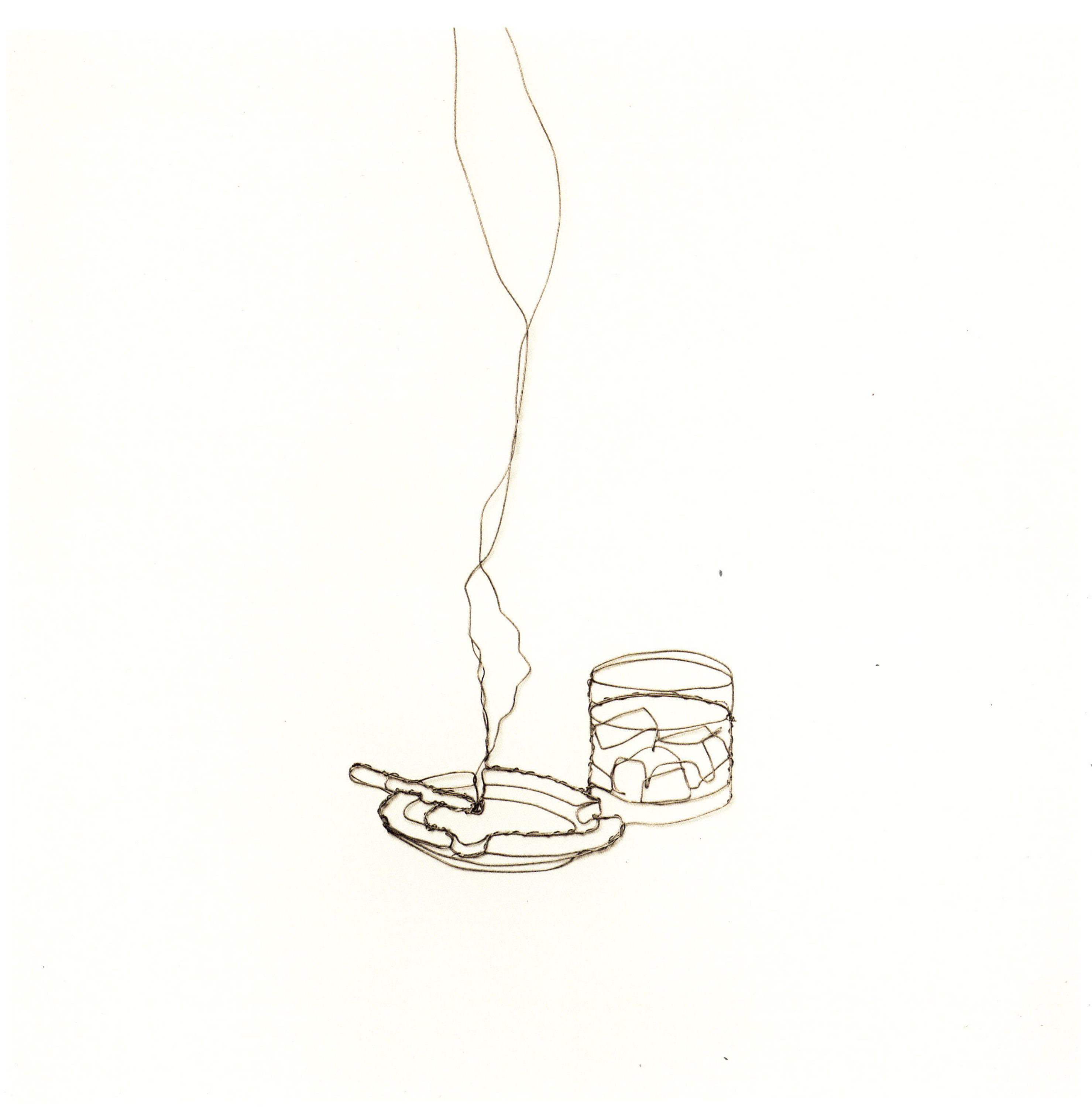

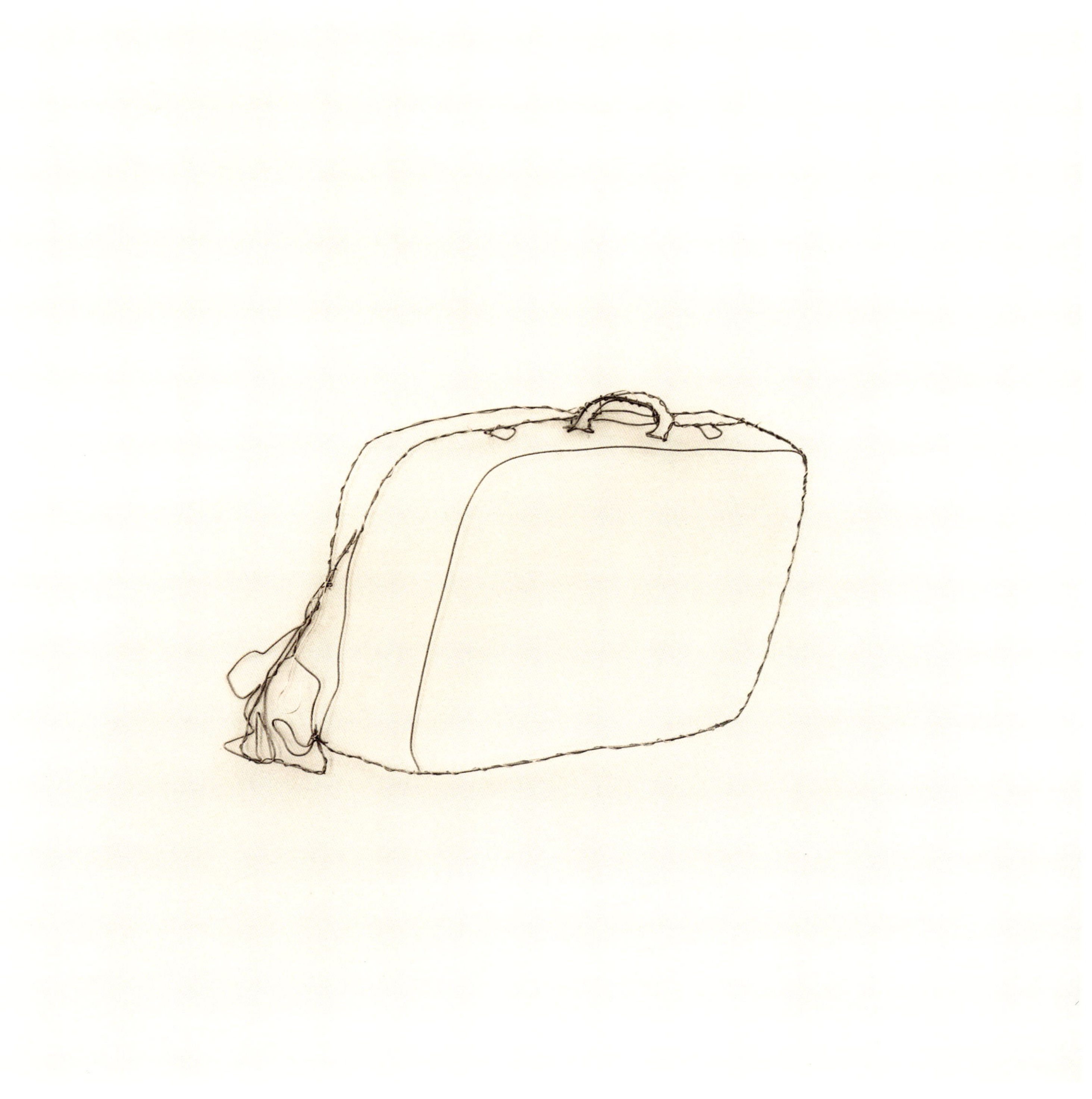

American Tourister (Suitcase)

Candle

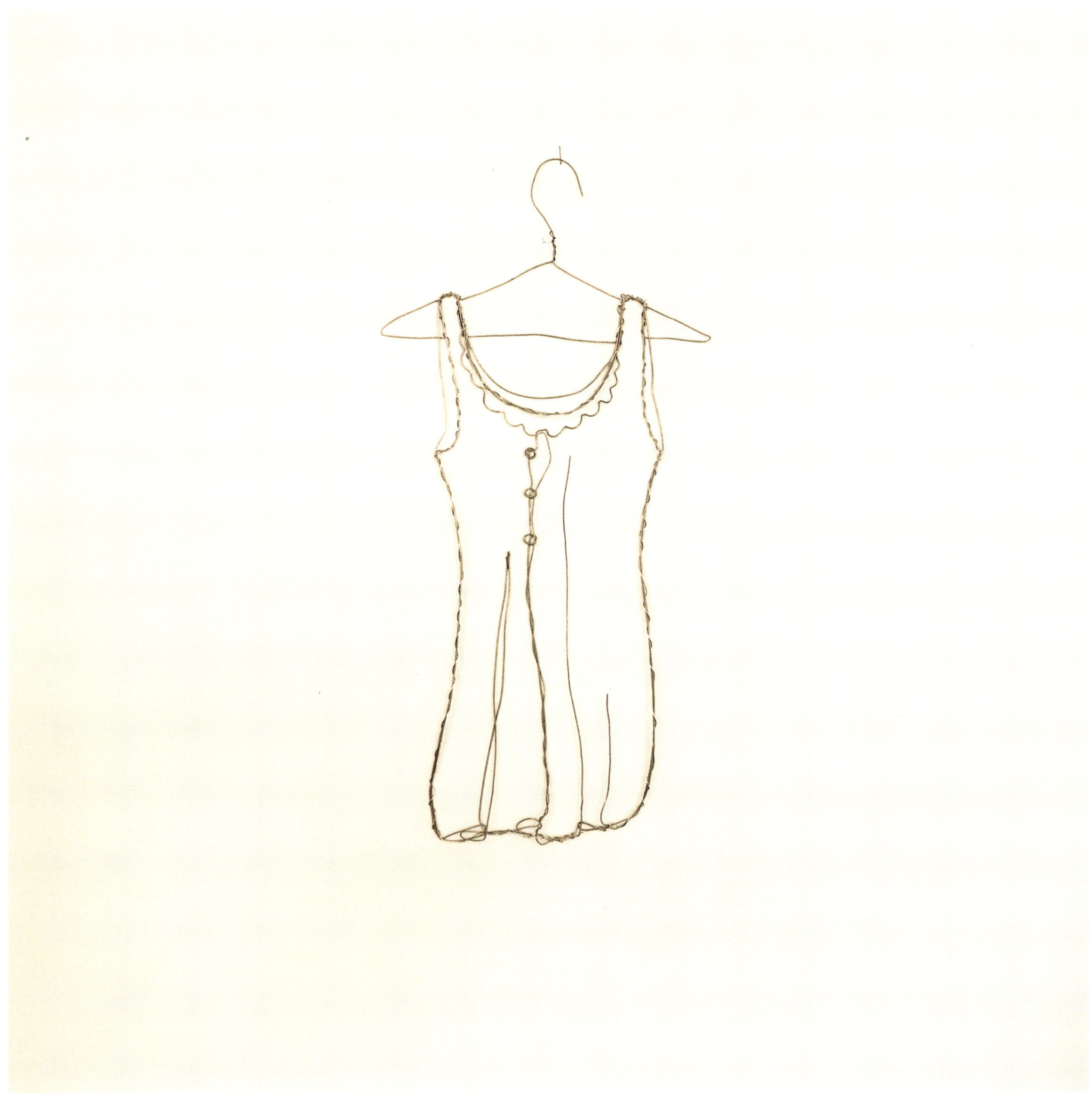

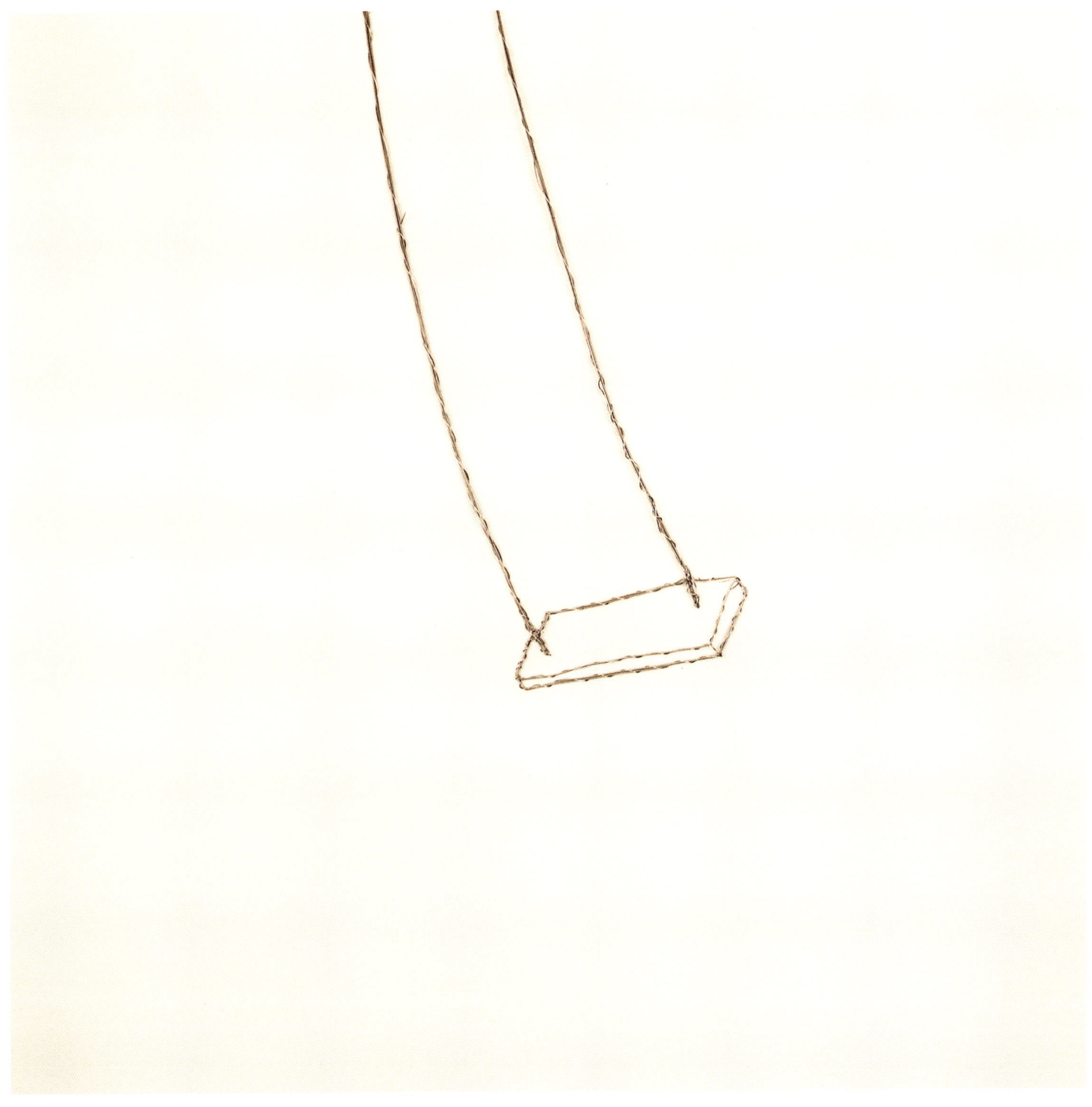

Wind (Swing)

SHADOWGRAMS (X-RAYS)

1993–94

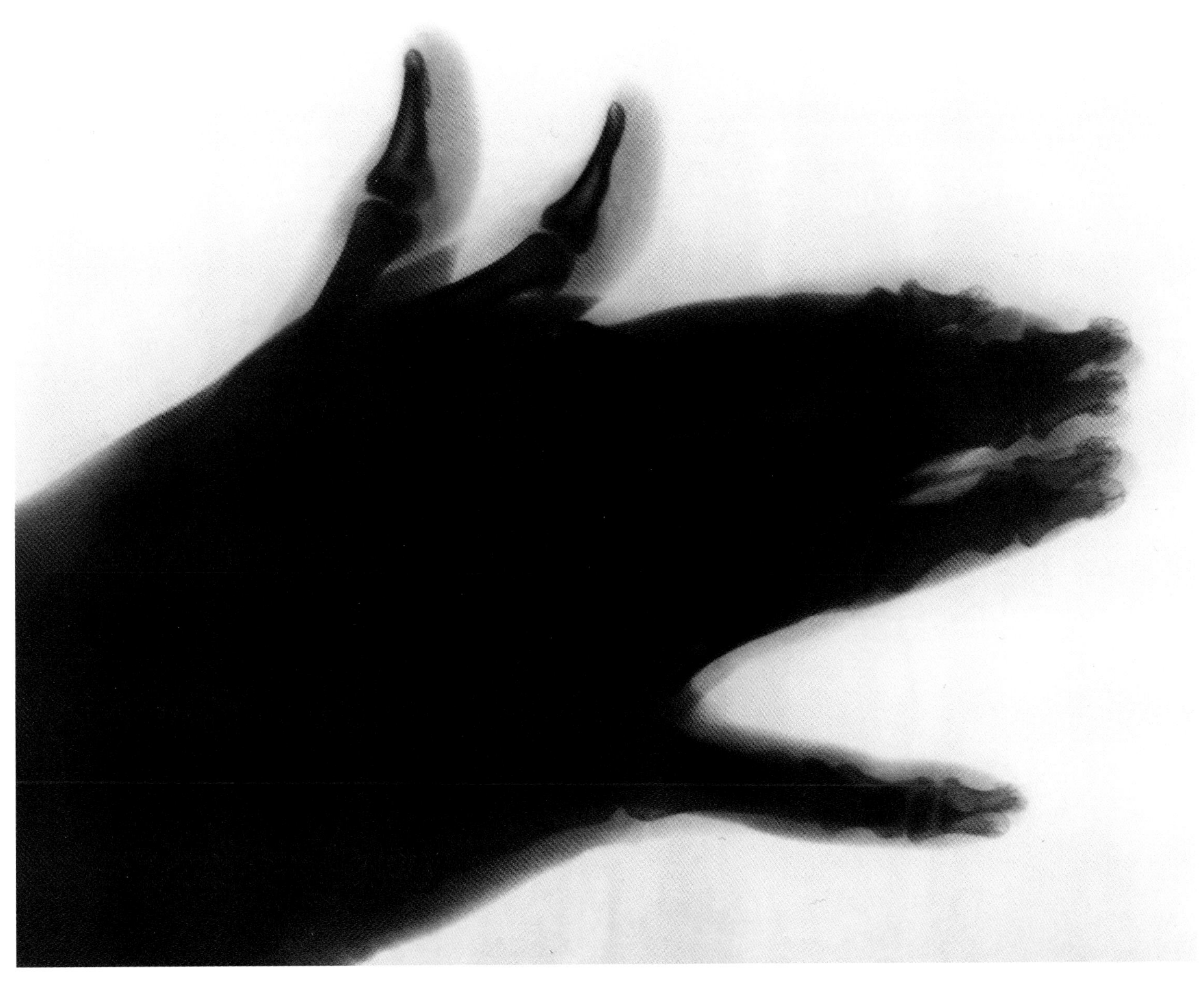

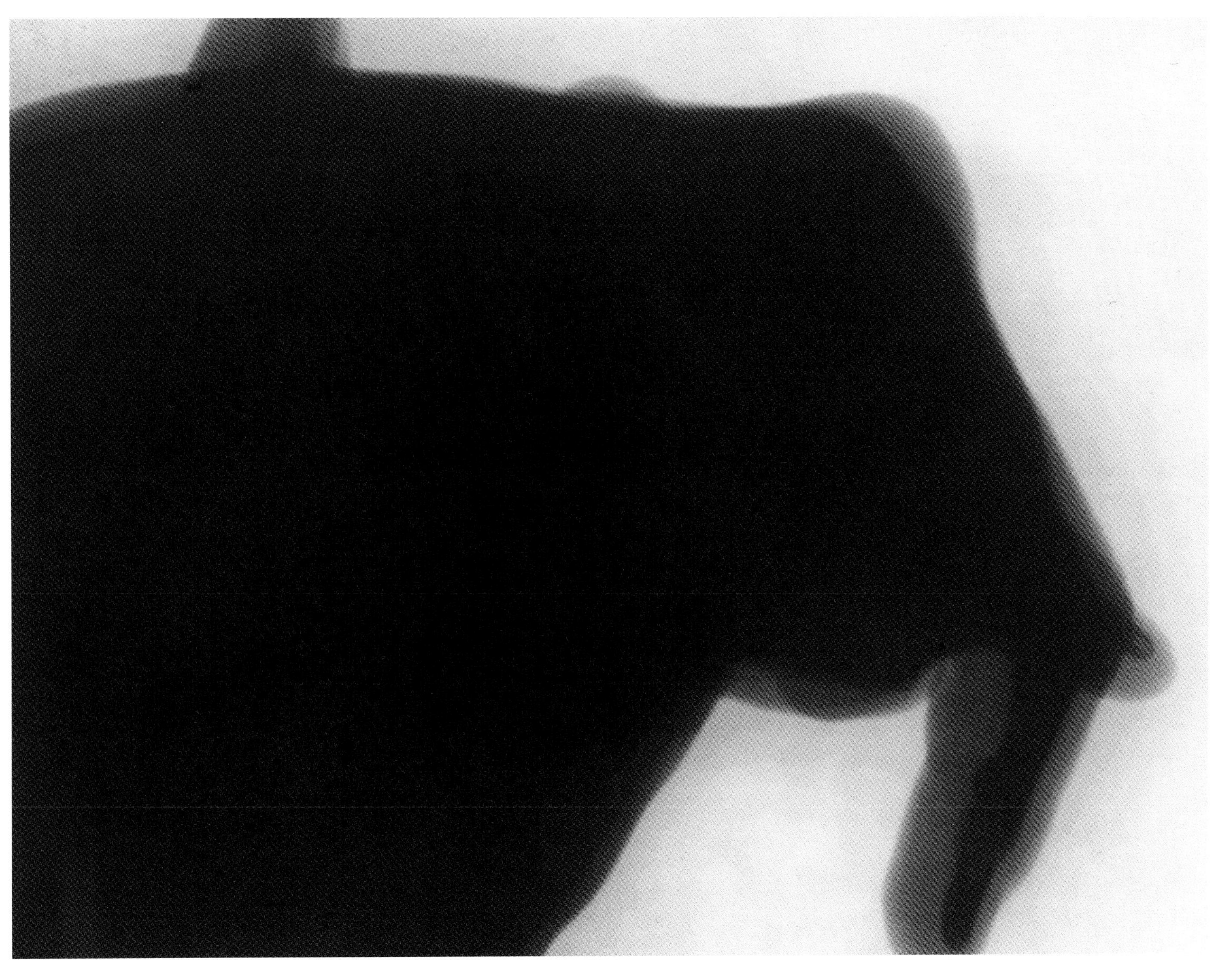

PICTURES OF THREAD

1995–98

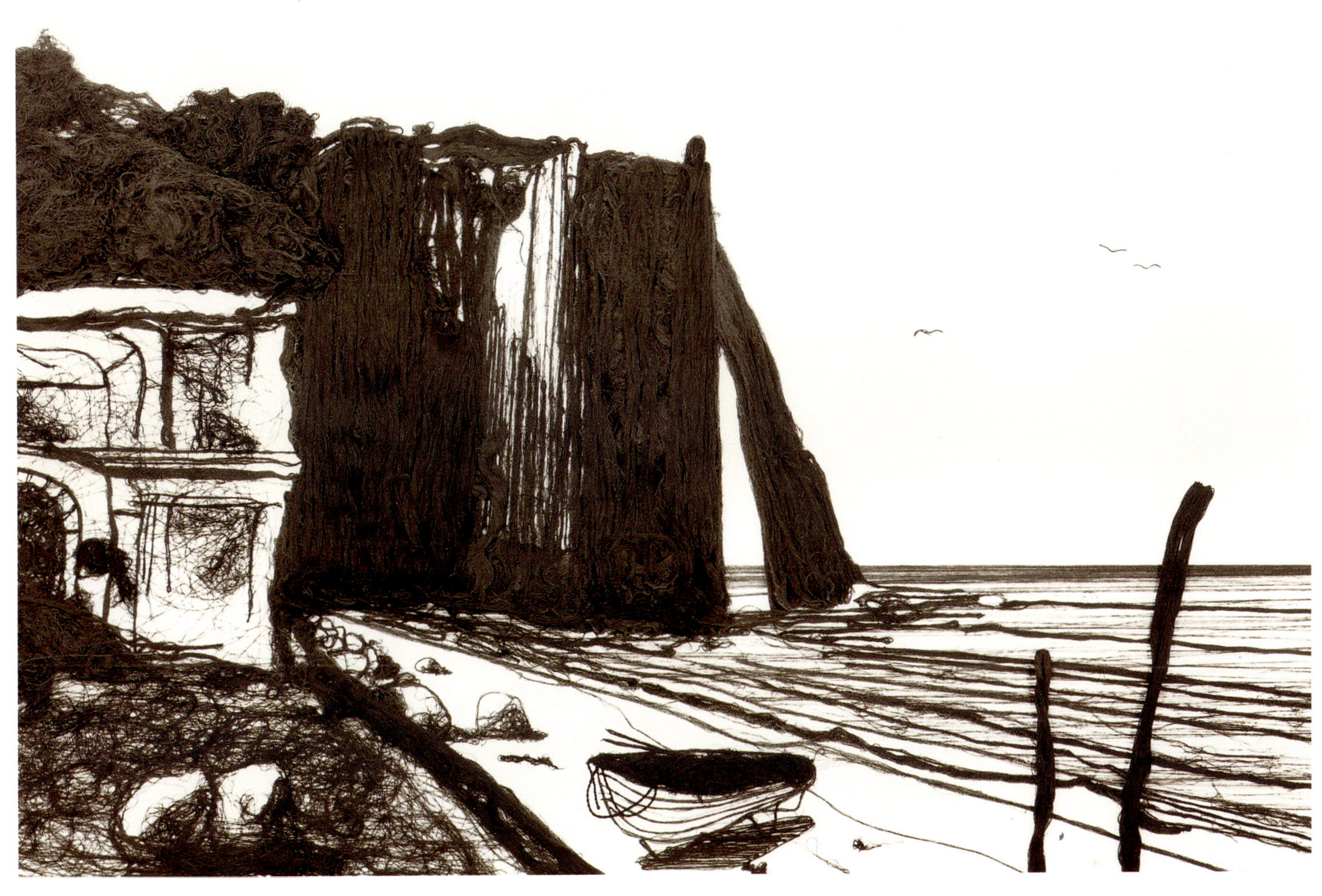

12,000 Yards (Etretat, after Courbet)

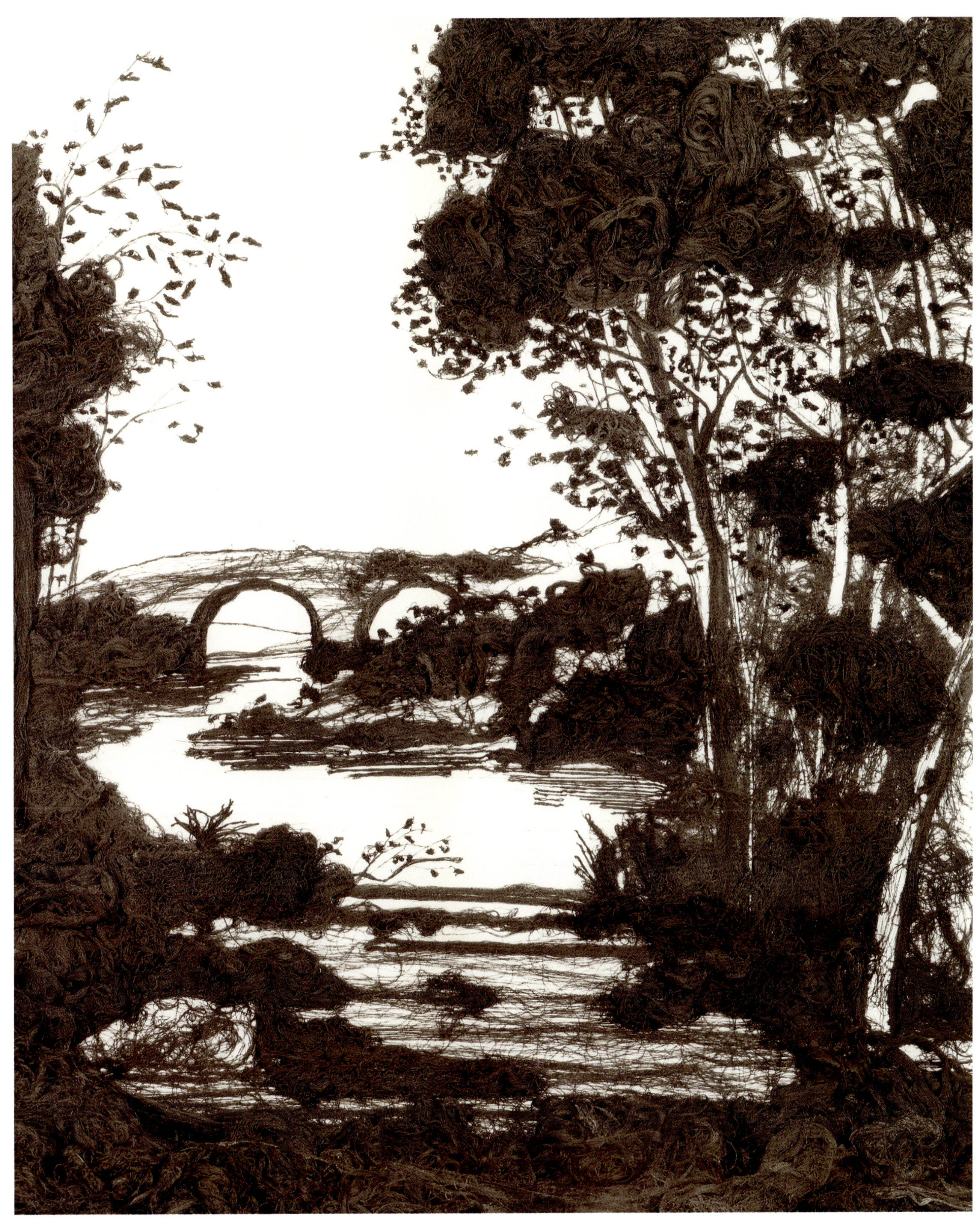

17,500 Yards (Landscape without an Angel, after Hagar and the Angel by Claude Lorrain)

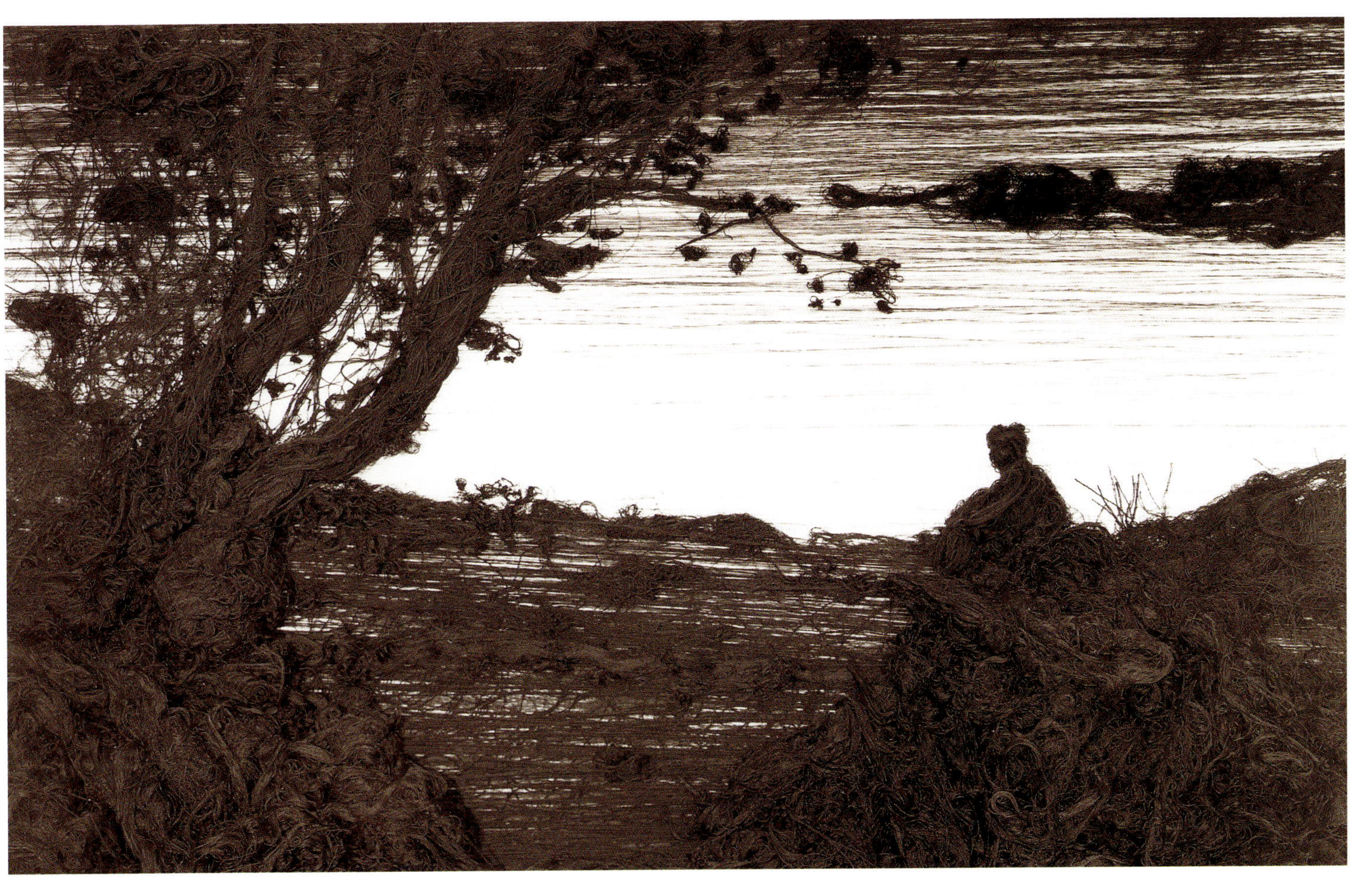

16,000 Yards (Le Songeur, after Corot)

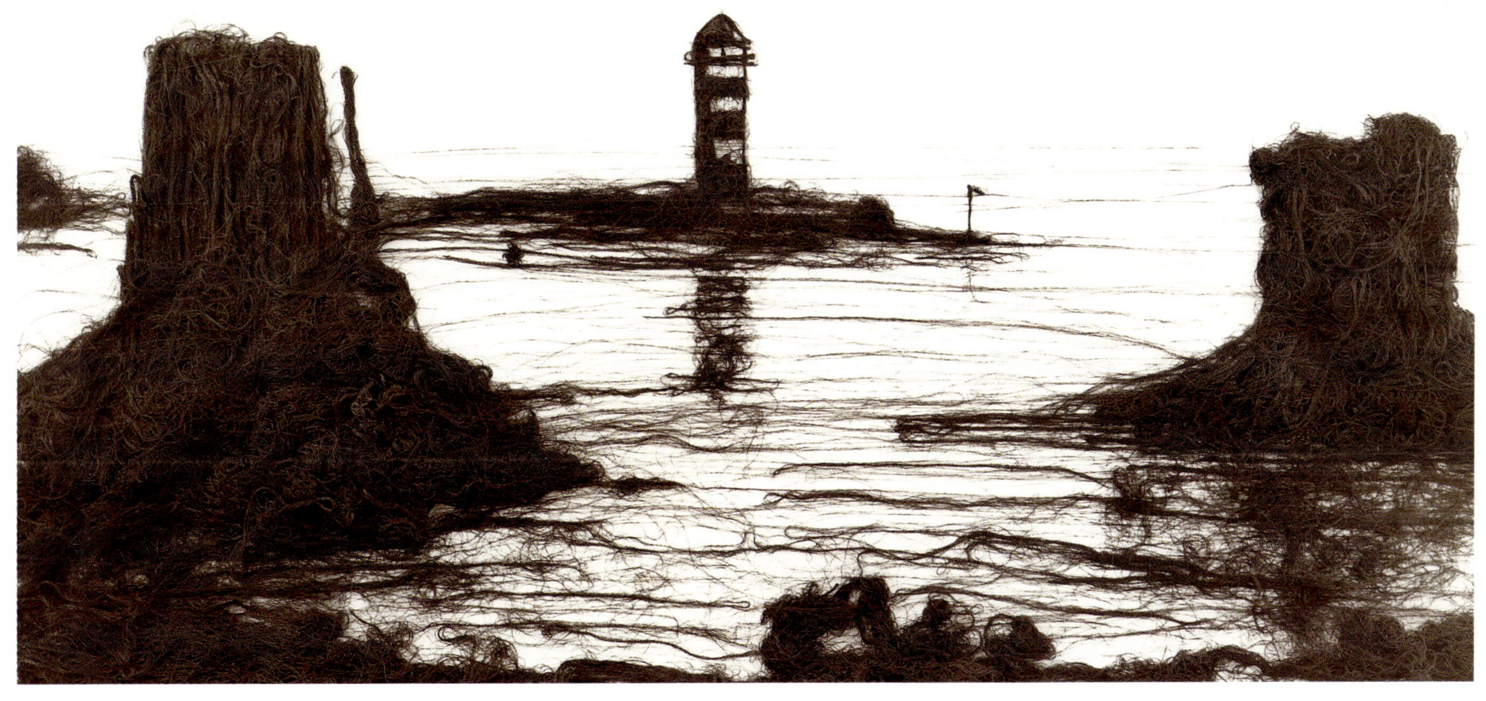

6,200 Yards (Lighthouse)

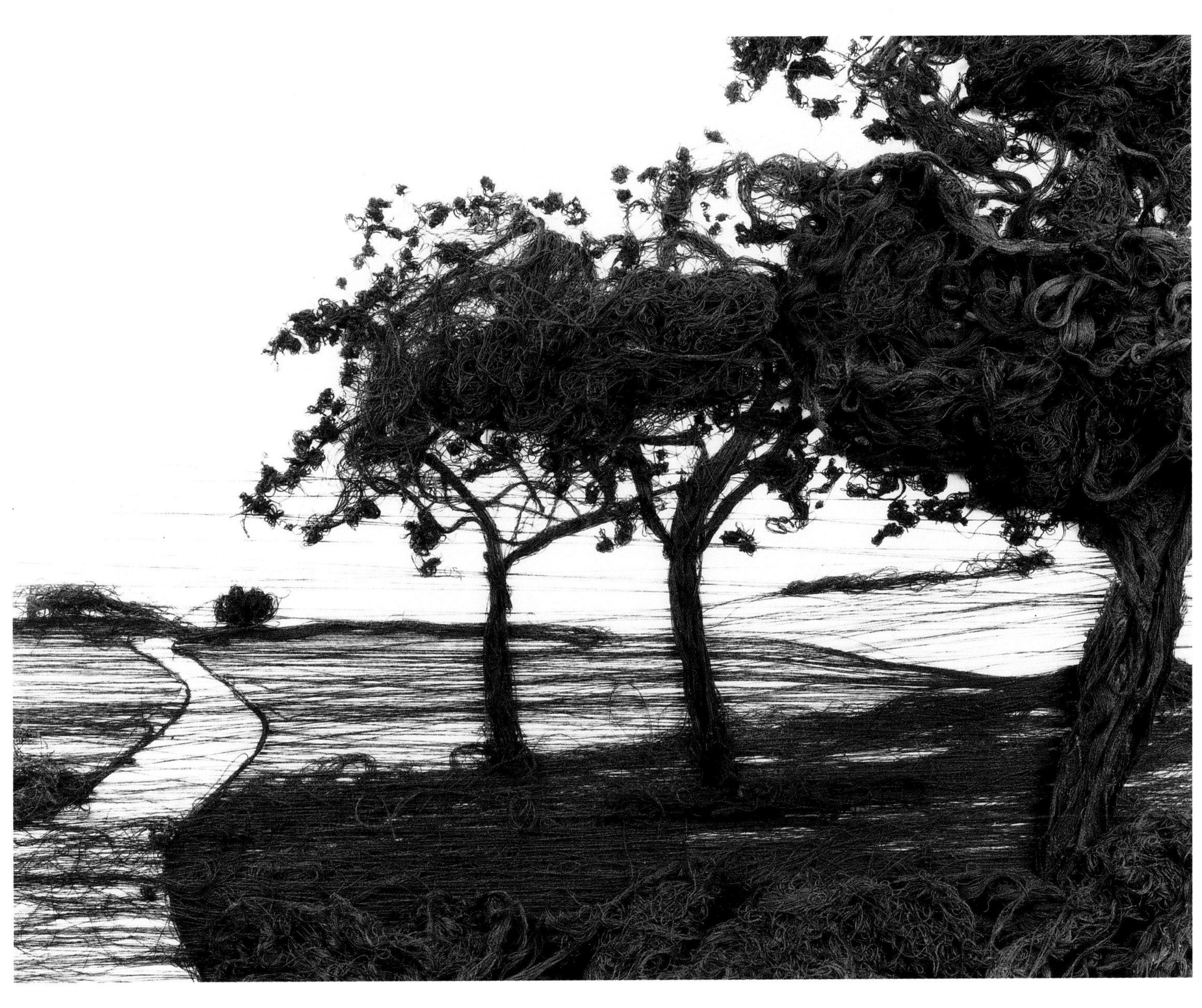

4,000 Yards (Apple Trees, after Gerhard Richter)

PICTURES OF HOLES

1997

Right: *702 Holes*

p. 100: *525 Holes*

p. 101: *637 Holes*

p. 102: *800 Holes*

p. 103: *848 Holes*

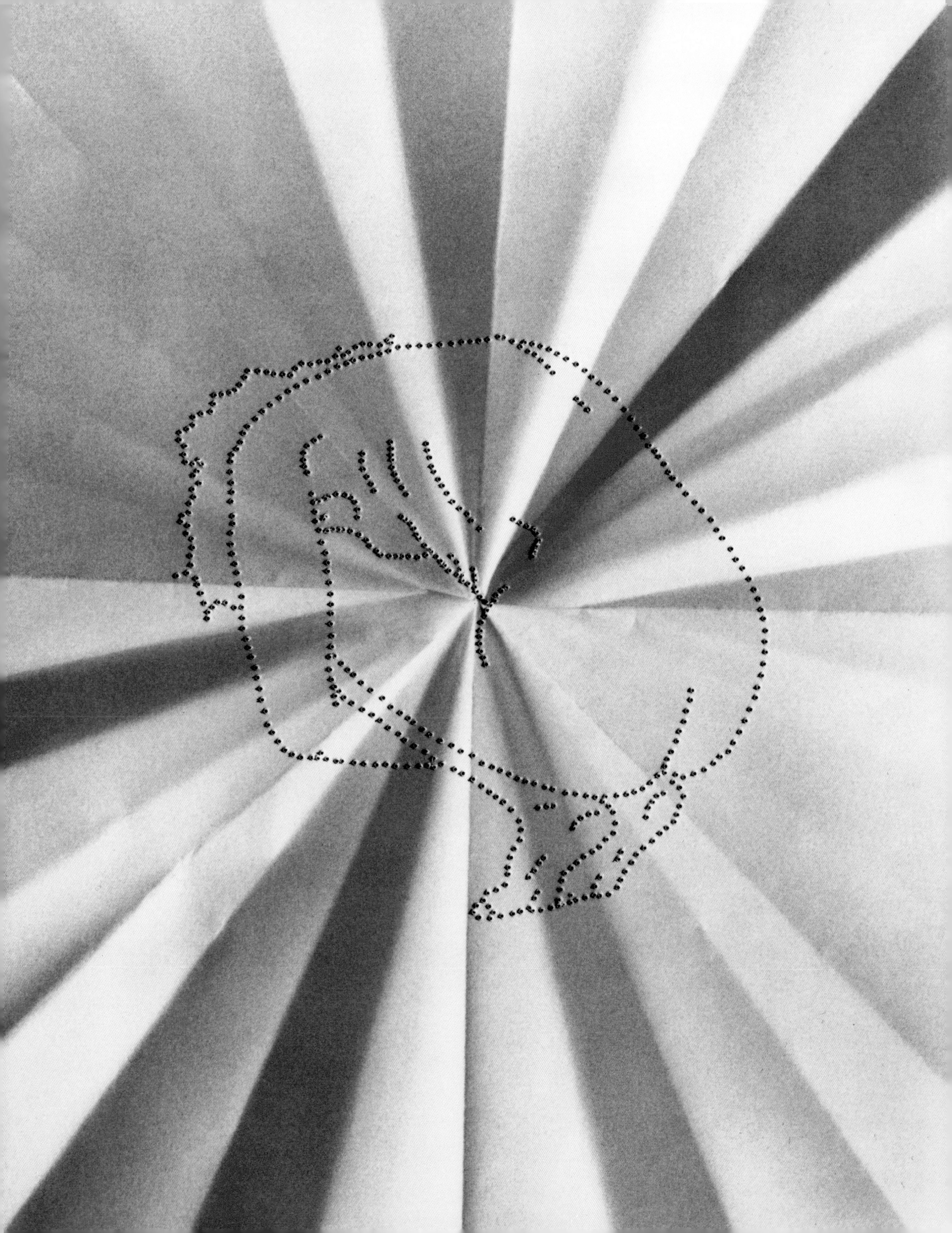

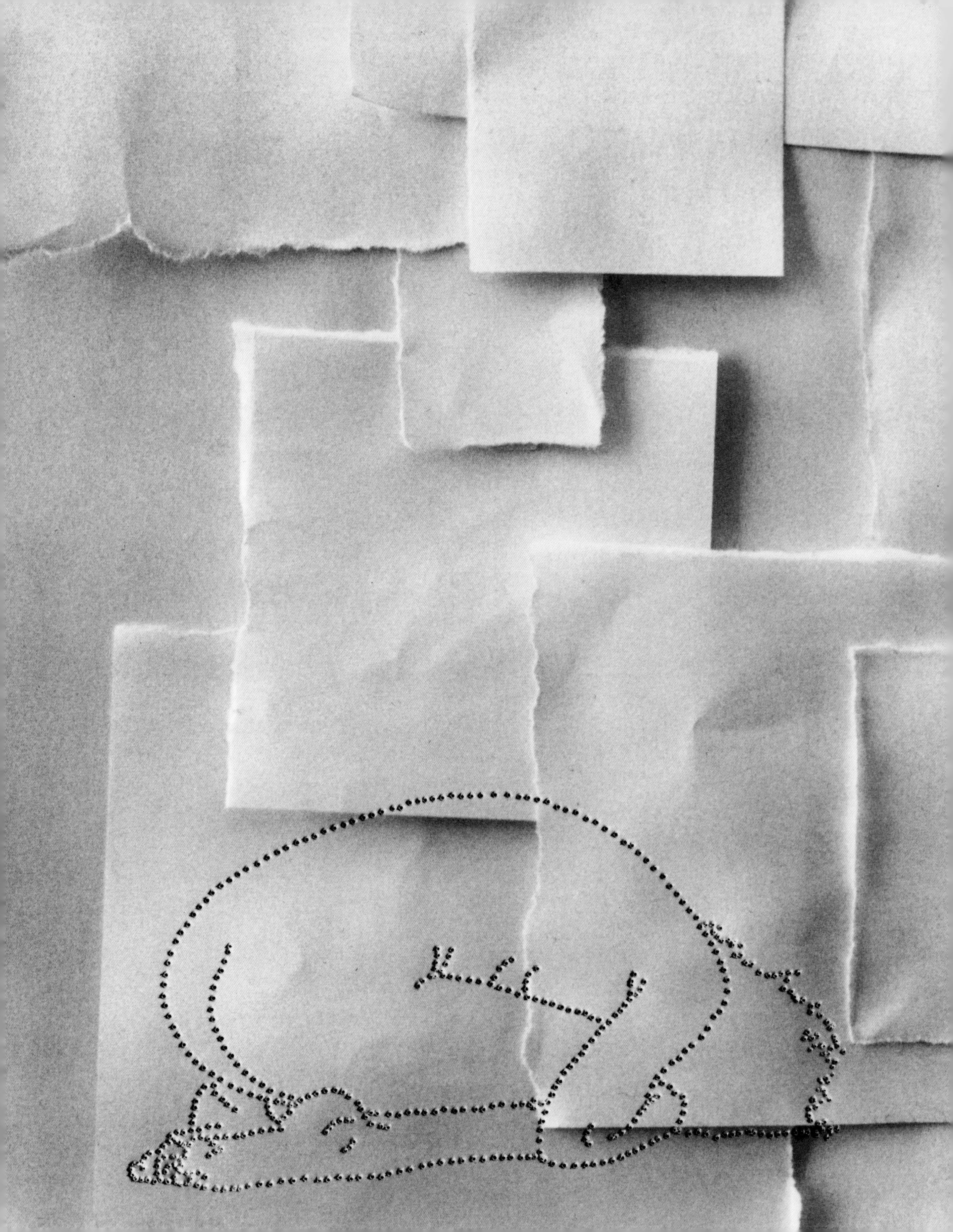

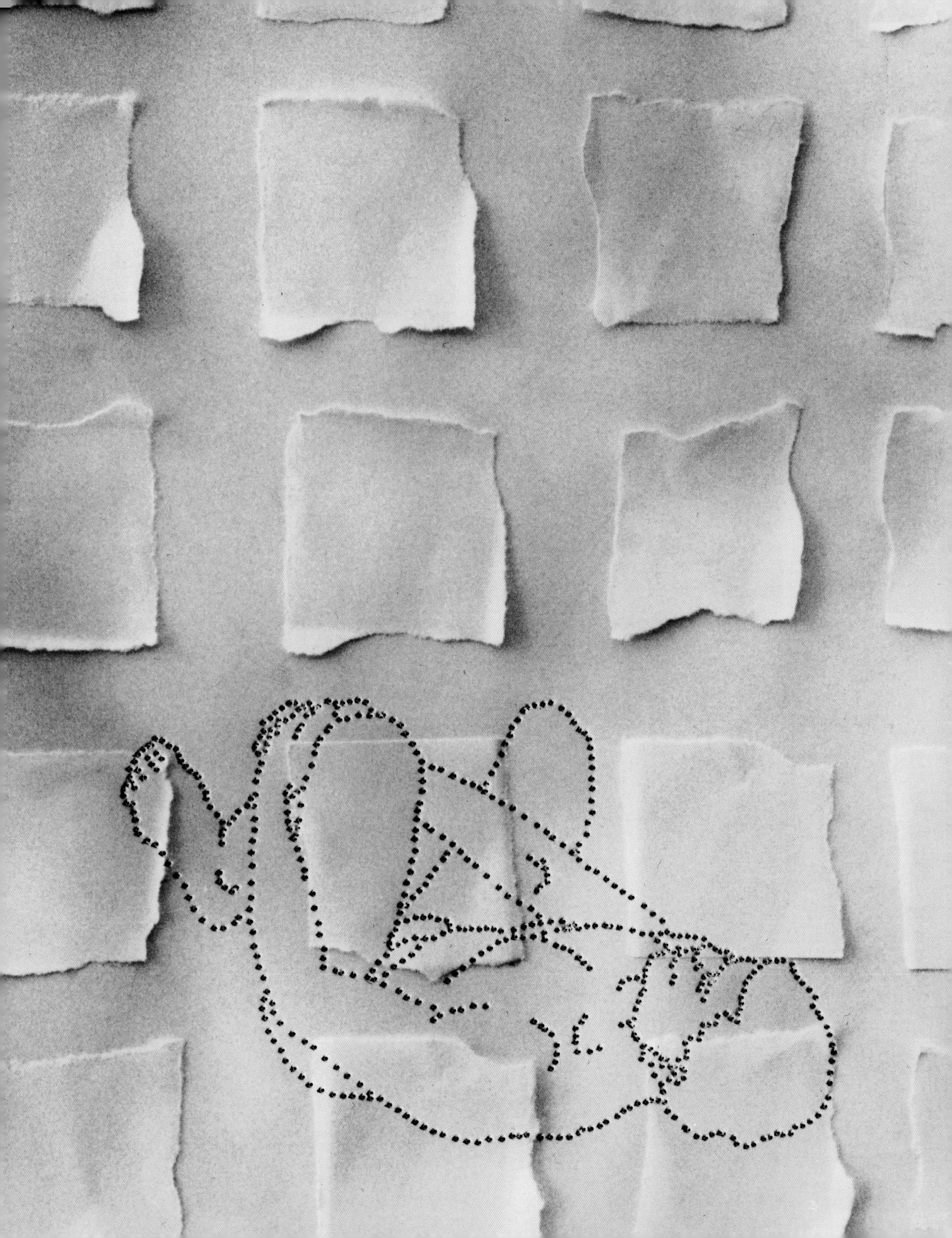

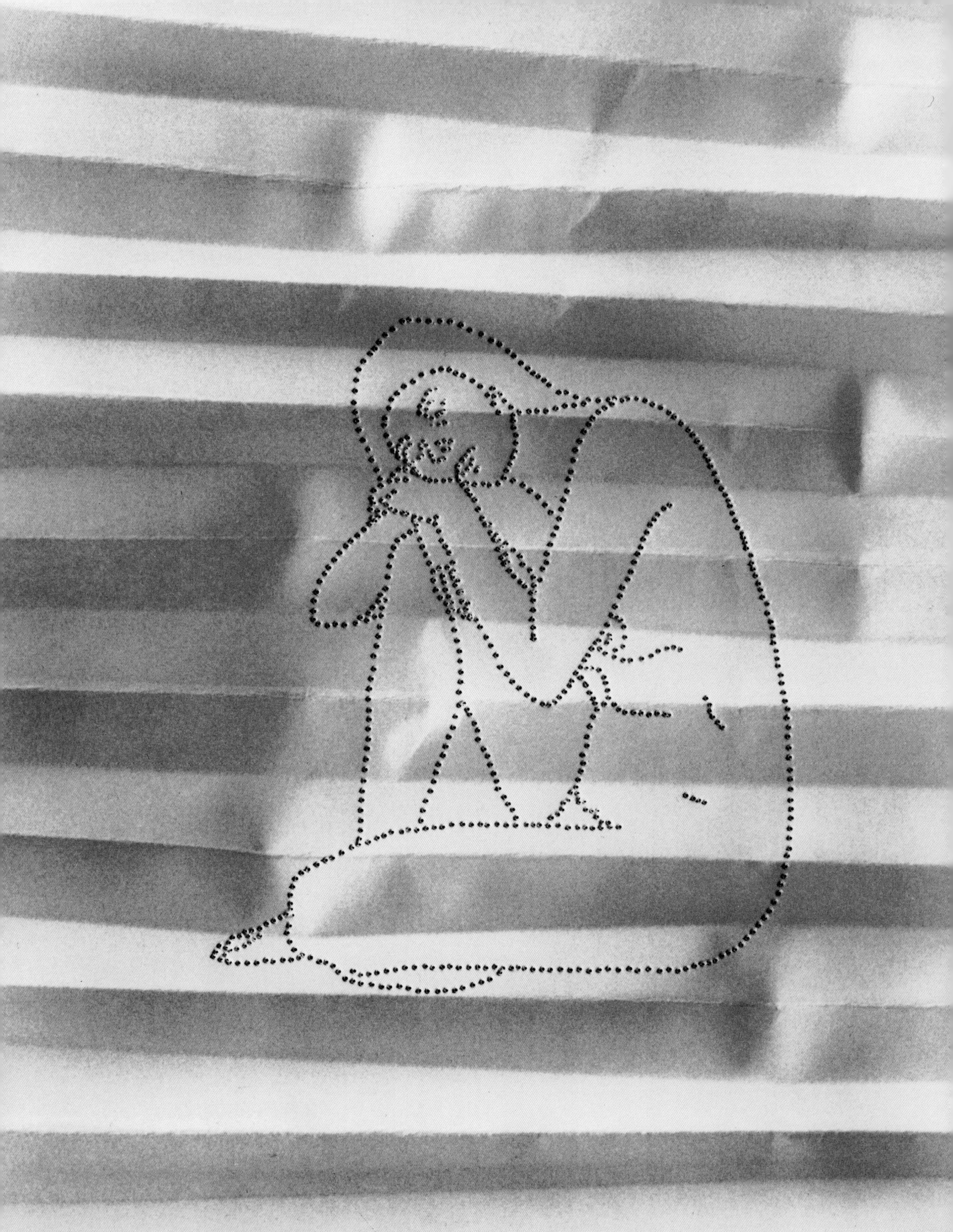

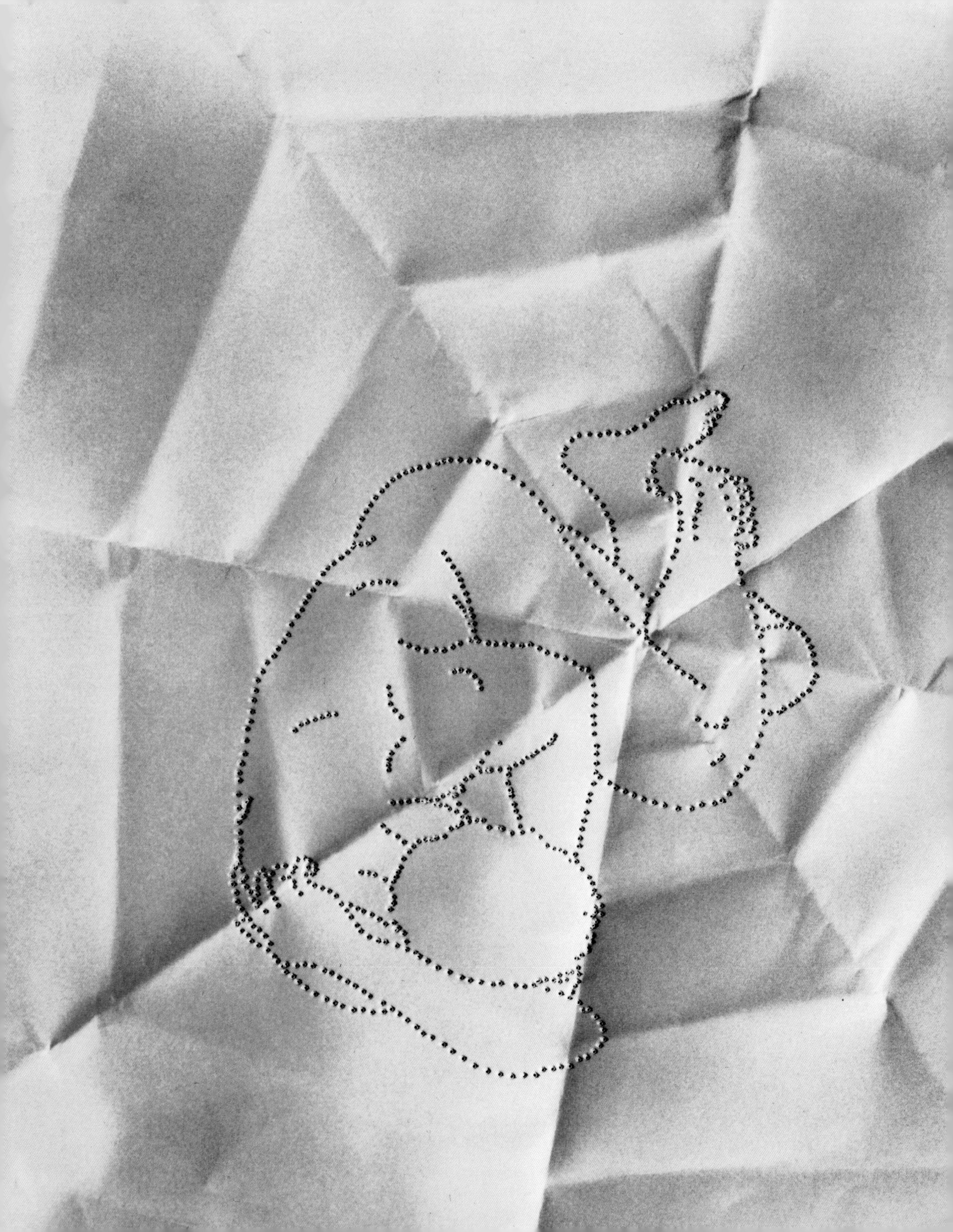

THE SUGAR CHILDREN

1996

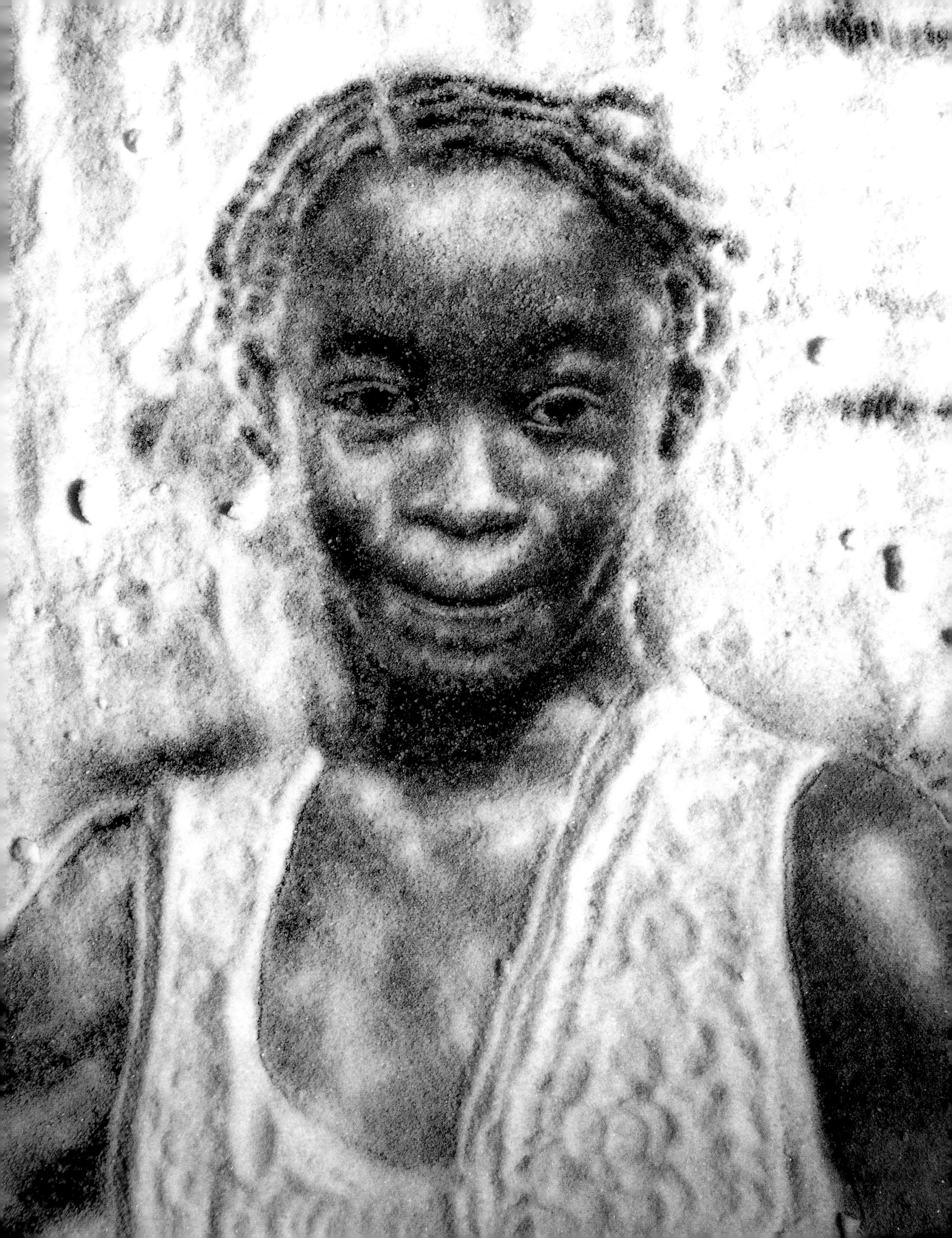

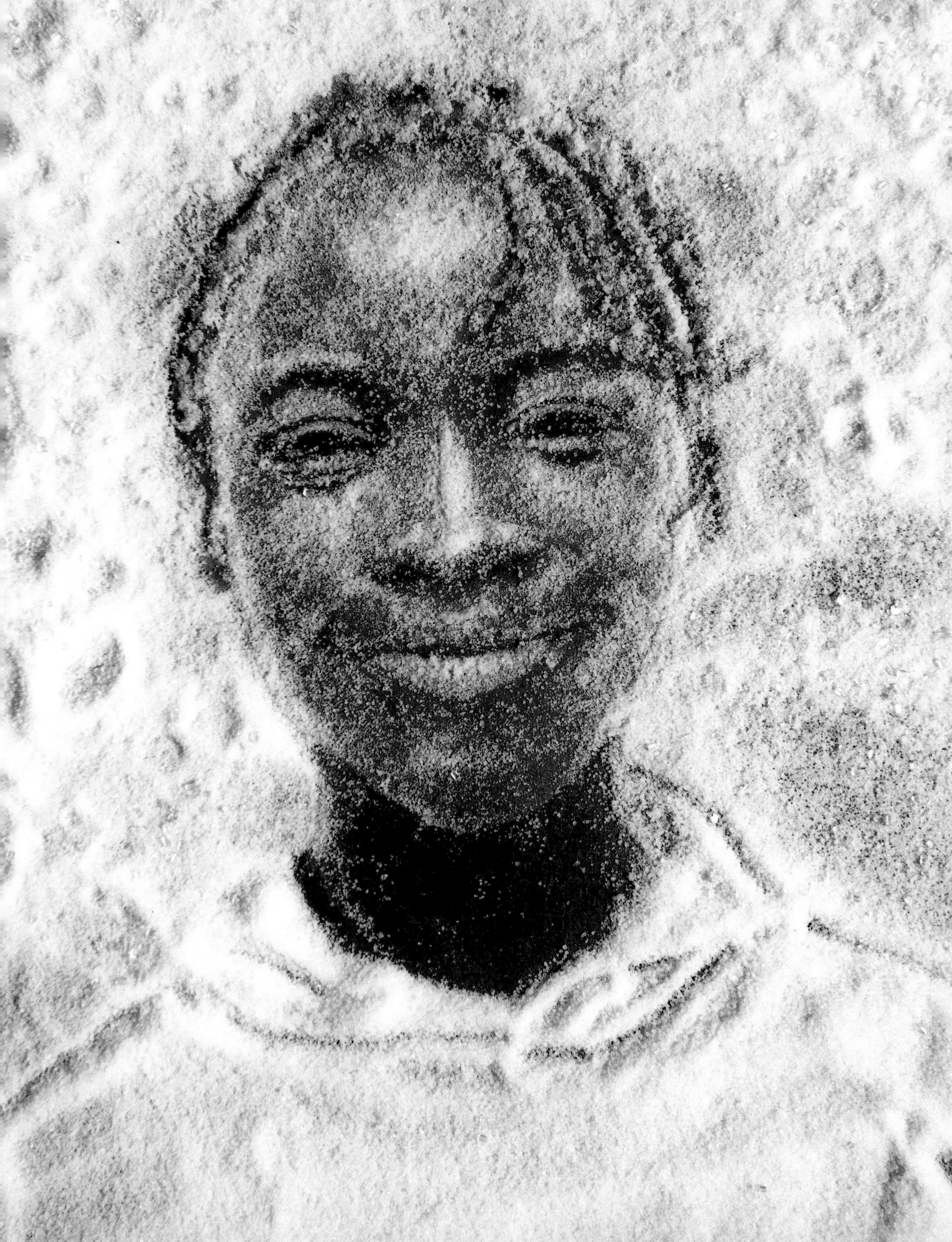

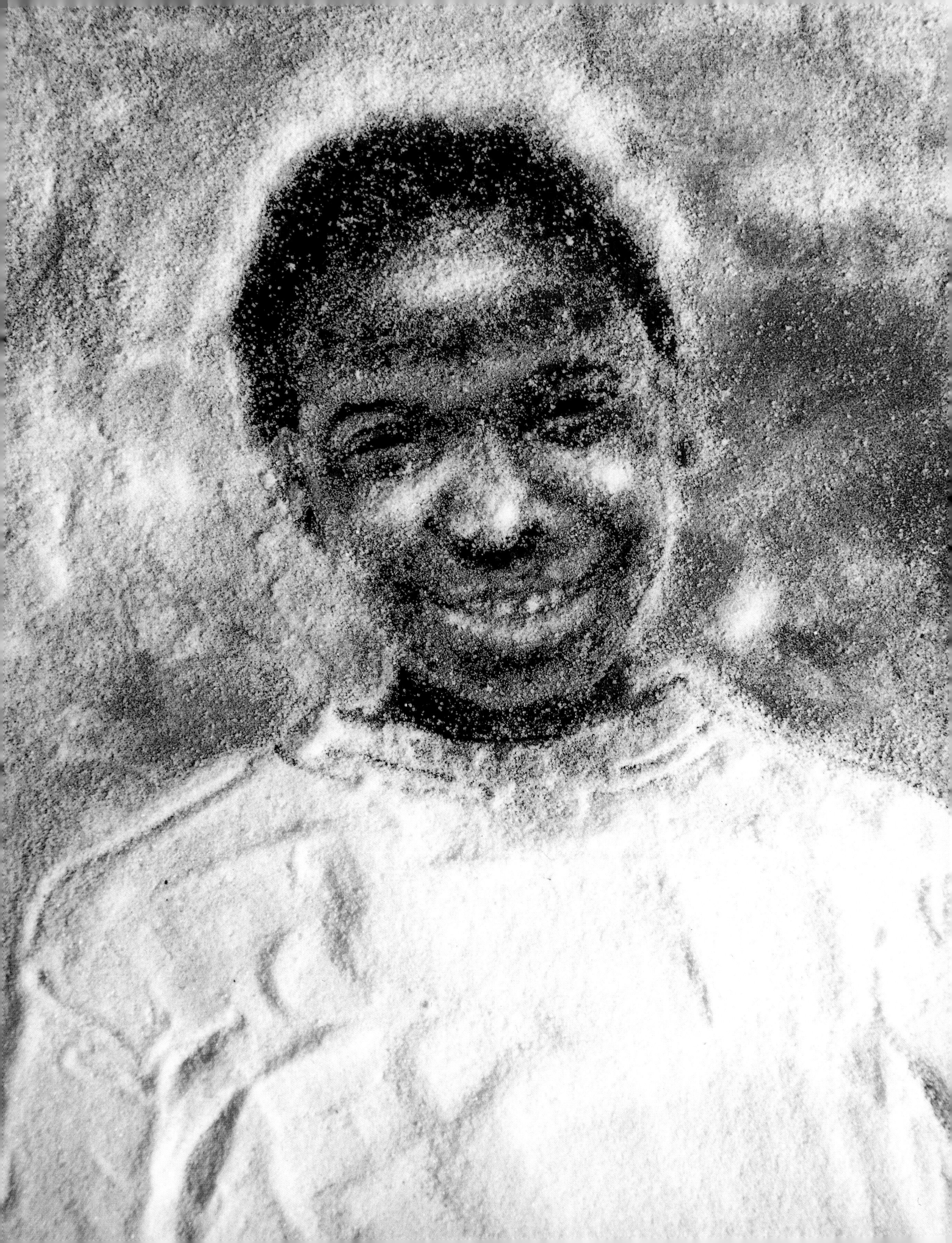

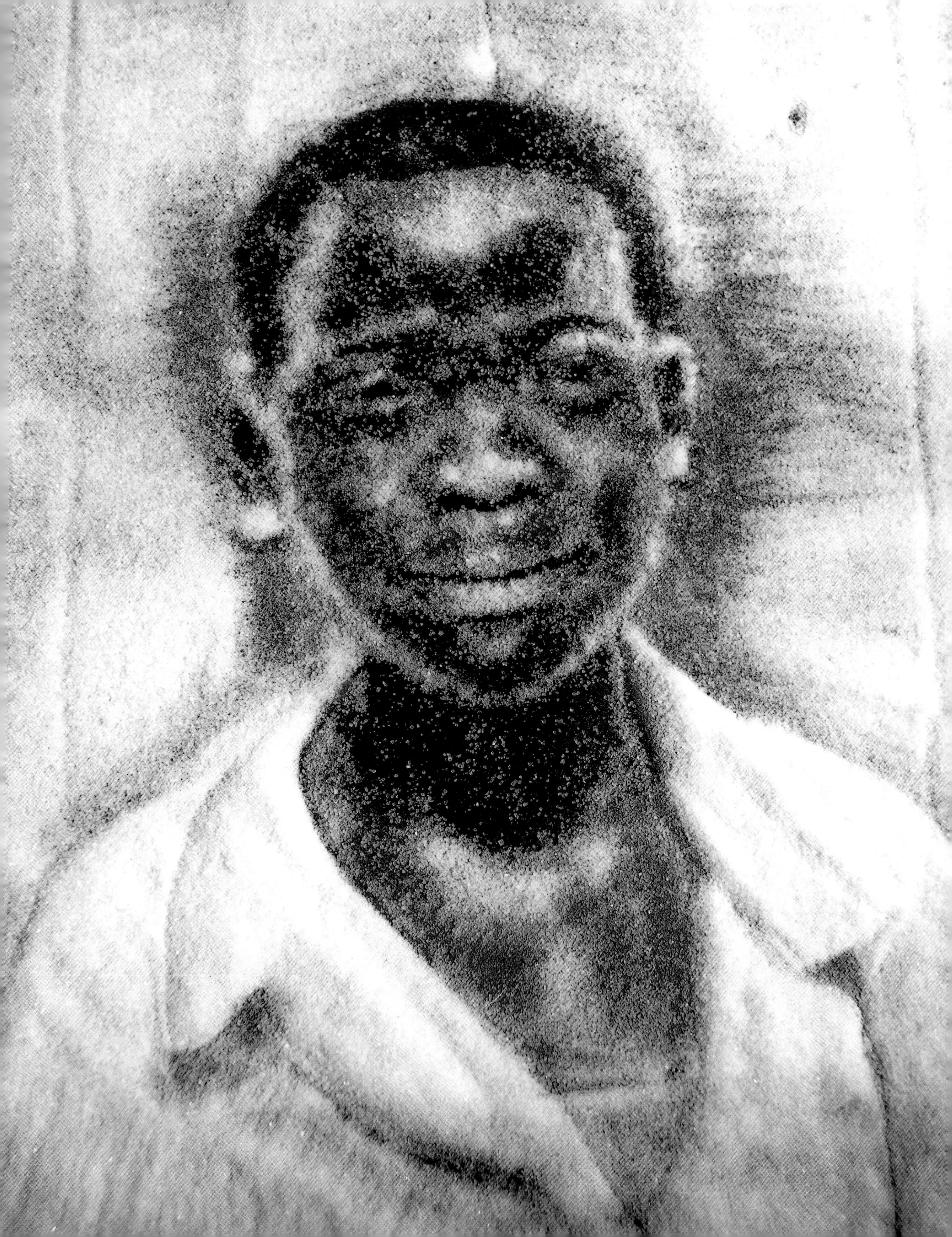

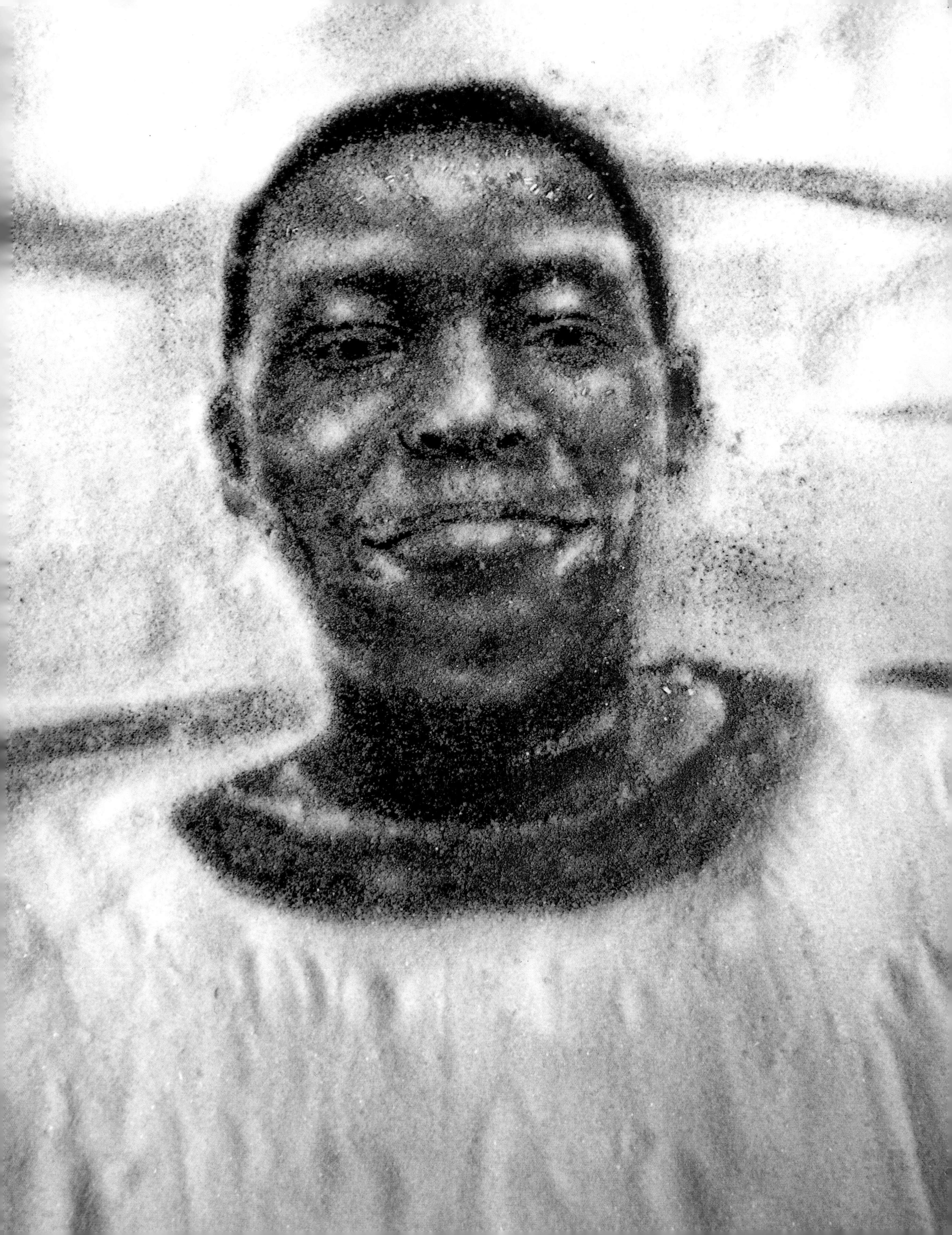

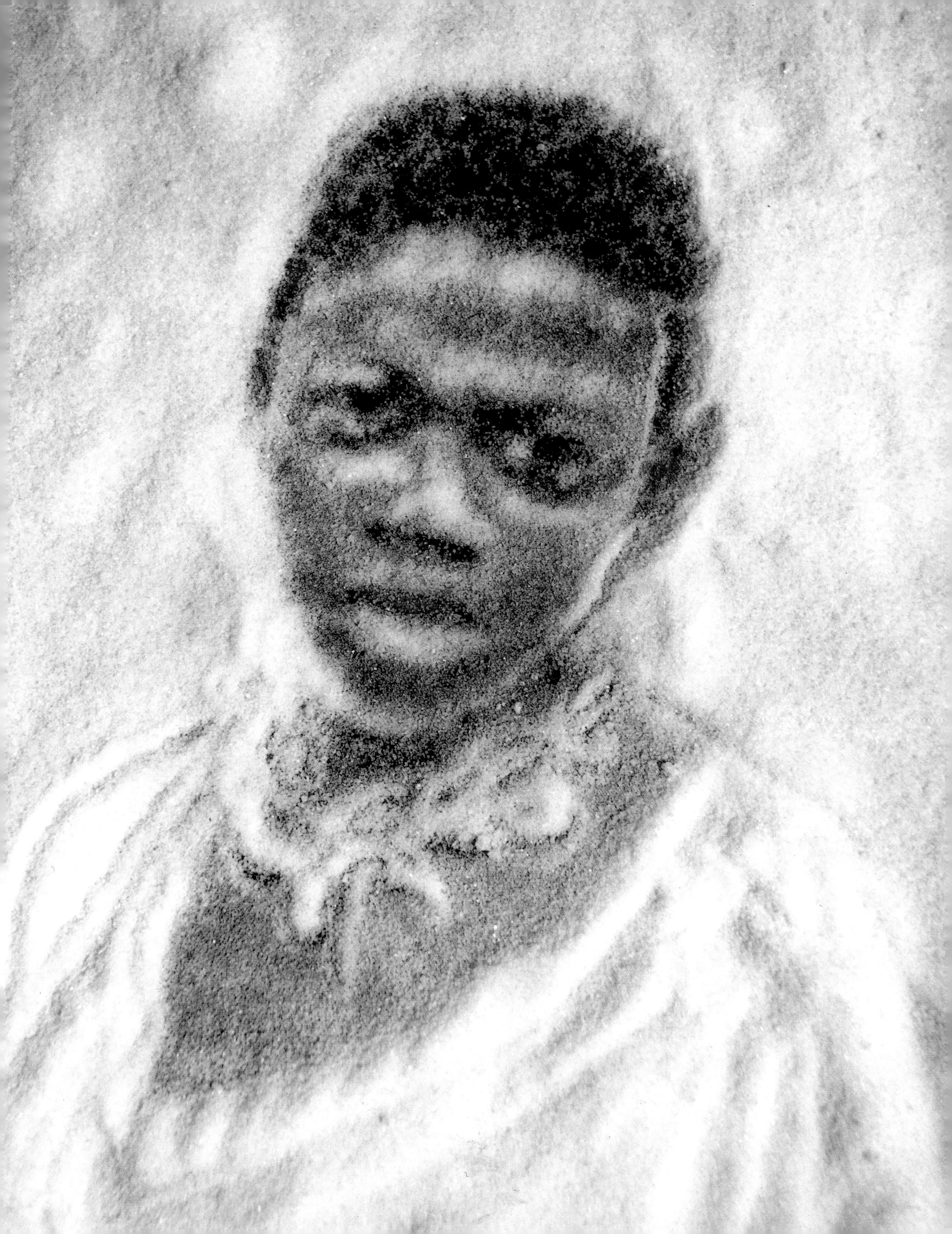

PRINCIPIA

1997

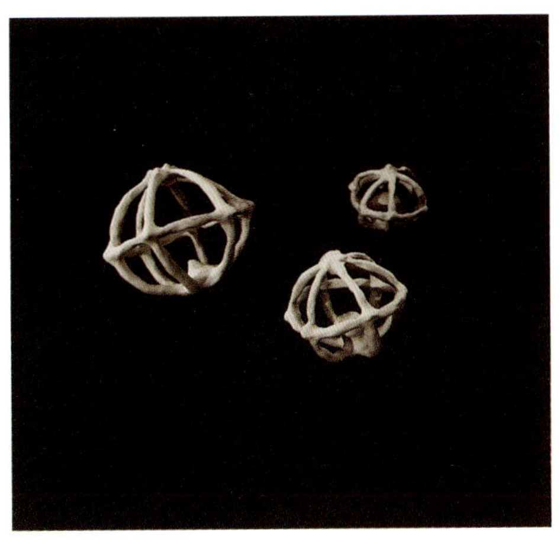
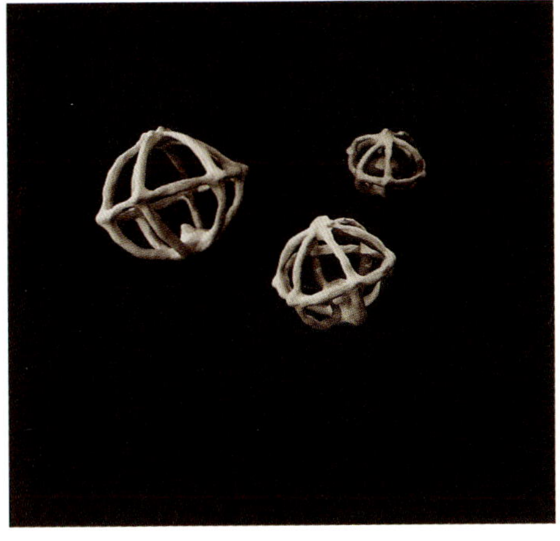

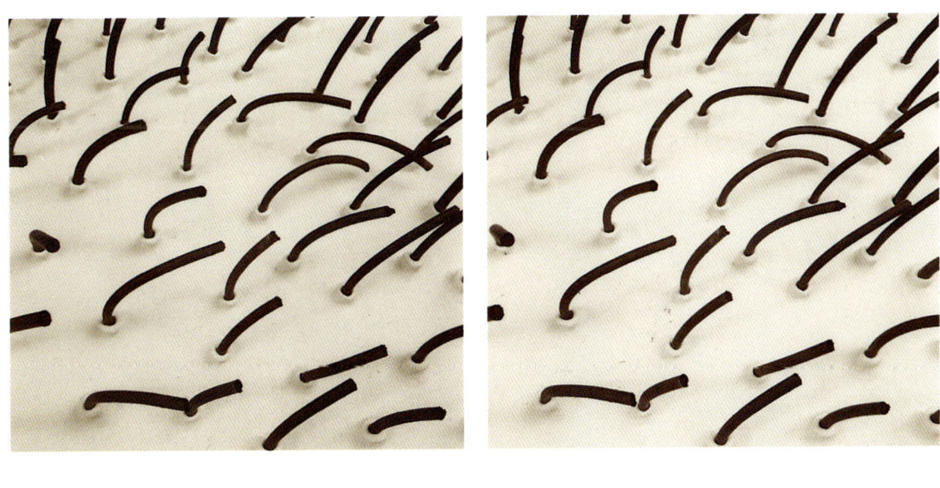

Principia 1: Three Naked Singularities

Principia 2: Facial Hair Magnified One Zillion Times

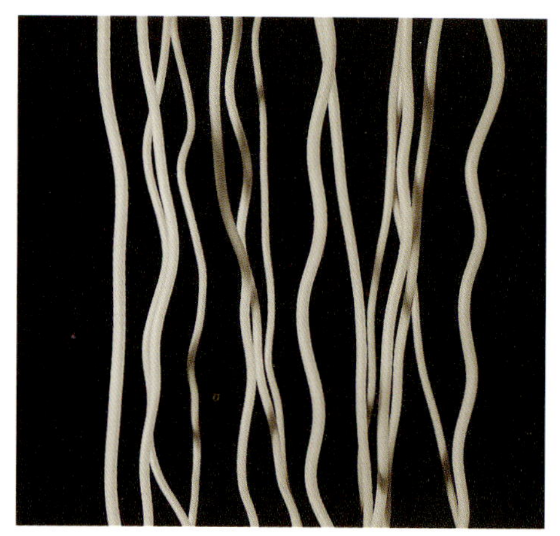

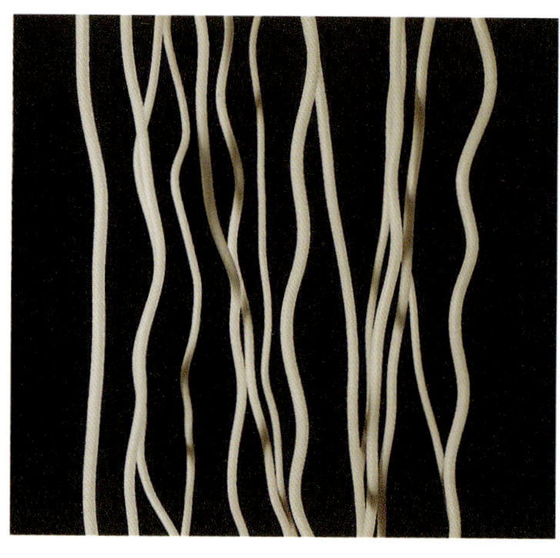

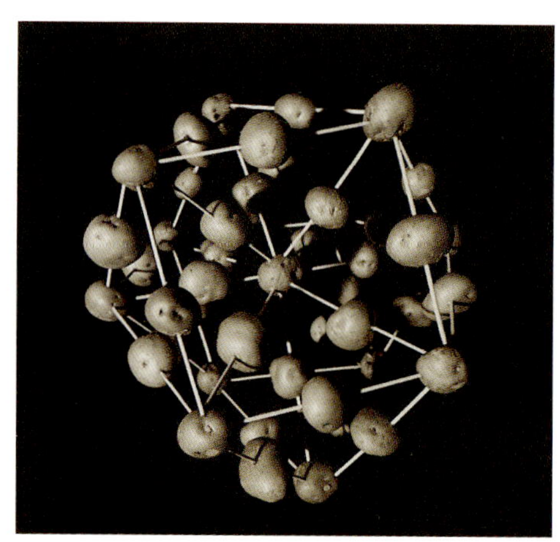

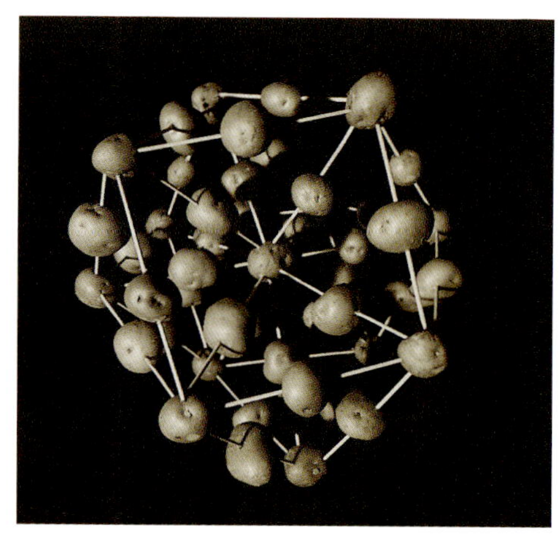

Principia 3: Vocal Cords Saying "Buon Giorno"

Principia 5: Goosebump Hormone

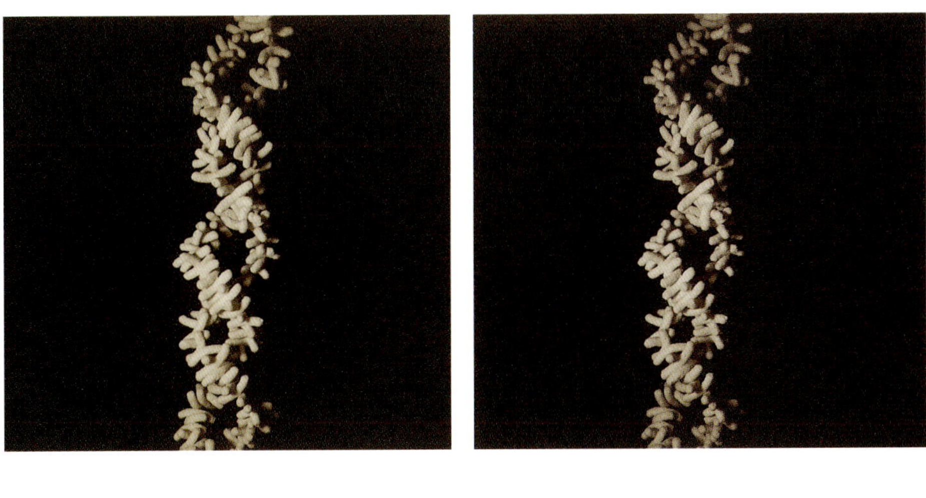

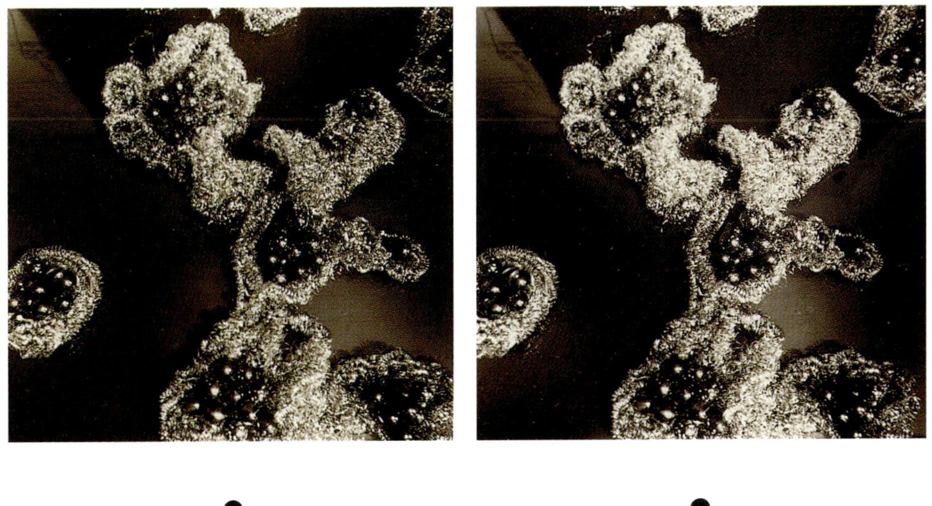

Principia 9: Loser Gene

Principia 10: Sloth Virus

PICTURES OF CHOCOLATE

1997–98

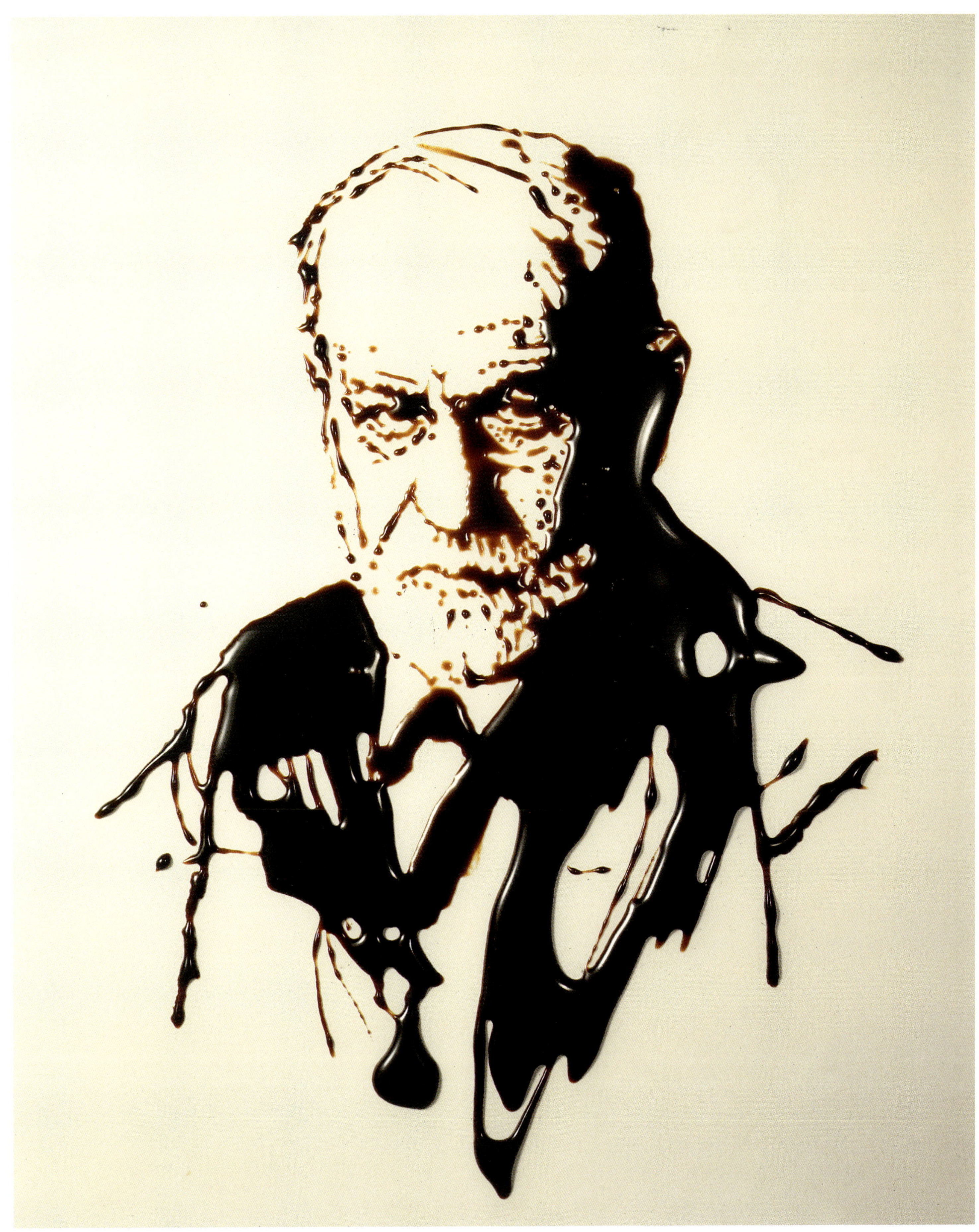

Sigmund

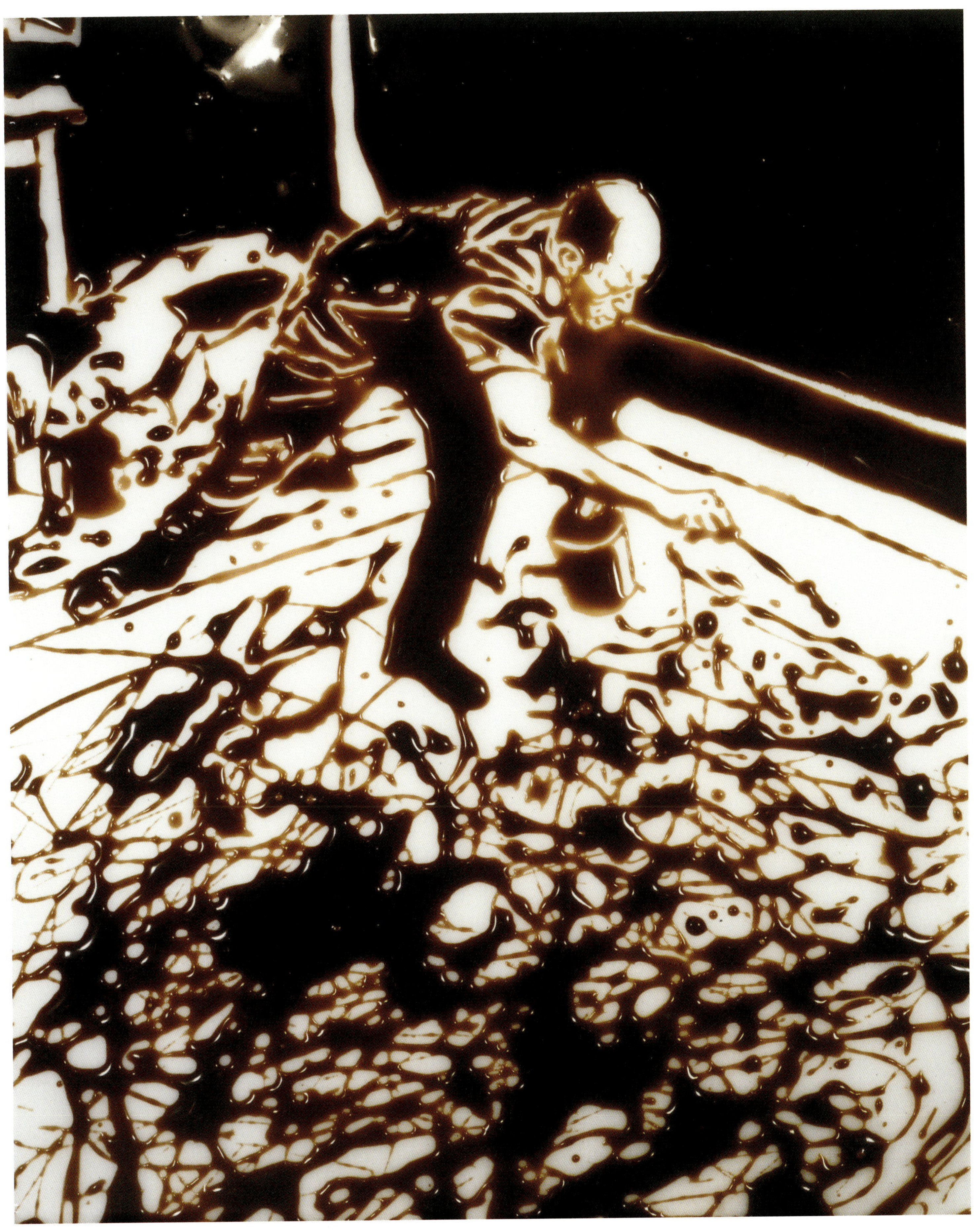

Action Photo I (After Hans Namuth)

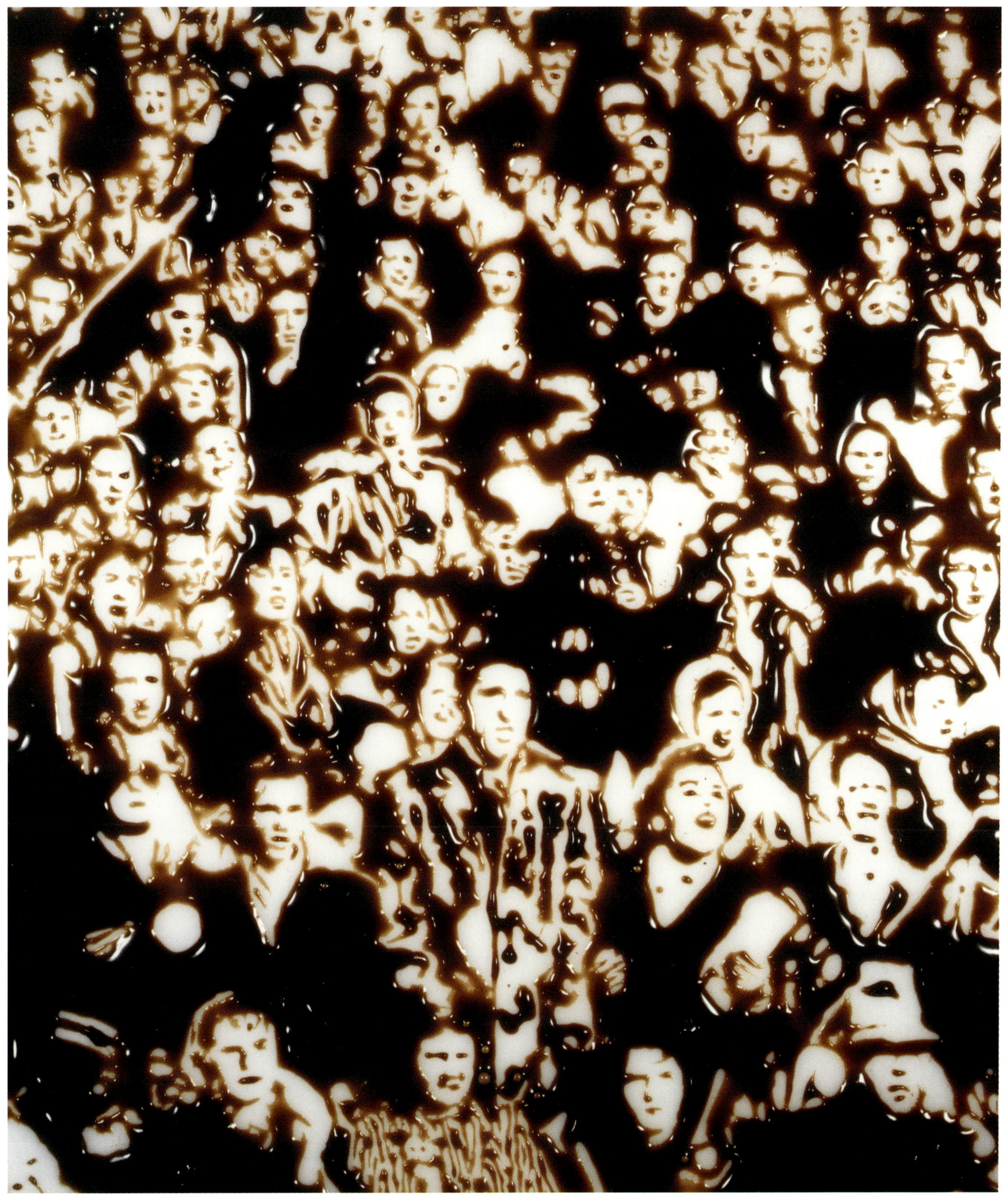

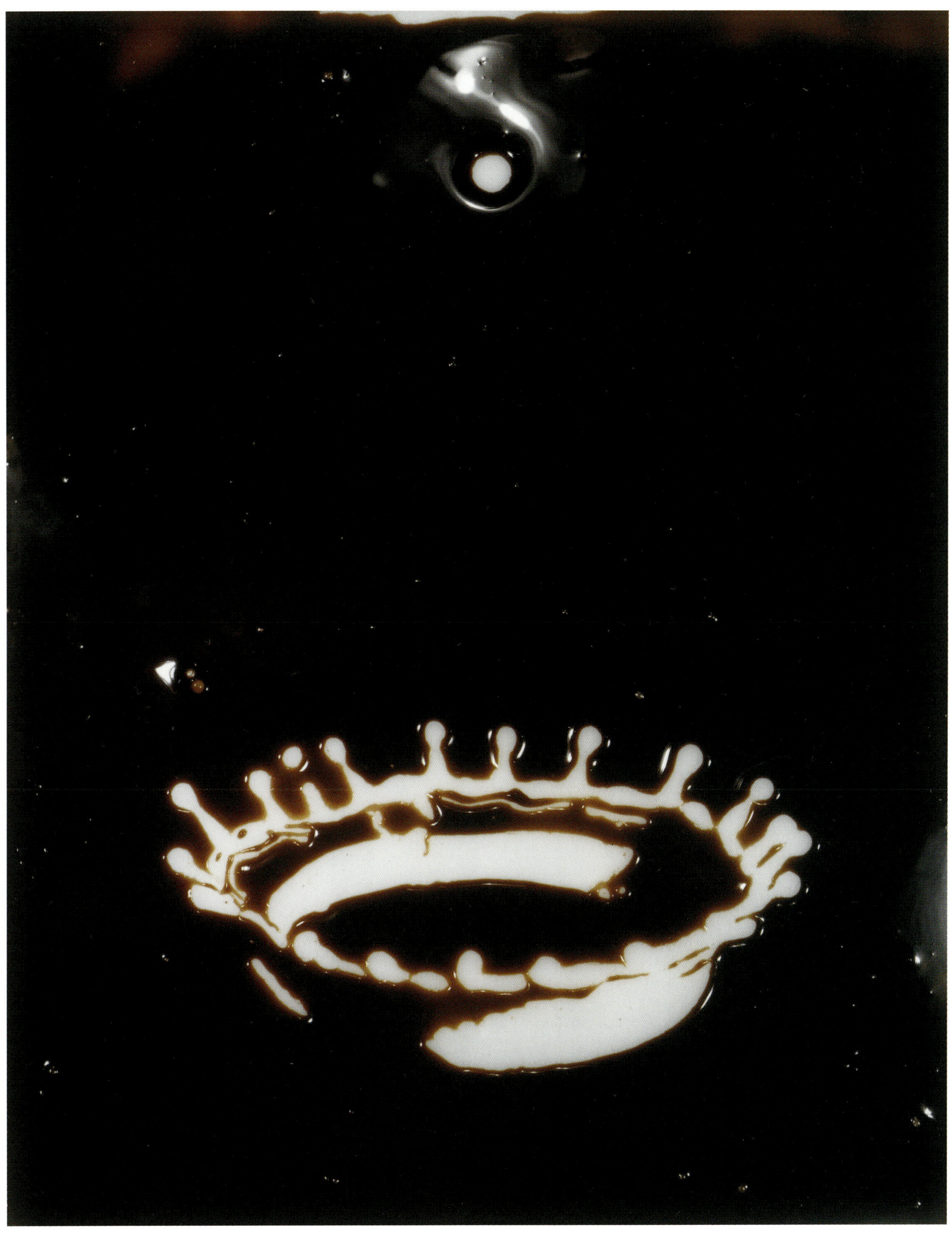

Milk Drop (After Dr. Harold Edgerton)

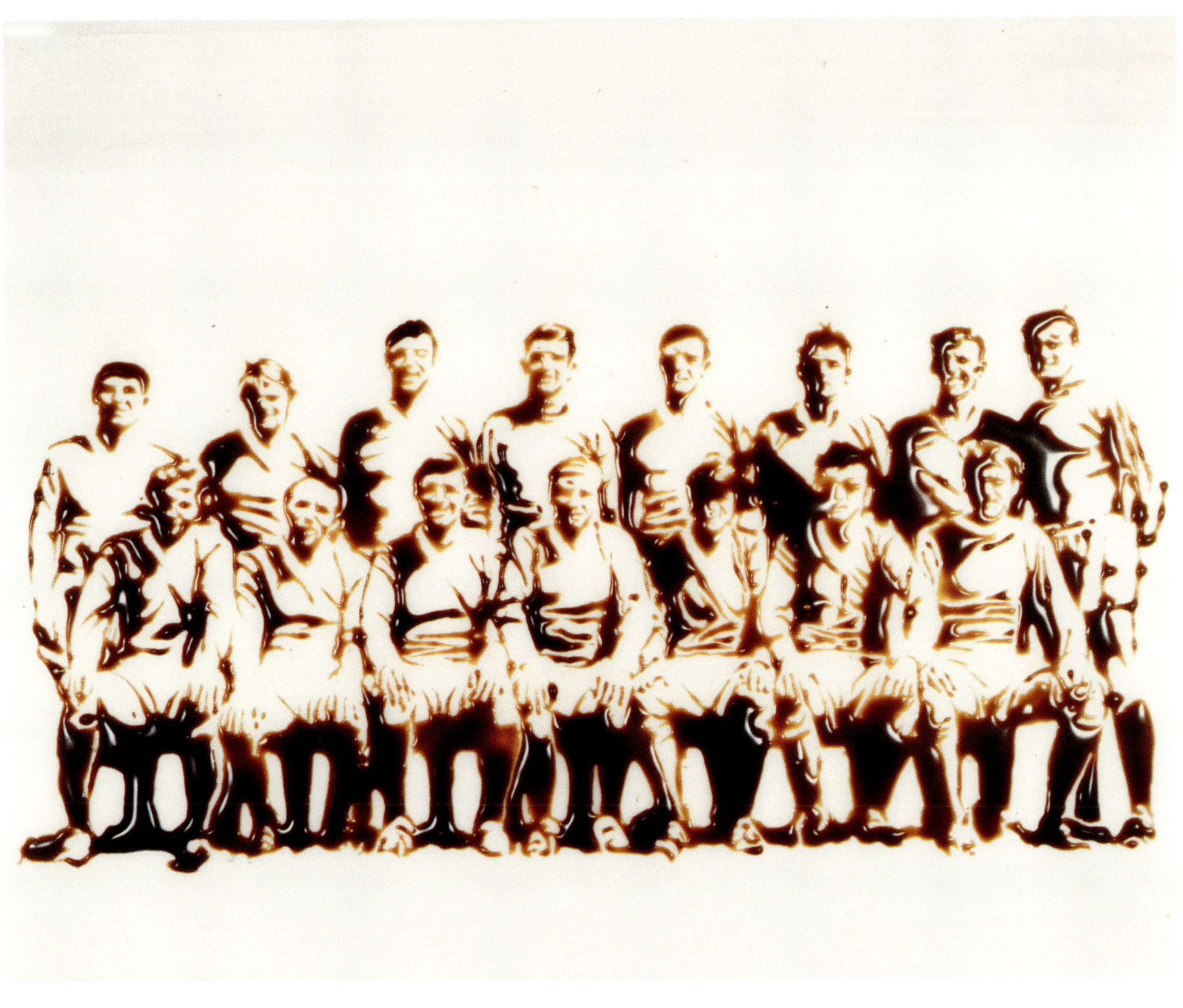

Team (soccer players)

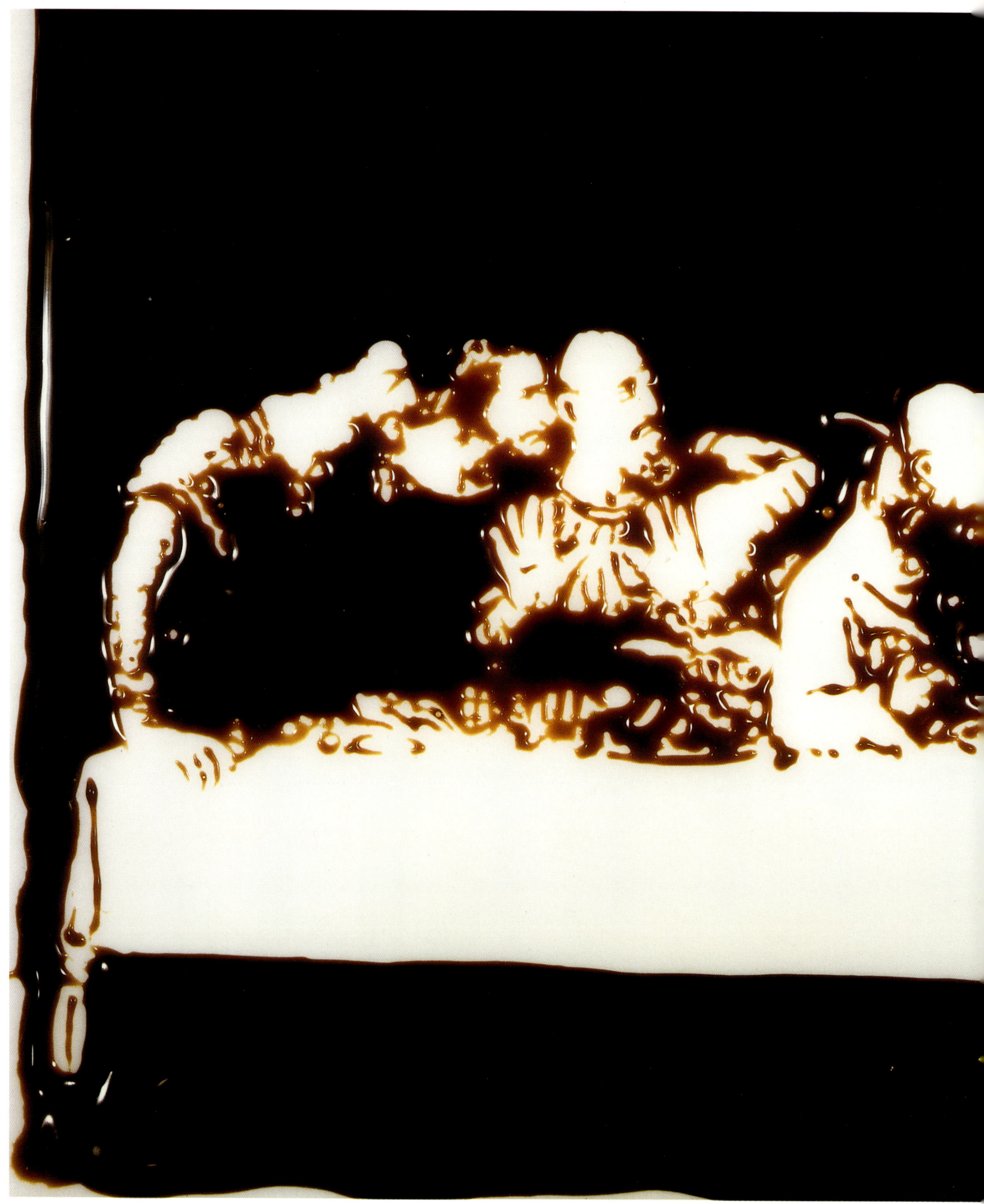

Milan (The Last Supper)

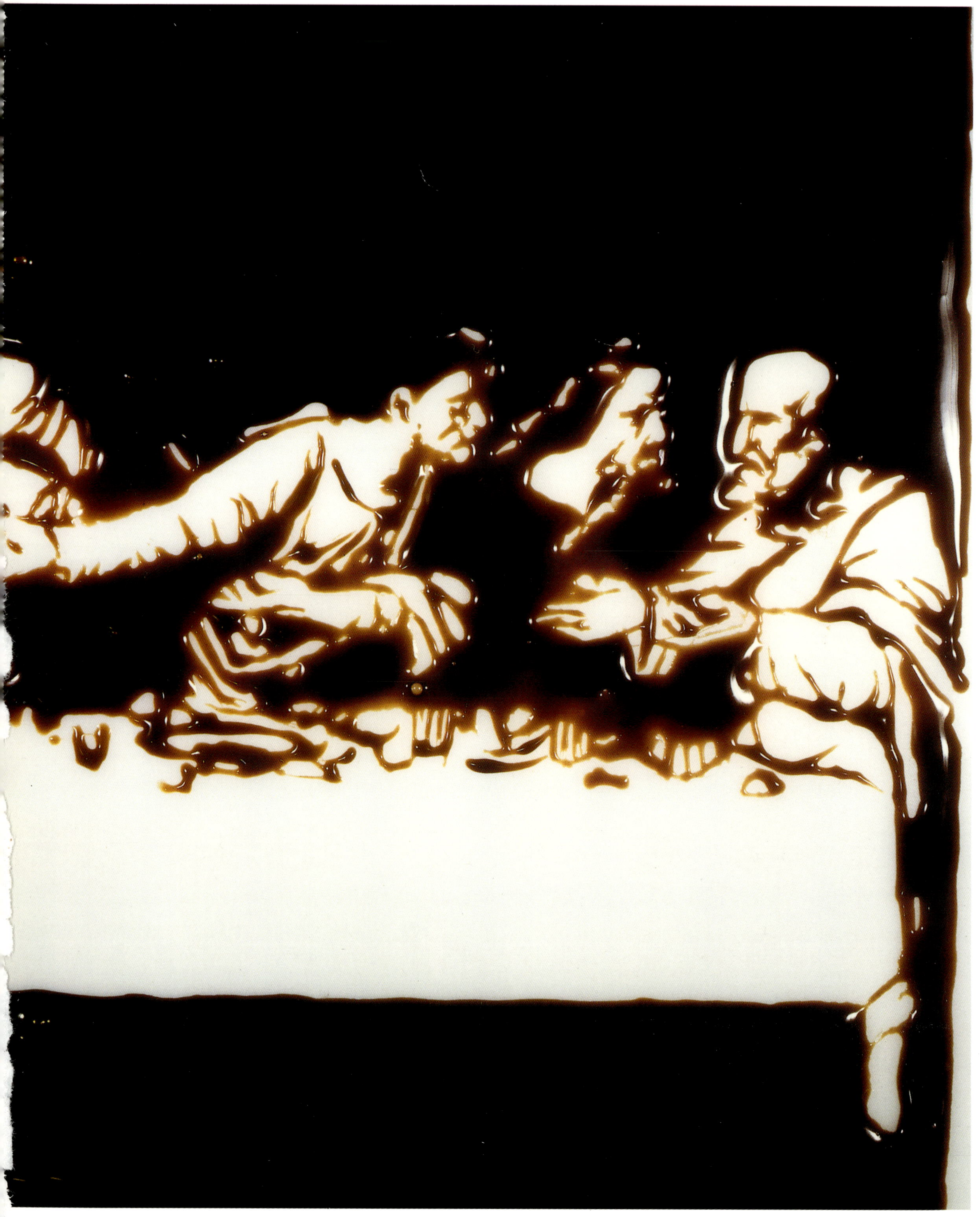

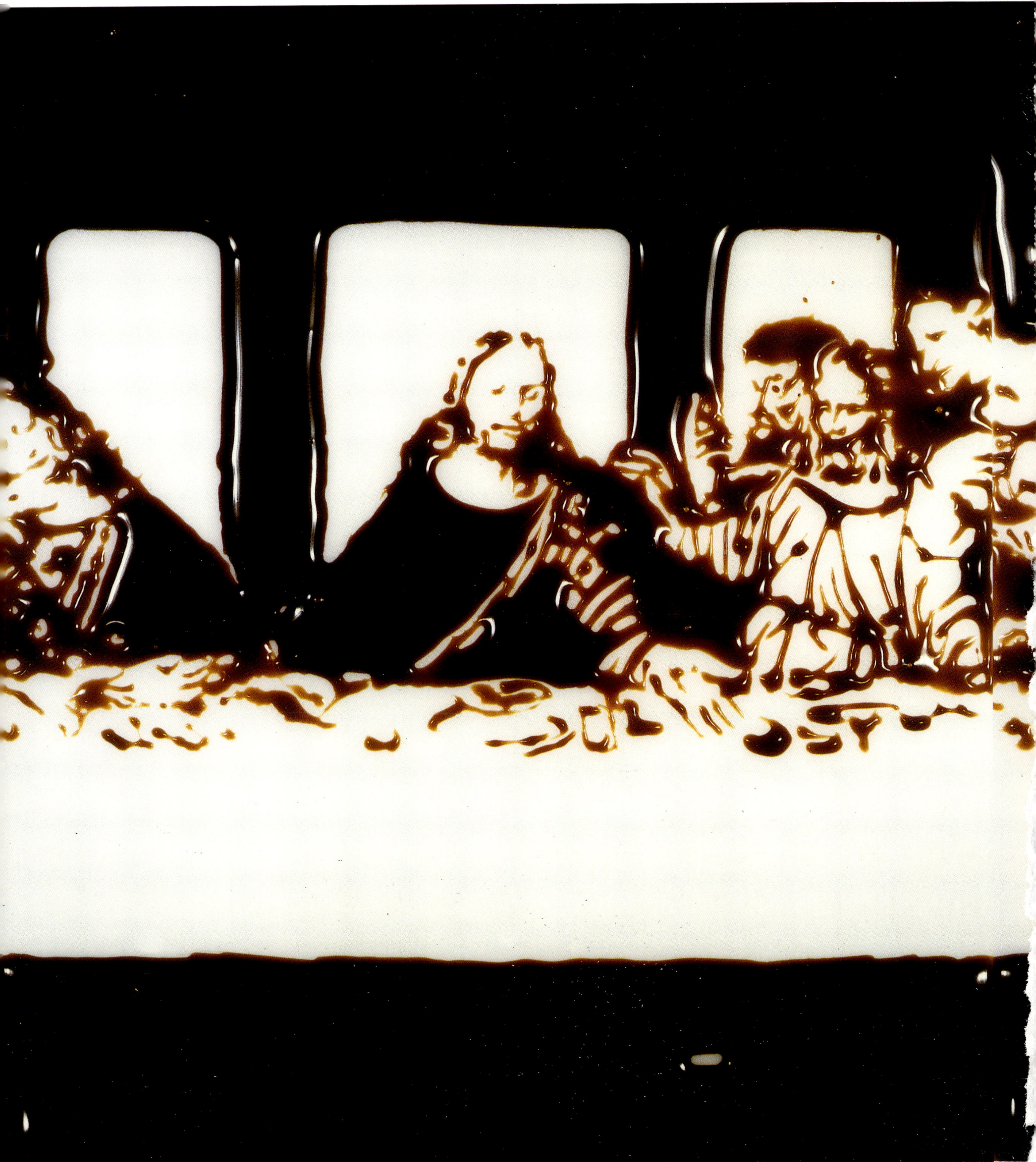

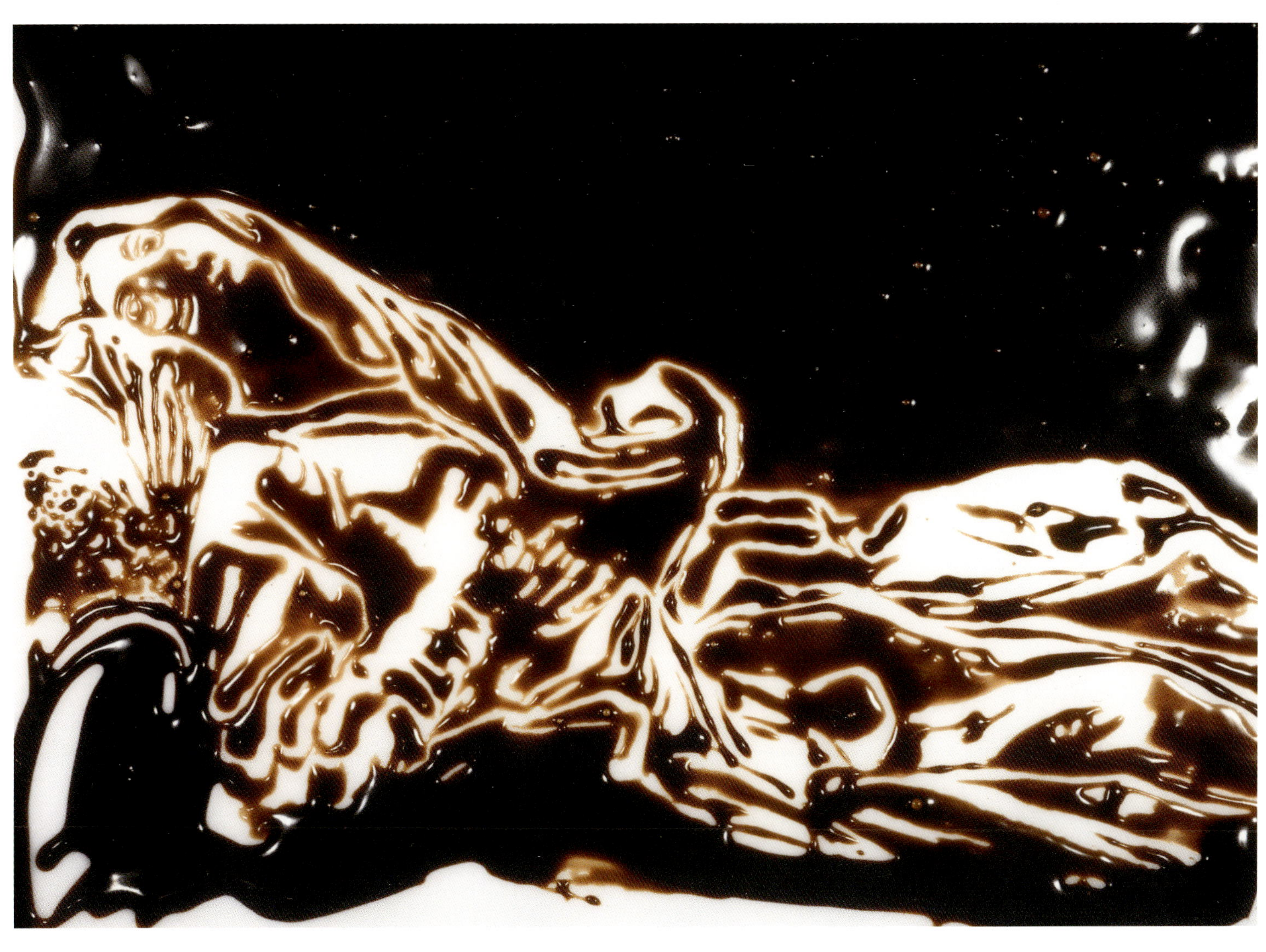

The Sacred Lodovica (After Bernini)

PICTURES OF SOIL

1997–98

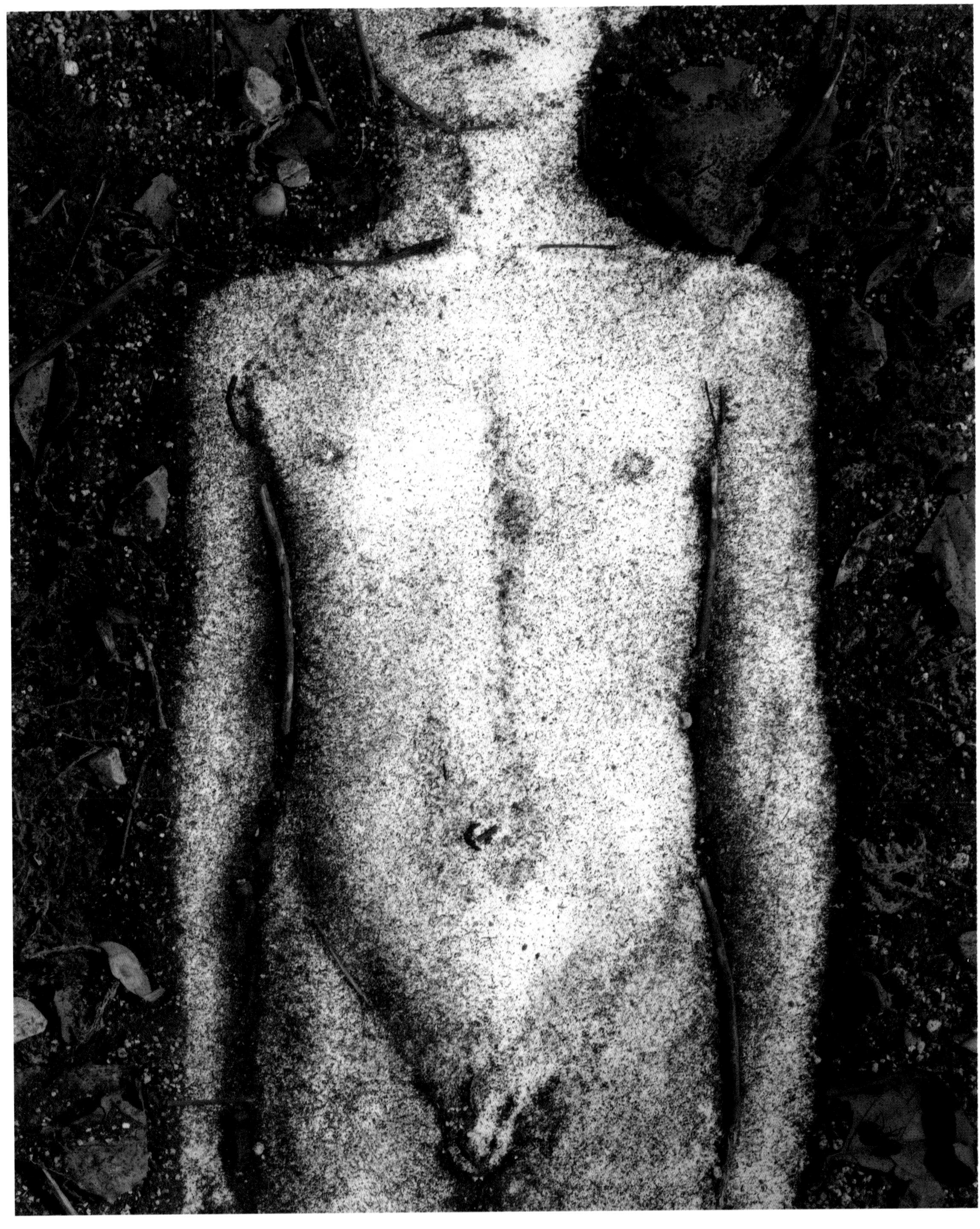

Youth (Gaspar)

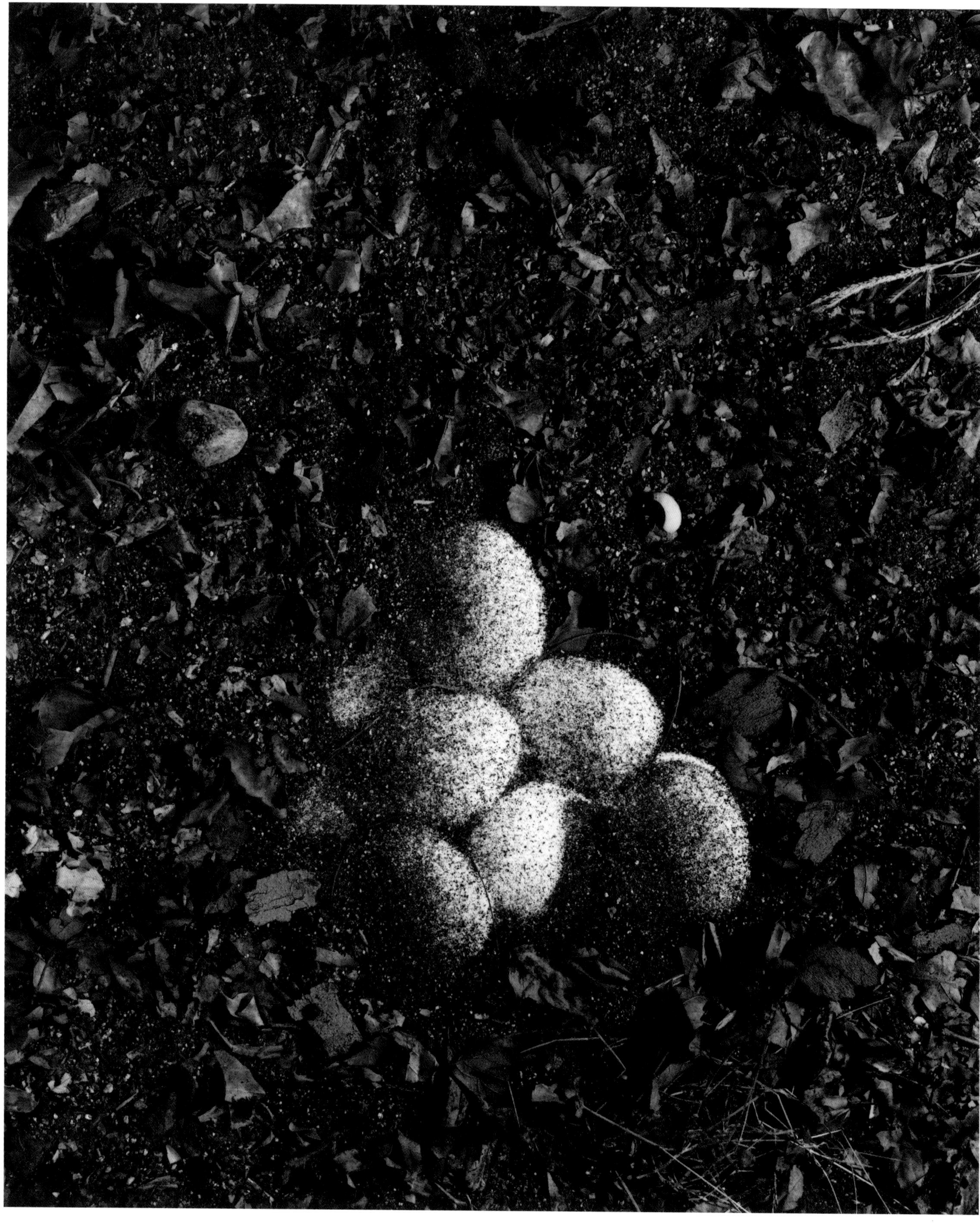

Eleven Eggs

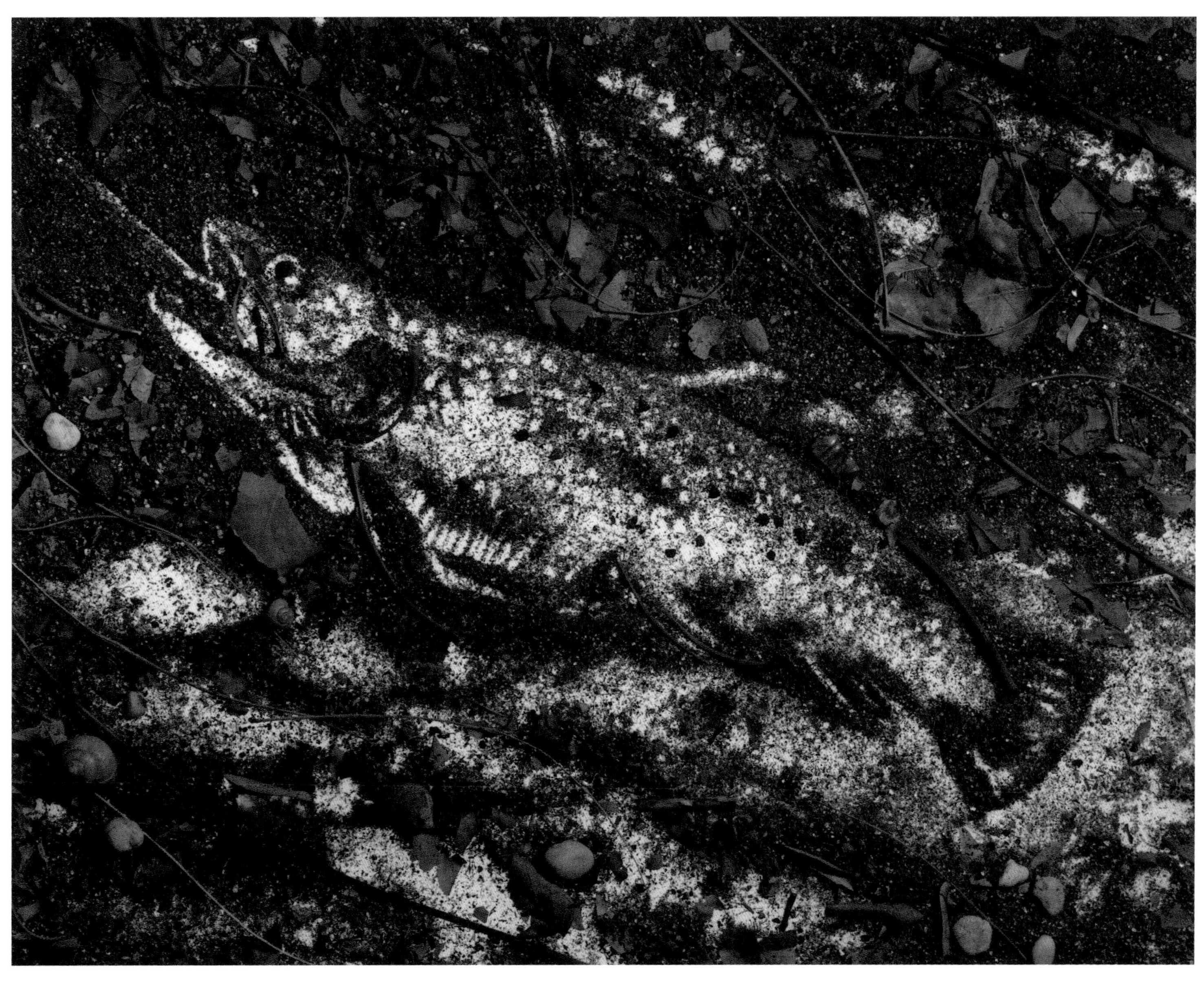

The Trout (After Courbet)

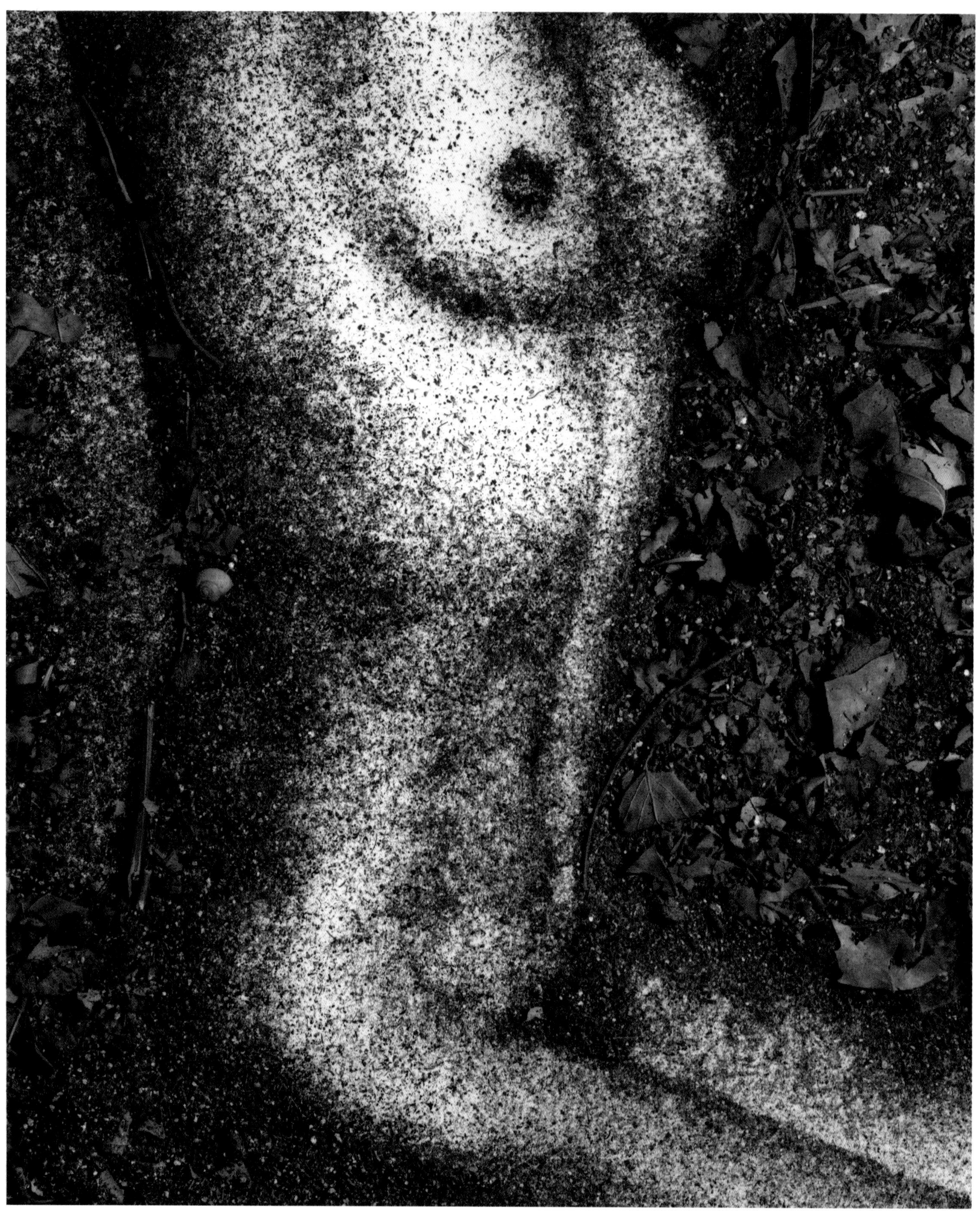

Torso (After Frantisek Dritkol)

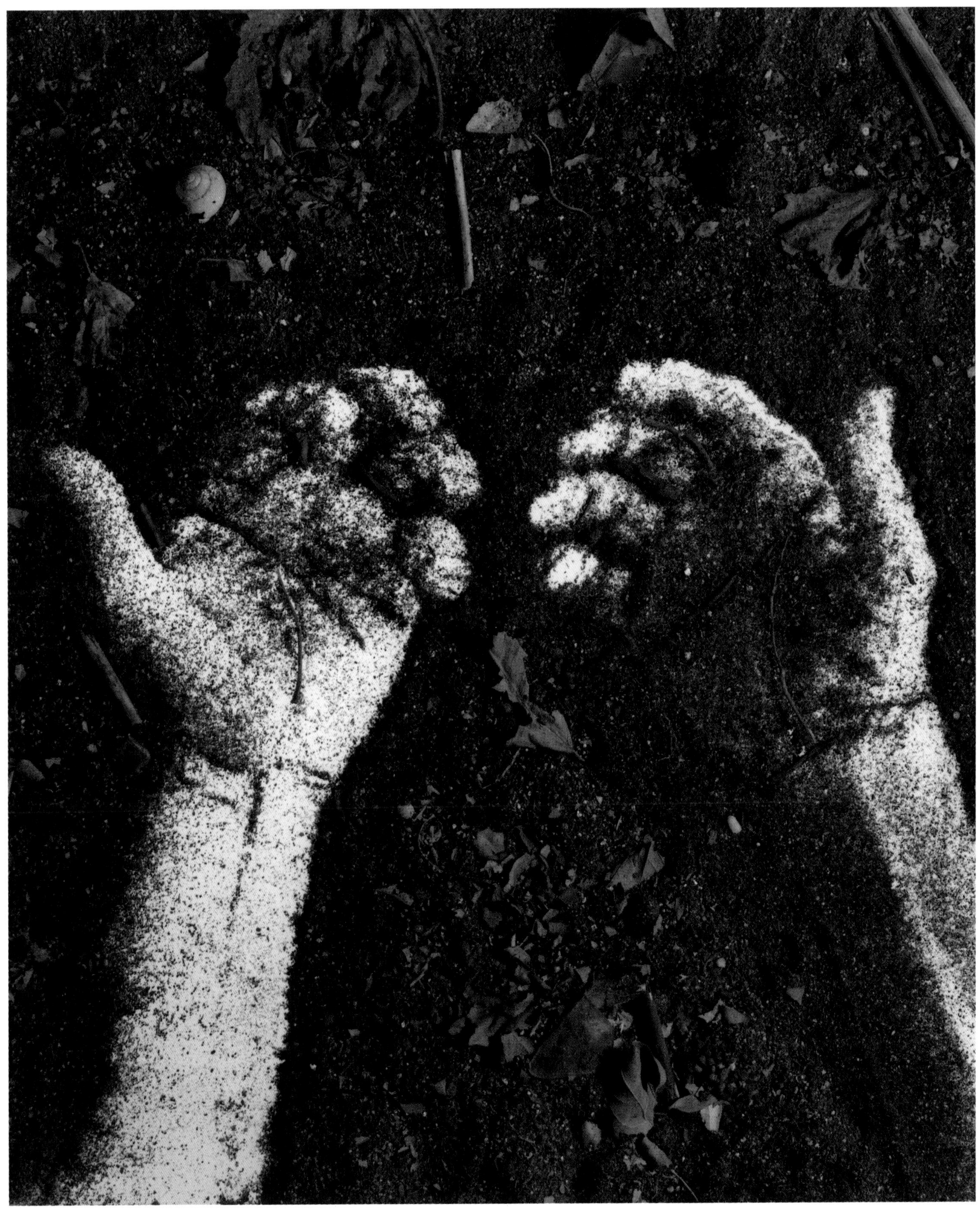

Hands

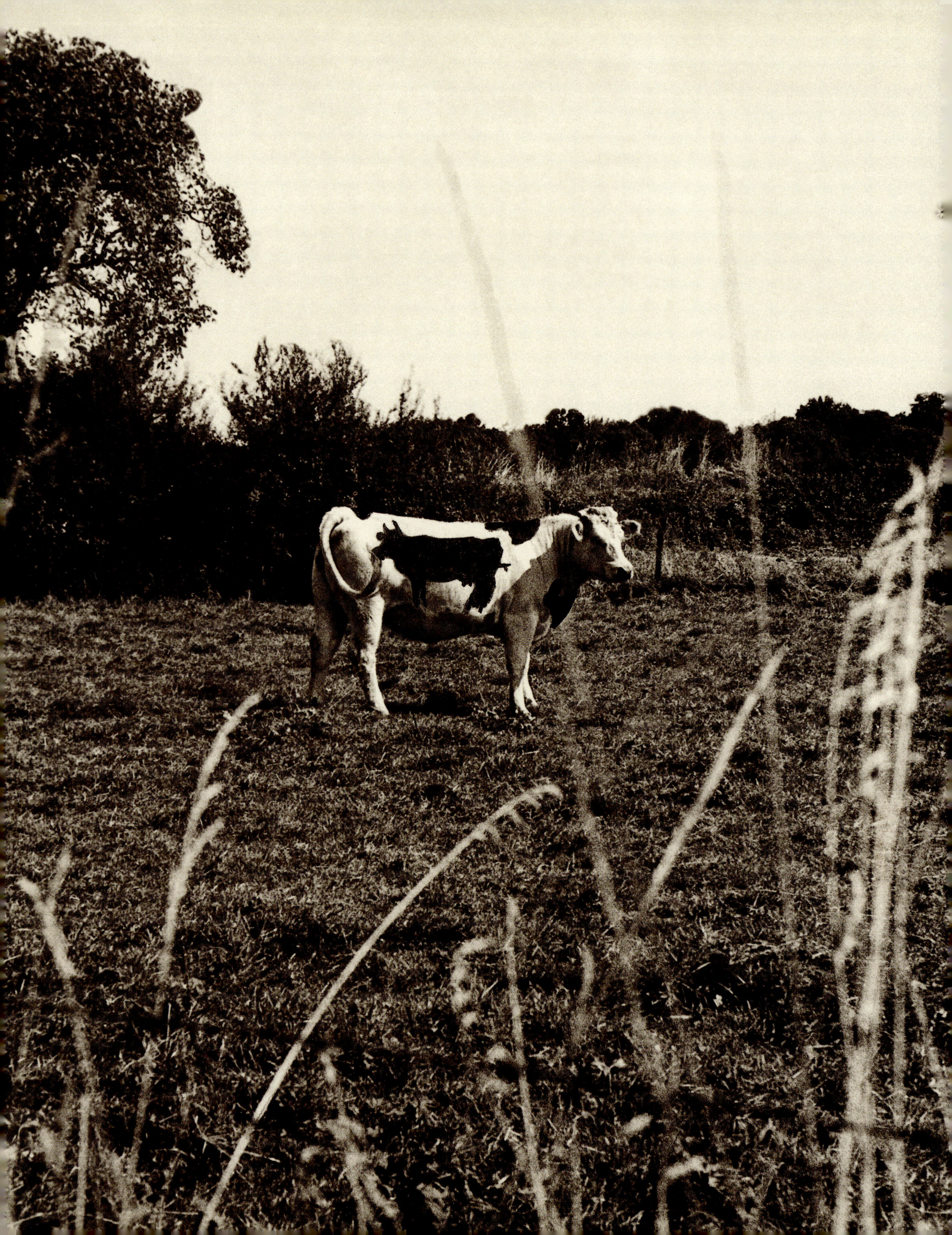

MARK ALICE DURANT

WHEN THE DUCK'S BEAK BECOMES THE RABBIT'S EARS: VIK MUNIZ AND THE ALPHABET OF LIKENESS

My mind is bent to tell of bodies changed into new forms.
—OVID

Miracles happen, not in opposition to nature but in opposition to what we know about nature.
—ST. AUGUSTINE

Things look like things, they are embedded in the transience of each other's meaning; a thing looks like a thing, which looks like another thing, or another. This eternal ricocheting of meaning throughout the elemental proves representation to be natural and nature to be representational.
—VIK MUNIZ

I pondered deeply, then, over the adventures of the jungle. And after some work with a colored pencil I succeeded in making my first drawing. My Drawing Number One. ... I showed my masterpiece to the grown-ups, and asked them whether the drawing frightened them. But they answered: "Frighten? Why should any one be frightened by a hat?" My picture was not a picture of a hat. It was a picture of a boa constrictor digesting an elephant. But since grown-ups were not able to understand it, I made another drawing: I drew the inside of the boa constrictor, so that the grown-ups could see it clearly. They always need to have things explained.
—ANTOINE DE SAINT-EXUPÉRY, *THE LITTLE PRINCE*

(A) Resembling Childhood

Mists gathered outside the house each evening, ephemeral tentacles slipped along roof gutters snaking their way into darkened rooms. In this part of the world the air is heavy during the day, at night it is chunky, humidity as palpable as cotton balls. A boy lies in bed staring at the ever-shifting moisture stain in the plaster ceiling directly above head upon pillow. Over the course of several weeks of these nightly morphing sessions, images grow in the clarity of their representation. As in time-lapse photography, an image reaches a fullness of recognition and then fades like a shriveling blossom. An ambiguous, scruffy outline begins to resemble the face of a clown, gradually the perimeter of the globular nose on the clown's

Vik Muniz, *Two Cows*, 1994, gelatin silver print, 11 x 14 inches.

face grows and reaches the arches of the painted eyebrows, the nose becomes a cratered planet. Several nights later a system of tiny capillaries appear, transforming the former nose into a spider's web. A week passes and the web has sagged beyond recognition but has settled comfortably into an image of a soccer net, complete with a miniature Pele, arms raised in the ecstasy of victory. The boy's night lessons are full of these transformations, a conjugation of forms; he internalizes and projects a pictographic language that is both ancient and modern, idiosyncratic and cultural. He even keeps a kind of visual diary that cumulatively chronicles the vast bestiary of his nocturnal observations.

The child owns nothing of the world, and as if to make up for this material poverty, the universe bestows all of its wonder. Under every rock, in each nervous shadow, and in the shape of every cumulus cloud there lies the dialectic of mystery and recognition. A child's relationship to the world is porous; the outside is animated by the child's imagination, and the child, in turn, is animated by the multitude of wonders that surrounds him. The difference between itself and things, both animate and inanimate, is less fixed than it is in the petrified certitude of adults. Occupying the space beneath the kitchen table while mom and dad, aunts and uncles and assorted grown-ups argue and laugh loudly, the child envisions the spindly disembodied legs as the multiple serpentine snouts of the beast that provides the heat for the child's underground hideaway. Who among us does not remember how something as fundamentally mute as a mud puddle could come alive as the primeval ooze? We filled our world with creatures and stories, and in turn these creations kept us company, helping us negotiate the foreign cultures of the tall people who owned everything.

Childhood is a blessing of unselfconsciousness. For a preciously short time in childhood we are unaware of ourselves as an image, we have not internalized the external gaze of authority. We own nothing, have no power, yet we are free. The foundational narrative of the West is found in the Book of Genesis; it is a story all about naming, authority, forbidden knowledge, and self-consciousness. In Eden, beyond being fruitful and multiplying, Adam and Eve had little to do after the naming of all things. They were, briefly, without shame; unaware of themselves as seen from the outside, they lived in harmony with all creatures great and small.

I believe the metaphor of the Peaceable Kingdom has everything to do with our lost childhood power of imaginative naming and our blissful ignorance of ourselves as an image. To add insult to injury, the unceremonious eviction from Eden came with the curse of self-consciousness, our beloved ancestors covered themselves with hastily tailored bits of clothing. This curse has resulted in a cultural lifetime of self-control, self-censorship, and estrangement from unadulterated wonder. We seldom, if ever, contentedly sit under the kitchen table as grown-ups.

There are other formative uncertainties that shade this specific boy's life, growing up in São Paulo, Brazil during the 1960s and '70s as the military holds the country hostage in a seemingly constant state of emergency. For the citizens of this blessed and cursed Amazonian kingdom, fixed positions vis-à-vis politics, culture, history, class, memory, and even the meaning of words are to be avoided. Sons and daughters, teachers and peasants, artists and union organizers, social workers and politicians often disappear without a trace. Between work and home, the dentist's office and a dinner date, or ripped from forgetful sleep, lives are interrupted without mercy. Explanations from the authorities are, of course, not forthcoming; one wonders whether a slip of the tongue or an unsuspecting friendship with an enemy of the state will transform one into a nonperson. Citizens taken into custody with books are doubly suspect: there are special interrogators reserved for those caught with the fruit of the tree of knowledge. As Edmund Burke wrote in 1757, "To make any thing terrible, obscurity seems in general to be necessary."[1] What can anything possibly mean when all meaning potentially threatens? A terror of absence settles on those that remain; the disappeared ones are, paradoxically, signifiers of the ultimate power of the state. Unavoidably, explicitly and through osmosis, these conditions encode themselves upon the boy's imagination, coloring his overpopulated internal landscape with an atmosphere of ambiguity.

The boy's parents are working class, his mother a switchboard operator, his father a bartender. One evening the father comes home, standing on the street calling his son to come out of the house. In the grainy light of the street lamp, his father stands holding the handles of a wheelbarrow in which rests a complete set of the Encyclopaedia Britannica, won in a game of billiards. Growing up in a house without books, this treasure trove of information will act as the mortar with which to build a bridge to the outside world. Starter encyclopedias usually go by the name of "Little Book of Wonders" or some such fancy. If we are lucky and/or predisposed to subtleties, at some point in childhood we realize that there are at least two types of "wonder" involved in such presentations. There is the thing itself presented in words and images, whether it be pictures of grazing giraffes or illustrations of water molecules. The second level of wonderment is generated by the realization that representations themselves are strange, quirky, difficult to identity, and that sometimes they reveal more about the processes of perception and the limits of communication than what is conveyed about the subject itself. This boy in particular is fascinated by the transformation of photographic and graphic illustrations into a semiotic gray area as a result of the cheap reproductions found on the impossibly thin pages of the Britannica. The tiny halftone photographs look like bad drawings and the murky graphics look like poor photographs. If the purpose of these images is to demystify the wonders of the world in direct, compact, and digestible fragments, they have the opposite effect for this artist-in-the-making, who finds ambiguity, mystery, and wonder in the muddy-gray tonalities of encyclopedic marginalia.

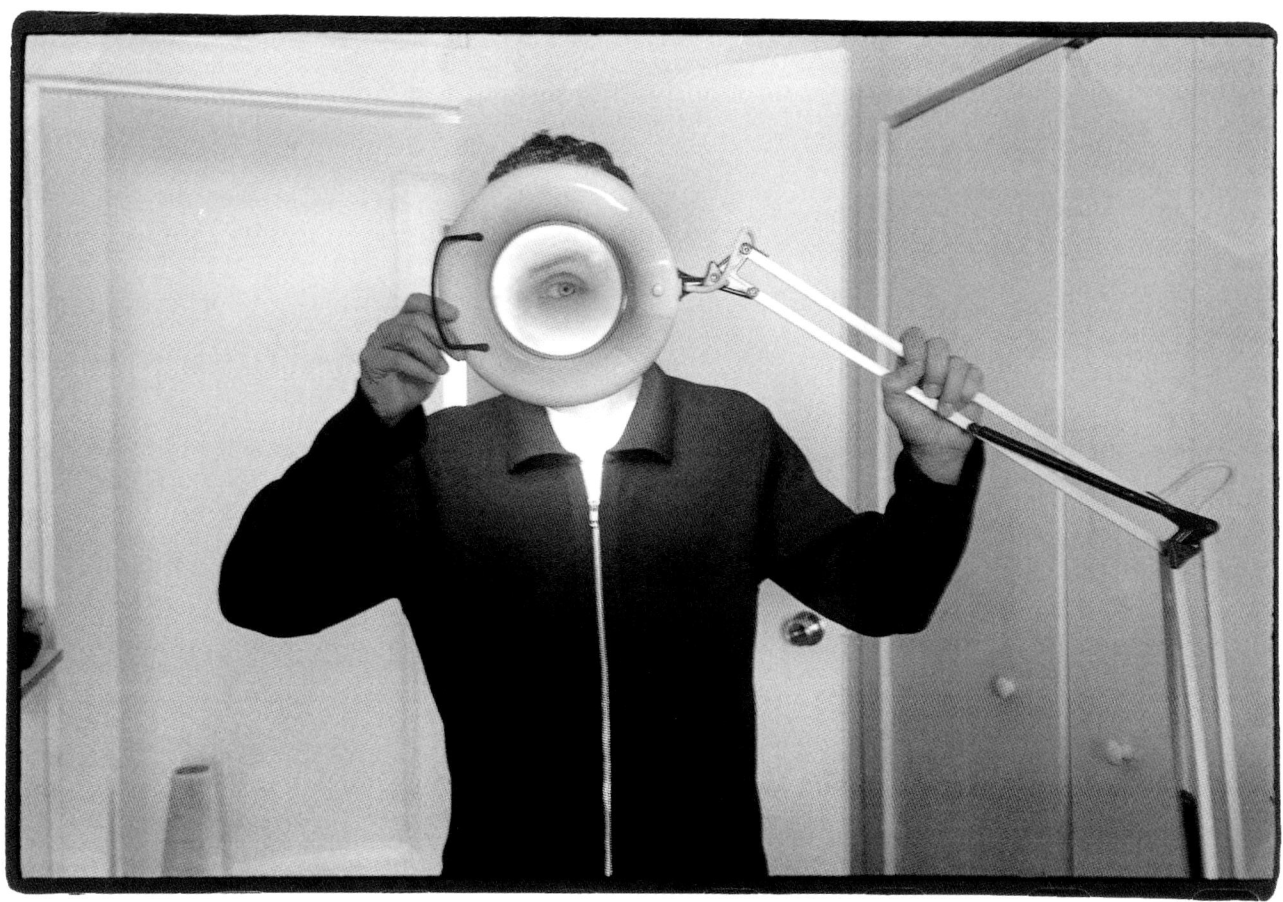

(B) Pictures in Stone

Vik Muniz is an artist who remains motivated by wonder and inexorably drawn toward ambiguity, who finds delight in the indeterminacy of images. He fancies himself a "low-tech illusionist" in search of perceptual sleight-of-hand that revels in its trickery but still retains the transformative power of magic. A quick review of a few items from his bag of tricks suggests the subversive play of the Muniz cabinet of wonders. Tufts of cotton are shaped like miraculous free-floating topiary, we know it is cotton, yet we see them as clouds, we know they are clouds but recognize them as praying hands. Another example is the image of thin graphitelike lines describing the outlines of a dripping faucet, but upon closer inspection we realize it is not a drawing but a photograph, and the photograph shows a length of twisted wire tacked to a white wall, a simple sculpture masquerading as a drawing. Thirdly, we think we recognize a well-known image from the collective memory archives, we silently mutter the name "Vietnam" under our breath, but we discover that the composition or the perspective seems to have soured, it is not exactly how we remember it. Again we are fooled, the image that plugged so readily into our repository is really a forgery, a handmade counterfeit, a drawing of a photograph that has been photographed. The Muniz archive is a collection of pictures imitating other pictures, an eccentric celebration of what he calls "the unbearable likeness of being," and the cumulative effect of his work maps out a rudimentary language of resemblances, an alphabet of likeness.

Vik Muniz in his studio, 1998. Photo: Mark Alice Durant.

"There are impossible scribblings in nature, written by neither men nor devils."[2] So states Roger Caillois in his fanciful yet compelling meditation on the origin of human aesthetics, *The Writing of Stones*. Caillois explores visual language in natural forms and in particular images as found in split and polished pieces of silica, agate, marble, or "picture stones" as they are known, which bear uncanny resemblances to every conceivable natural phenomenon and human invention. As Marguerite Yourcenar observed in her introduction, contrary to accusations of anthropomorphism, Caillois proposed that human aesthetics were but part of a larger universal order of beauty. Found in polished "picture stones" are representations of both organic and inorganic structures, landscapes and castles, portraits and holy apparitions. Caillois suggests that humans learned about representation through images that already existed in nature.

> *These [models of nature] consist of subtle and ambiguous signals reminding us, through all sorts of filters and obstacles, that there must be a pre-existing general beauty vaster than that perceived by human intuition — a beauty in which man delights and which in his time he is proud to create. Stones — and not only they, but roots, shells, wings and every other cipher and construction in nature — help to give us an idea of the proportions and laws of that general beauty about which human beauty must be mere one recipe among others ...*[3]

Simply put, the visual workings of nature were our first art teacher; lesson one involved discovering images in natural forms that resembled our experience of the world. Before a Neanderthal proto-Rembrandt etched an antelope on the cave wall, perhaps he noticed a water stain that reminded him of his favorite meal. This recognition gave him pleasure for it stirred feelings of desire, violence, and satiation, and then he noticed — quite dimly, for he was a Neanderthal after all — that the water stain/antelope image would look better if he scratched a circle where the eye would be and maybe if he extended the antlers just so, the overall impression would be more lifelike, which to his mind was good. This is an apocryphal tale of the first artistic collaboration in which our lowbrowed ancestor began the long road of aesthetic evolution by attempting to imitate and improve upon a preexisting iconography created by natural forces. In this way, Caillois believes that representation itself is first and foremost "natural," and human culture's obsession to identify and re-create images is a primordial impulse.

(C) It Looks a Lot Like Life

> *To see life; to see the world; to eyewitness great events; to watch the faces of the poor and the gestures of the proud; to see strange things — machines, armies, multitudes, shadows in the jungle and on the moon; to see man's work — his paintings, towers, discoveries; to see things thousands of miles away, things*

hidden behind walls and within rooms, things dangerous to come to; the women that men love and many children; to see and to take pleasure in seeing; to see and be amazed; to see and be instructed.[4]

So proposed Henry R. Luce in 1936 to establish a pictorial magazine named *Life* for the American masses. Human beings have had many art teachers throughout the millennia. In the modern world, photography has been an instructor like no other, and *Life* magazine has been the syllabus. After coming to the United States in 1983, Vik Muniz found a copy of *The Best of Life* at a garage sale outside of Chicago. Still negotiating the rudiments of English, photographic images were the primary language for his introduction to American Culture. Luce's adviso "to see and take pleasure in seeing; to see and be amazed; to see and be instructed" found an eager student in Muniz. As represented in *Life* magazine, American culture seems oddly choreographed and melodramatic, a place seemingly without hierarchies of historical importance: a hula-hoop gyrates adjacent to a mushroom cloud and an assassination on the streets of Saigon segues into hippies on Haight Street.

Some years later in 1989, Muniz attempts to recall from memory these iconographic moments from American history in his own *Best of Life* series. What is revealed, among other things, is how insidiously Henry Luce's family album has seeped into our nation's collective consciousness. *Life's* images have become the anchors to *our* memory. Photographs are, paradoxically, both fragmentary and iconographic: they represent moments severed from the linearity of time, yet they promise an almost seamless access to the world. When we look at a photograph we generally say "This is my mother," not "This is a picture of my mother." This difference is crucial in understanding the seductive power of representation that photography holds. Photography is a magician who seldom slips up, whose illusions are always perfect, thereby never calling attention to the trick of turning an animated three-dimensional world into a two-dimensional static object. In his photographic transformations, Muniz aims to destabilize photography's evidentiary power by deliberately undermining the truth of its communication. The smudgy and awkward charcoal drawings Muniz dredged up from his memory banks cannot but remind us of the source: images such as theater audiences uniformly wearing 3-D glasses, a naked Vietnamese girl running down an incinerated road, or the summary execution of a suspected enemy on a Saigon street are all lodged deeply in our personal and collective memories. After photographing these memory renderings, Muniz printed them with a dot-screen pattern to mimic even more closely the original image. In *The Best of Life* series, he suggests that although these images may be seared in our consciousness, they exist solely in the rarefied realm of the symbolic, devoid of their original power. Perversely, his strategy seems to resuscitate these images, as if in their falseness they take on a new power to disturb. Like a renegade conjurer who reveals the machinations of illusion, or as when someone tries a magic trick that doesn't work, something is revealed about the fundamentally hallucinatory quality of photographic representation.

I want to make the worst possible illusion that will still fool the eyes of the average person ... Illusions as bad as mine make people aware of the fallacies of visual information and the pleasure to be derived from such fallacies. These illusions are made to reveal the architecture of our concept of truth. They are meta-illusions.

— VIK MUNIZ [5]

Upon moving to New York in 1984, Muniz began making sculptural objects, many of which toyed with perceptual differences between two- and three-dimensional representation. Three works from the late 1980s illustrate how he often combined photographs with objects that both contradicted and completed one another to create a conceptual whole. In *Tug of War* (1988) two photographs bracket and are connected by an actual piece of rope that hangs flaccidly between the two struggling adversaries. We get the joke without hesitation, yet there is something endearingly futile about the herculean effort being made, not only to pull the line taut, but also to make the concept visually seamless. *Cogito Ergo Sum* (1989) presents a photographic image of tangled and knotted electrical wire within a frame. Actual wire carrying current is plugged into the socket in the wall below the frame, a light fixture rises above the frame, and in a gesture of delusional grandeur, the image illuminates itself. In *Arrangements* (1989), Muniz choreographed sixteen black-and-white photographs of the same Canadian goose in the pattern of a migrating flock. Again the illusion of visual logic is laid bare: we immediately comprehend the formula for meaning, recognizing the pattern from nature while simultaneously understanding its fabrication. This playful self-referentiality echoes the work of photographic conceptual artists such as Robert Cumming, Bruce Nauman, and John Baldessari.

As transitions between image and object, operating in the liminal space between flatness and depth, Muniz found himself attracted to the photographic documents of his sculptural pieces more than the objects themselves. The photographs conveyed the conceptual rigor of the sculpture, yet added the hermetic lightness and the perceptual economy of photography. In 1991, with a fast-approaching exhibition deadline and little money to spend on materials, Muniz purchased a lump of plasticene and a few rolls of black-and-white 35mm film. Muniz shaped the plasticene into various fantastical figures, photographing each one before remolding the same material into another figure. This process resulted in approximately sixty photographed figures, or "individuals" as Muniz came to consider them; five dozen humble and quirky sculptures whose only proof of their short and charmed existence was the photographic document, which was also their portrait, their death mask, if you will. Muniz gave each one a human name — *Veronica, Bob, Phil, Carrie, Amanda,* etc. — and when time came for the exhibition, he exhibited the photographs along with empty pedestals which served as memorials for the lost presence of these poor, departed souls. Symbolically, Muniz was also bidding farewell to sculpture and embracing photography as the sole vehicle for his ideas.

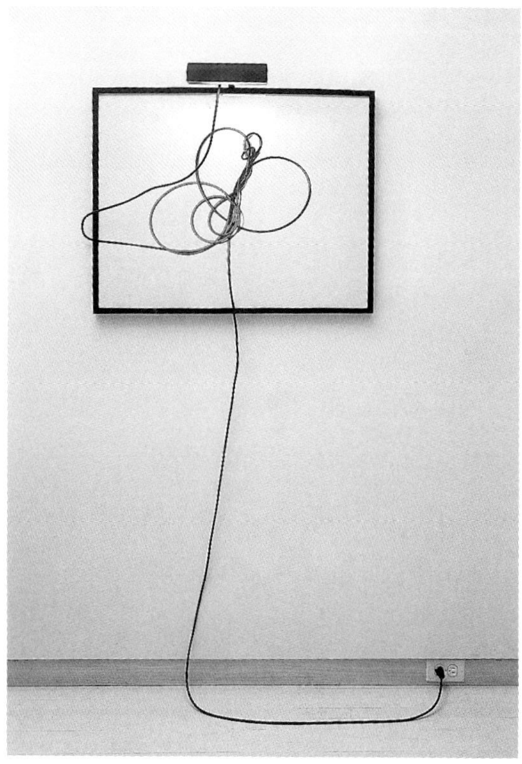

Vik Muniz, *Cogito Ergo Sum*, 1989, silver print, cord, and light fixture, 68 x 31 x 8 inches. Collection Gerald Talbert, New York.

Vik Muniz, *Tug of War*, 1988, silver print and rubber, 50 x 9 inches. Collection Barbara Schwartz, New York.

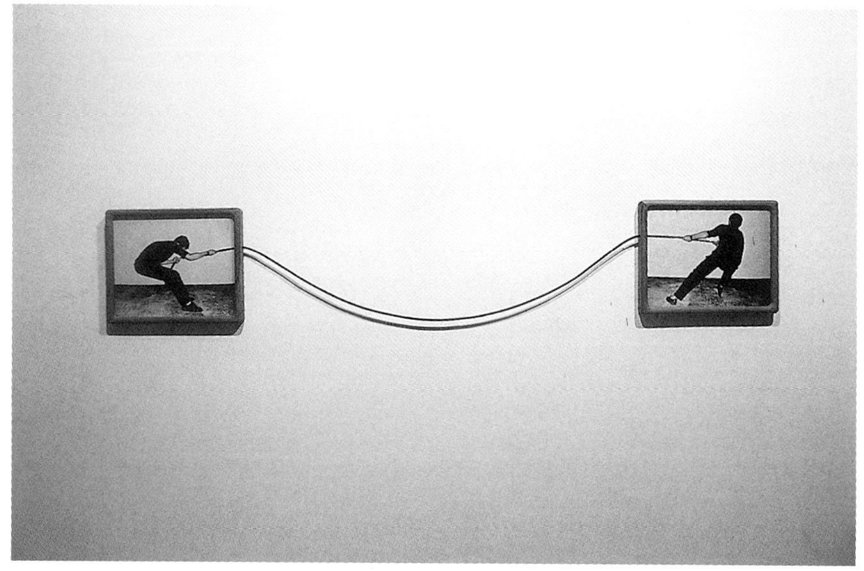

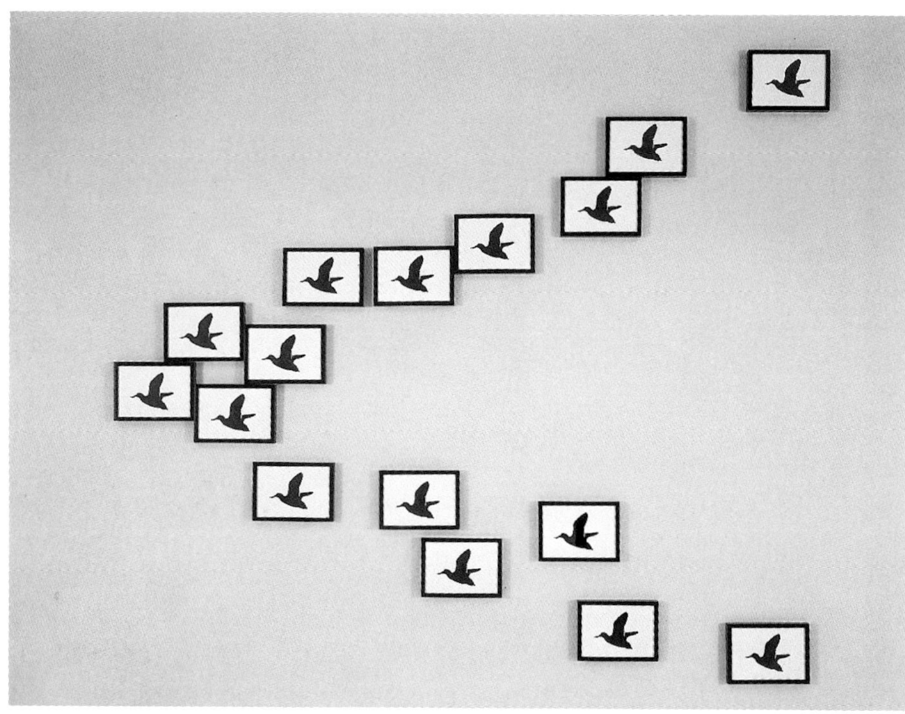

Vik Muniz, *Arrangements*, 1989, 16 gelatin silver prints, each 5 x 7 inches. Collection Doug and Nancy Starn, New York.

(D) I've Looked at Clouds From Both Sides Now

The cloud pictures (*Equivalents*) from 1993 are visually accessible yet resonate deeply with ideas from and referrals to art history and art theory. Looking at these pictures one might remember laying on one's back, splayed in a meadow, thickly whipped white cumulus billowing overhead. One is hypnotically involved in the fauna of imagination, a process of perceptual transformation occurs as the eyes scan the heavens, coming to rest on a recognizable formation. As the bunny cloud becomes the Elmer Fudd apparition, we participate in an endless and seemingly random game of recognition and association. This memory/image of cloudgazing, whether it be actual or just a cultural trope, represents a kind of benevolent collaboration between the individual and the grand coincidences of nature. Is a recognizable apparition in the clouds any less miraculous than Jesus in a tortilla, a monumental face on Mars, or Etruscan ruins as they appear in a polished agate? What are these moments of reciprocity between natural phenomena and human perception? Again, to quote Caillois:

> *I see the origin of the irresistible attraction of metaphor and analogy, the explanation of our strange and permanent need to find similarities in things. I can scarcely refrain from suspecting some ancient, diffused magnetism; a call from the center of things; a dim, almost lost memory, or perhaps a presentiment, pointless in so puny a being, of a universal syntax.*[6]

The cloud pictures also recall Alfred Stieglitz's images of atmospheric skies that he first exhibited in 1922. Initially titled *Songs of the Sky* and subsequently renamed *Equivalents*, Stieglitz pointed his camera skyward and later remarked, "My photographs are a picture of the chaos in the world, and of my relationship to that chaos. My prints show the world's constant upsetting of man's equilibrium, and his eternal battle to establish it."[7]

In terms of the history of the medium, much has been made of Stieglitz's accomplishment with this body of work, in the sense that he utilized photography conceptually, establishing a method of working that was fundamentally different from slavishly mimicking the aesthetics of painting as was fashionable for the Pictorialist photographers of his day. Nor was he concerned with using photography to document social realities, as in the work of Lewis Hine, for example. For Stieglitz, his cloud pictures were like no others since photography's inception, free of painterly and sociological constraints. He believed them to be powerful, transcendent, and liberating images for himself, the viewer, and finally for photography itself.

While at the end of the twentieth century it is nearly impossible for an artist to make such metaphysical claims for his work without irony, Muniz is interested, in a more humble way, in the idea of negotiating meaning out of chaos. But meaning in a contemporary sense is not found in transcendent metaphors, and chaos is not to be located in the endlessly shifting

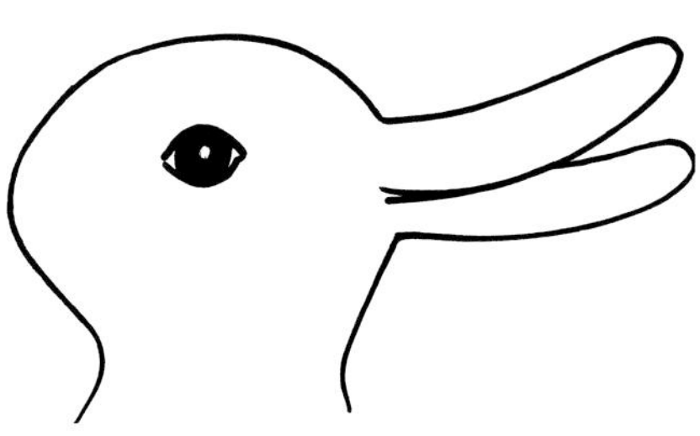

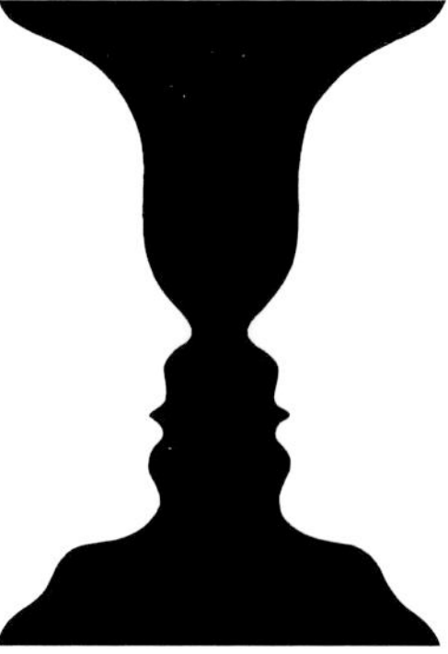

shapes of nature but the ever-accumulating image archive of our personal and collective histories. For a modernist like Stieglitz, the heroic struggle for the artist was to find visual equivalents and natural analogues for internal states. Muniz is interested in something a bit less romantic: his images are experiments and hypotheses concerning the psychology of perception. He is not interested in the nature of the physical world but in our perceptual reaction to our image-saturated culture.

In *Art and Illusion*, E. H. Gombrich poses the fundamental question to representation: "Is it possible to see shape apart from its interpretation?" At the beginning of this hugely influential text, he presents a simple black-and-white illustration, an image that on one hand looks like a rabbit with swept-back ears and on the other a duck with beak slightly parted. We can fall back and forth between the two readings, yet it seems impossible to see both simultaneously.

> *True, we can switch from one reading to another with increasing rapidity; we will also "remember" the rabbit while we see the duck, but the more closely we watch ourselves, the more certainly we will discover that we cannot experience alternative readings at the same time. Illusion, we will find, is hard to describe or analyze, for though we may be intellectually aware of the fact that any given experience* must *be an illusion, we cannot, strictly speaking, watch ourselves having an illusion.*[8]

A tuft of cotton resembles a cloud that resembles a man in a gondola that reminds us of Stieglitz. In the process of switching our perceptual framework between the varying positions, we can almost feel the muscles of seeing and perceiving, we watch ourselves watching and are delighted in the magic of it. The psychology of perception is complex indeed and Gombrich proposes various theories, including a kind of perceptual trial and error in which everything we see either confirms or contradicts what we already know. Human consciousness, therefore, never ceases probing and testing its environment, moving from the general to the particular in the process of identification. This perceptual switchboard, it seems to me, is the structure for the subversive play of not only the cloud pictures but the entirety of the Muniz archive in which he exchanges the thing for an illusion of the thing, thereby forcing the viewer to experience the process of vision.

"Optical confusions" and ambiguous images: (above, left) a duck becomes a rabbit, depending on the viewer's perspective; (above, right) Rubin's vase.

(E) An Icon Erased with the Slurp of a Tongue

Muniz is fond of telling a story about a Buddhist monk he met at the Asia Society in New York City who was publicly constructing an elaborate mandala out of sand. Day after day Muniz would visit the site, becoming hypnotically involved in watching the painstaking, methodical, and meditative ritual of pouring colored grains of sand in intricate patterns. The image of the mandala evolved from an accumulation of gestures as the monk's hands gracefully hovered over the ground, wispy trickles gathering in a web of stunning simplicity. The mandala was finally complete after a week of intensive labor, and as the monk raised himself off the floor and gazed upon his creation, another monk arrived with a broom and dustpan. The creator of the mandala appeared unfazed by this almost Dada-like anti-art performance, and Muniz shuffled over to inquire how the monk could so peacefully accept the destruction of the beauty of his labor. As might be expected, initially the monk replied philosophically, claiming the process and labor were, in and of themselves, their own rewards. Prodded further, the monk continued to elaborate on the theme of letting go of materialism, that things of this world have no intrinsic value. Muniz the Mischievous questioned the monk more pointedly and finally, with a conspiratorial smile slowly gathering on his lips, the monk slyly pulled a camera from inside his robes saying, "At least I'll have the photos."

In the case of the photographs of Vik Muniz, one might be awed by the serenity or question the sanity of a man who would spend up to two weeks constructing an image out of sugar, dirt, or thread. Muniz moves every grain of soil and sugar crystal, he endlessly unwinds spools in intricate patterns only to photograph the resulting image once and then unceremoniously dump the product of his labor into the trash bin. The apparent simplicity of his images obscures the excruciating detail and laboriousness of the making. Muniz employs a tiny vacuum apparatus, cotton swabs with glue, tweezers, and brushes to rearrange and build density, highlight, and shadow out of bits of wood pulp and soil; granules of sugar are transported one by one as if by an oversized and single-minded ant intent on making accurate the visage of a child. Imperceptible behind the whimsical accessibility of his work is a ravenous visual intelligence – he is forever shifting, sifting, making the strange recognizable and the familiar monstrous in a dialectic of connection and estrangement. In his world of material, process, and illusion, Muniz – in the words of critic Andy Grundberg – "revels in the unstable territory between object and image, material and representation, fact and metaphor."[9] That unstable territory is like the suspended moment before a first kiss, full of mystery and the giddy anticipation of revelation.

The Sugar Children series (1996) was inspired by a vacation-trip Muniz made to the Caribbean island of St. Kitts, where he met the children of workers in the sugar growing and processing industry, which along with tourism is the primary economic engine of the local economy.

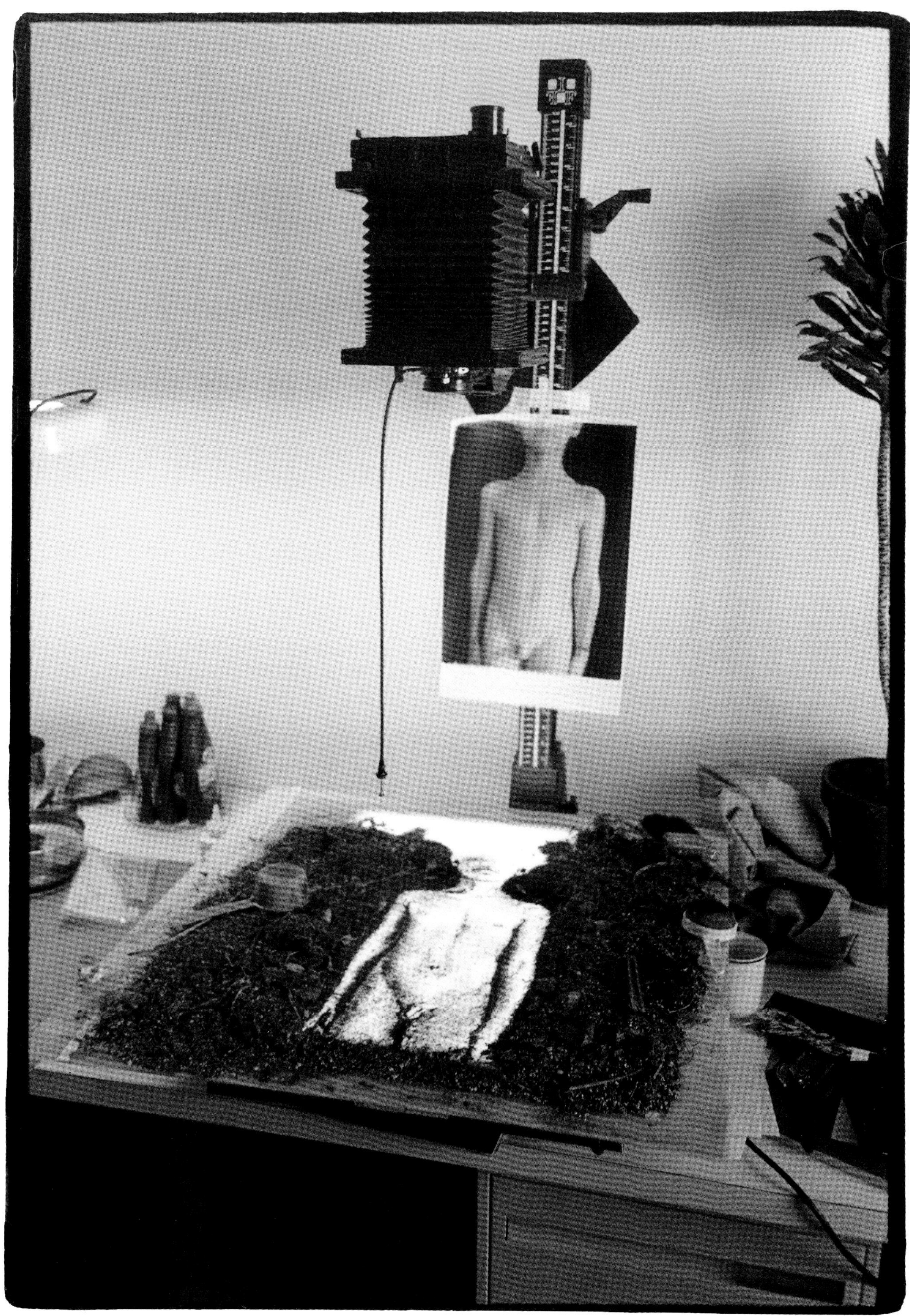

Vik Muniz's studio, 1998. Photo: Mark Alice Durant.

Muniz spent much of his time hanging out with the kids of St. Kitts, getting to know them and making photographic portraits. The titles from this series indicate the personal rather than sociological investment Muniz had in his relationships with these children: *Big James Sweats Buckets*, *Valicia Bathes in Sunday Clothes*, and *Jacynthe Loves Orange Juice* are examples of the intimacy between artist and subject. It is stating the obvious to observe that becoming cane-cutters in the sugar fields is the most likely fate for these children. The irony of utilizing the sweet substance of their servitude to portray them is not lost in these images. Yet there is something more than a glib political/conceptual equation at work here. The sugar pictures are heartbreakingly beautiful, simultaneously rough and ephemeral, full of the light of childhood yet almost too delicate to last. Folds of granular whiteness gather on black paper, the grains of sugar mock the monetary and reproductive value of the silver grains of the photographic process. It is as if the production of sugar threatens to drain away the sweetness and presence of these children's spirit, and that the "refined" product is somehow haunted by the ghost of their labor, past, present, and future.

There is a strong element of the performative in many of Muniz's works, especially in the *Chocolate* and *Thread* series. Photography and performance art have a long history together: artists have often relied on photographs not only as evidence of an activity, but photographic documentation can also function as a kind of visual currency to distribute ideas about time-based artmaking. One need only to think of the image of Joseph Beuys "explaining art to a dead hare," or Chris Burden's crucifixion on a VW Bug to see how photography and performance are inextricably bound in the creation of a kind of anticelebrity yet heroic aura around the artist. In opposition to the aura of rebellion that inflates so much of performance photography, the *Thread* series in particular flattens out the performative in service of the pictorial. Eight hundred to 21,000 yards of thread are unspooled like a continuous line, building density, volume, perspective, detail, shadow, texture, and contour. From across the room, one identifies these images as, perhaps, nineteenth-century nature studies and landscape exercises, but on closer inspection we find that our assumptions are incorrect. Our expectations of subject matter and material are confounded: these are photographs that look like drawings but are in fact documents of a durational performance. We view a scene, a pastoral perspective represented in thread, and we are brought to think about an unseen action in which the artist, over a period of days and weeks, unfurled thousands of yards of thin cotton line upon a lightbox, creating an illusion of a traditional pen-and-ink landscape.

The first image made in the *Pictures of Chocolate* series was a portrait of Sigmund Freud. As with *The Sugar Children*, Muniz wanted to increase the sensory palate of his imagery, and was struck by how chocolate in particular seemed to have a seductive power over many people. Freud seemed a natural beginning for a group of images that could be erased with a vigorous slurp of the tongue. Drawing with chocolate (Bosco, actually) proved to be a unique

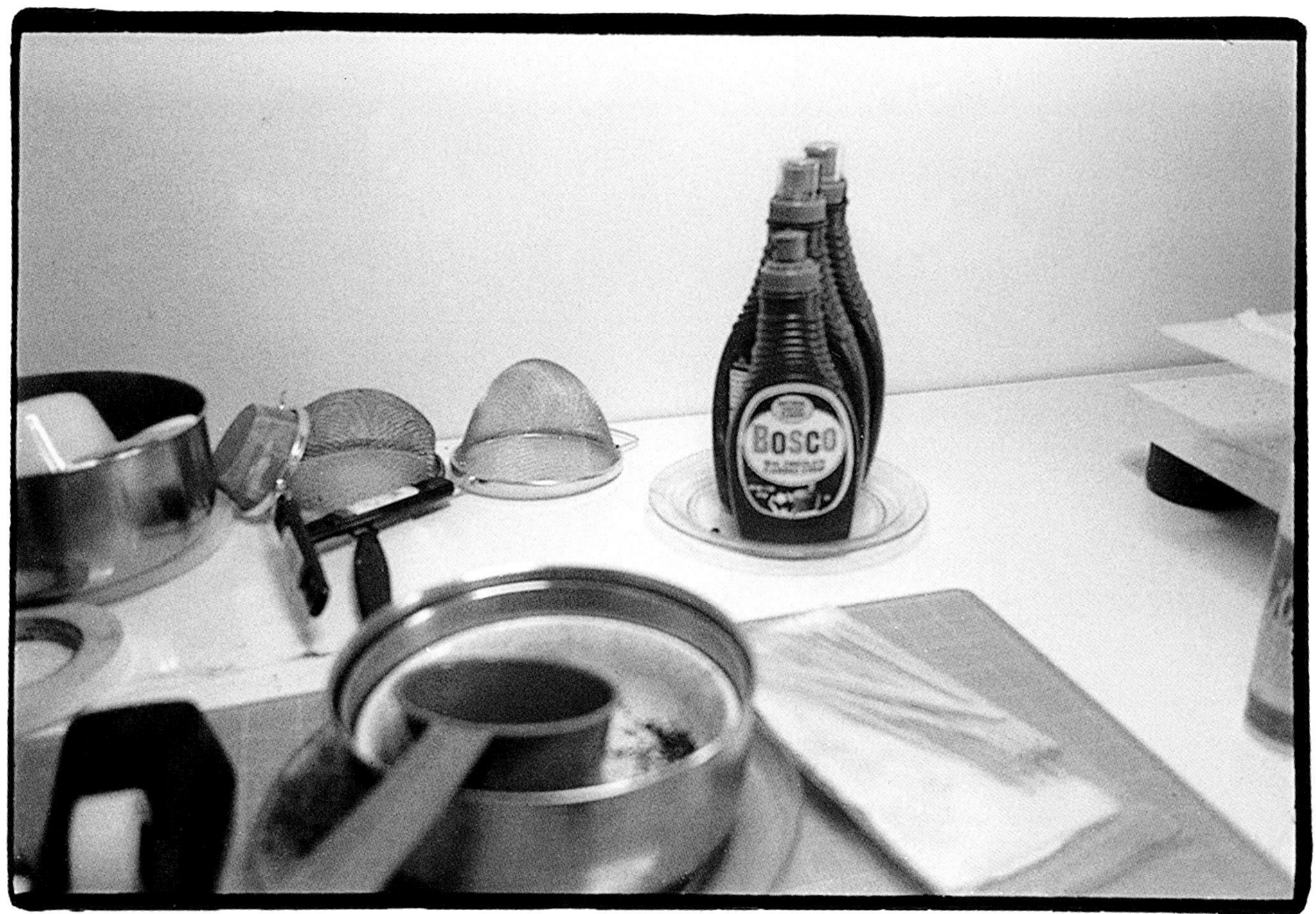

challenge; if the image was not drawn and photographed quickly, the liquid would lose its glossy wetness. It was also necessary for the first time to photograph in color, as the liquid chocolate resembled a film-noirish blood when rendered in black-and-white tonalities.

In dripping and glistening chocolate, Muniz has cleverly re-created several images of Hans Namuth's portraits of Jackson Pollock working in his studio. These images were originally published in *Life* magazine and exerted tremendous influence on the image of the artist in the popular imagination. These images remain symbols of the artist as a tragic figure heroically struggling with his internal demons, recording the metaphysical battle on the surface of the canvas. Namuth's photographs have become iconographic documents of painting as existential performance. In Muniz's revisionist history, although the images are blown up, monumentally forcing the photographs to function on the scale of painting, he gently revises the overblown seriousness of the myth of the rugged male artist spilling his guts onto virginal canvas. Muniz empties the historical image of its stale content, causing us to gleefully respond to the simple wonders of pictures: how one can draw with chocolate, how a photograph can look like a painting, how some things look like other things, which in turn look like still other things.

Vik Muniz's studio, 1998. Photo: Mark Alice Durant.

Muniz reminds us that all pictures are illusory and therefore fundamentally miraculous: seeing is believing. Intellectuals and skeptics can scoff at the gullible masses and their devotions to such apparitions as the Virgin of Guadalupe as it forms in the window condensation of an office building. I, for one, think we should humbly accept miracles wherever and whenever they are given. Representation is the altar of communication between our internal landscape and the external chaos of things that are not us. When we perceive something, even if it is illusory, we activate the intricate machinations of comparison, and in that process lies the interconnectedness of all things. In the genetic structure of our imagination we intuitively understand that the familiar and the aberrant, the human and the animal, the intimate and the dispersed are variations in a kaleidoscope of forms. Even when we sort out difference, we do so through a dialectic of recognition and wonder, thereby creating a correspondence between divine creation and humanity's humble imitations.

Notes

1. As quoted in Michael Taussig, *The Nervous System* (New York: Routledge, 1992), p. 2.
2. As quoted by Marguerite Yourcenar in her introduction to Roger Caillois, *The Writing of Stones* (Charlottesville: University Press of Virginia, 1985), p. xix.
3. Caillois, *The Writing of Stones*, p. 2.
4. *The Best of Life* (New York: Time-Life Books, 1973).
5. Vik Muniz in conversation with Charles Stainback, this volume, p. 16.
6. Caillois, *The Writing of Stones*, p. 104.
7. As quoted in Dorothy Norman, *Alfred Stieglitz: An American Seer* (New York: Random House, 1973), p. 161.
8. E. H. Gombrich, *Art and Illusion* (Princeton: Princeton University Press, 1969), pp. 5–6.
9. Andy Grundberg, "Sweet Illusion," *Artforum* (September 1997), p. 104.

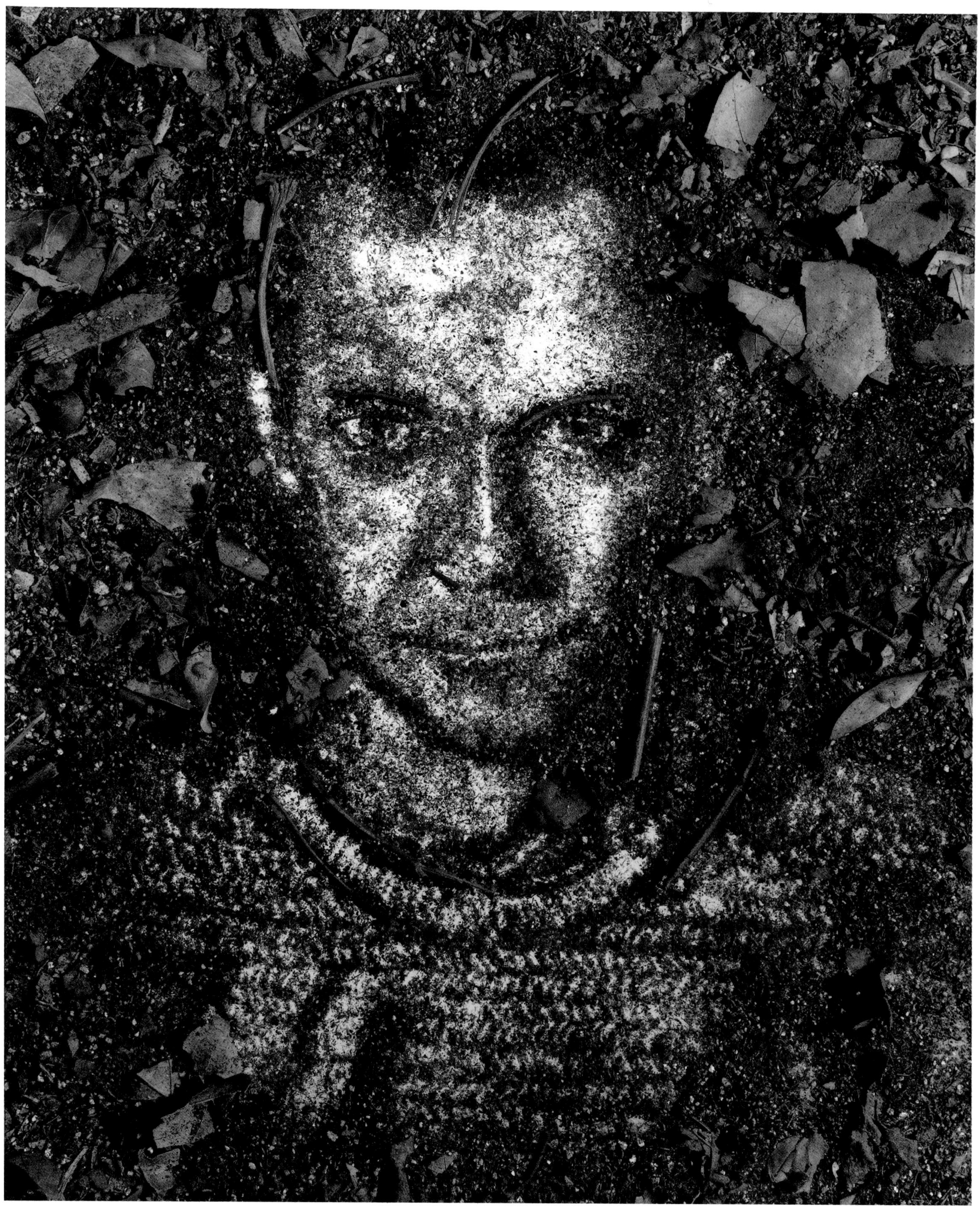

Vik Muniz, *Vik*, 1998, gelatin silver print, 20 x 24 inches.
Collection Betty and Lester Guttman, Chicago.

LIST OF WORKS

The Best of Life

1988-90
Gelatin silver prints
Each 11 x 14 in.

Memory Rendering of Man Stopping Tank in Beijing
Collection Maison Européenne de la Photographie, Paris

Memory Rendering of Kiss at Times Square
Collection Jacqueline d'Amercourt, Paris

Memory Rendering of 3-D Screening
Collection The Linc Group, Chicago

Memory Rendering of Saigon Execution of Vietcong Suspect
Collection The San Francisco Museum of Modern Art

Memory Rendering of Tranbang Child
Collection The Metropolitan Museum of Art, New York

Memory Rendering of the Man on the Moon
Collection The Metropolitan Museum of Art, New York

Memory Rendering of John Lennon in Manhattan
Collection William J. Hokin, Chicago

Individuals

1992–93
Gelatin silver prints
Each 20 x 16 in.

Veronica
Private Collection, Turin

Equivalents

1993
Toned gelatin silver prints

Dürer's Praying Hands
24 x 20 in.
Collection The Museum of Fine Arts, Boston

Teapot
20 x 24 in.
The West Family Collection, Oaks, Pennsylvania

The Rower
20 x 24 in.
Collection Juan Uslé and Victoria Civera, New York

The Snail
20 x 24 in.
Collection Rena Bransten, San Francisco

Kitty Cloud
24 x 20 in.
The West Family Collection, Oaks, Pennsylvania

Pictures of Wire

1993-97
Gelatin silver prints
Each 20 x 16 in.

Parcel, 1994
Collection David Leigh, New York

Faucet, 1994
Collection The Museum of Fine Arts, Houston

Fiat Lux (Lightbulb), 1994
Collection REFCO Group, Chicago

Cage, 1995
Collection Heidi Steiger, New York

Paper and Wire 1, 1995
Collection Gary Schneider, San Francisco

Relaxation, 1994
Collection Leo Malca, New York

American Tourister (Suitcase), 1995
Collection Lars Bohman, Stockholm

Candle, 1996
Collection Leo Malca, New York

Summer, 1996
Private Collection, Los Angeles

Wind (Swing), 1996
Collection The Art Institute of Chicago

Shadowgrams (X-rays)

1993–94
Gelatin silver prints

Coyote
48 x 60 in.
Collection Henry Buhl, New York

Indian Elephant
48 x 60 in.
Collection the artist

Pictures of Thread

1995–98
Toned gelatin silver prints
Each 20 x 24 in.

12,000 Yards (Etretat, after Courbet), 1998
Private Collection, Paris

17,500 Yards (Landscape without an Angel, after Hagar and the Angel by Claude Lorrain), 1998
Collection David Leigh, New York

16,000 Yards (Le Songeur, after Corot), 1996
Collection The San Francisco Museum of Modern Art

6,200 Yards (Lighthouse), 1995
Collection Jack Banning, New York

4,000 Yards (Apple Trees, after Gerhard Richter), 1998
Collection Martin Eisenberg, New York

Pictures of Holes

1997
Gelatin silver prints
Each 16 x 20 in.

702 Holes
Collection Gilberto Chateaubriand/Museu de Arte Moderna, Rio de Janeiro

525 Holes
Private Collection, São Paulo

637 Holes
Private Collection, São Paulo

800 Holes
Collection Gilberto Chateaubriand/Museu de Arte Moderna, Rio de Janeiro

848 Holes
Collection the artist

The Sugar Children

1996
Gelatin silver prints
Each 14 x 11 in.

Valentina, the Fastest
Collection The MacArthur Foundation

Valicia Bathes in Sunday Clothes
Collection The Museum of Modern Art, New York

Jacynthe Loves Orange Juice
Collection The Art Institute of Chicago

Little Calist Can't Swim
Collection The National Museum of American Art, Smithsonian Institution, Washington, D.C.

Big James Sweats Buckets
Collection The Metropolitan Museum of Art, New York

Ten Ten's Weed Necklace
Collection Fondation Cartier pour l'Art Contemporain, Paris

Principia

1997
Toned gelatin silver prints
Collection the artist

Principia 1: Three Naked Singularities
Principia 2: Facial Hair Magnified One Zillion Times
Principia 3: Vocal Cords Saying "Buon Giorno"
Principia 5: Goosebump Hormone
Principia 9: Loser Gene
Principia 10: Sloth Virus

Pictures of Chocolate

1997–98

Sigmund
60 x 48 in.
Collection Tete Pacheco, São Paulo

Action Photo I (After Hans Namuth)
60 x 48 in.
Collection Eileen and Peter Norton, Los Angeles

Individuals
60 x 48 in.
Collection Progressive Corporation, Cleveland

Milk Drop (After Dr. Harold Edgerton)
60 x 48 in.
Private Collection, France

Team (soccer players)
48 x 84 in.
Collection Scott Cook, New York

Milan (The Last Supper)
60 x 144 in.
Collection Vicky and Kent Logan, Tiburon, California

The Sacred Lodovica (After Bernini)
48 x 60 in.
Collection the artist

Pictures of Soil

1997–98
Gelatin silver prints
Each 20 x 24 in.

Binoculars
Collection Ann Schaffer, Vermont

Youth (Gaspar)
Collection David Leigh, New York

Eleven Eggs
Collection The Metropolitan Museum of Art, New York

The Trout (After Courbet)
Collection The Metropolitan Museum of Art, New York

Torso (After Frantisek Dritkol)
Collection Gilberto Chateaubriand/Museu de Arte Moderna, Rio de Janeiro

Hands
Collection Cindy Sherman, New York

Vik
Collection Betty and Lester Guttman, Chicago

VIK MUNIZ

Born 1961 in São Paulo, Brazil
Lives and works in New York

Solo Exhibitions

1998
Galeri Lars Bohman, Stockholm
Galeria Módulo, Lisbon
"Seeing Is Believing," International Center of Photography, New York
Rena Bransten Gallery, San Francisco

1997
"Pictures of Thread," Wooster Gardens, New York
Galeria Camargo Vilaça, São Paulo
Dan Bernier Gallery, Los Angeles

1996
"The Sugar Children," Tricia Collins Contemporary Art, New York
Galeria Casa de Imagen, Curitiba, Brazil
"The Best of Life," Wooster Gardens, New York
"Pantomimes," Rena Bransten Gallery, New York

1995
"The Wire Pictures," Galeria Camargo Vilaça, São Paulo

1994
"Representations," Wooster Gardens, New York

1993
"Equivalents," Tricia Collins Contemporary Art, New York

1992
"Individuals," Stux Gallery, New York

1991
Gabinete de Arte Rachel Arnaud, São Paulo
Galerie Claudine Papillon, Paris

1990
Meyers/Bloom Gallery, Santa Monica, Calif.
Stephen Wirtz Gallery, San Francisco

1989
Stux Gallery, New York

Selected Group Exhibitions

1998
24th Bienal Internacional de São Paulo
"Antropofagia Urbana," Paço das Artes, São Paulo
"The Garden of the Forking Paths," Kunstforeningen, Copenhagen; traveled to Oslo and Helsinki
Coleção Gilberto Chateaubriand/ Museu de Arte Moderna, Rio de Janeiro
Haus der Kulturen der Welt, Berlin
"Das Mass der Dinge," Ursula Blickle Stiftung, Kraichtal, Germany
"The Cottingley Fairies and Other Apparitions," Leslie Tonkonow, New York
"La Collection II," Fondation Cartier pour l'Art Contemporain, Paris
"Internality Externality," Galerie Lelong, New York

1997
"New Photography XIII," Museum of Modern Art, New York
"New Faces and Other Recent Acquisitions," Art Institute of Chicago
"Assi Esta la Cosa," Centro Cultural Arte Contemporaneo, Mexico City
"Une Fleur des Photographes: L'Arum," Musée National de la Coopération Franco-Américaine, Chateau de Biérancourt, France
"Pool," Rena Bransten Gallery, San Francisco
"Photographie d'une Collection Caisse des Dépôts et Consignations," 13 Quai Voltaire, Paris
"One Line Drawing," UBU Gallery, New York
"Colleción Ordónez Falcón de Fotografia," IVAM Centro Julio González, Valencia, Spain
"Artistes Latino-Américains," Daniel Templon, Paris
"20 Years, Almost," Robert Miller Gallery, New York
"Hope," National Arts Club, New York
"Ut Scientia Pictura," Paolo Baldacci Gallery, New York

1996
"Wesenchau: Disingenuous Images," Galerie Renee Ziegler, Zurich
"Bis," Galeria Camargo Vilaça, São Paulo
"The Subverted Object," UBU Gallery, New York
"Recent Acquisitions," Metropolitan Museum of Art, New York
"Inclusion/Exclusion," Kunstlerhaus, Graz, Austria
"Some Assembly Required," Art Institute of Chicago
"Novas Aquisiçoes," Collection Gilberto Chateaubriand/Museu de Arte Moderna, Rio de Janeiro
"Shadow Play," San Jose Institute of Contemporary Art, San Jose, Calif.
"Material Matters," A.O.I. Gallery, Santa Fe, N.M.

1995

"Changing Perspectives," Contemporary Art Museum, Houston

"Panorama da Arte Contemporanea Brasileira," Museu de Arte Moderna, São Paulo/Museu de Arte Moderna, Rio de Janeiro

"Mostra America," Fundação Cultural de Curitiba, Curitiba, Brazil

"Recent Acquisitions," Los Angeles County Museum of Art

"The Photographic Condition," San Francisco Museum of Modern Art

"The Cultured Tourist," Center for Photography, Woodstock, N.Y.

"Blindspot," The MAC, Dallas Artist Research and Exhibition

"Garbage," Thread Waxing Space, New York

1994

"Single Cell Creatures," Katonah Museum of Art, Katonah, N.Y.

"Crash," Thread Waxing Space, New York

"Up the Establishment: Reconstructing the Counterculture," Sonnabend Gallery, New York

"Garbage," Real Art Ways, Hartford, Conn.

"Jetlag," Gallerie Martina Detterer, Frankfurt

1993

Tom Cugliani Gallery, New York

"The Alternative Eye: Photography for the 90s," Southern Alleghenies Museum, Loreto, Pa.

"Time to Time," Castello di Rivara, Turin

"Sound," Museo d'Arte Moderna, Bolzano, Italy

"Post-Verbum," Palazzo della Regione Bergamo

1992

"Life Size: Small, Medium, Large," Museo d'Arte Contemporaneo Luigi Pecci, Prato, Italy

"Multiples," Alldrich Museum of Art, Ridgefield, Conn.

"Detour," International House, New York

"The Collection," Centro per l'Arte Contemporaneo Luigi Pecci, Prato, Italy

"Les Enfants Terribles," Wooster Gardens, New York

"Gallery Artists," Galerie Claudine Papillon, Paris

"Theoretically Yours," Regione Autonoma della Valle d'Aosta, Aosta, Italy

1991

"Mike Kelley/Vik Muniz/Jim Shaw," Real Art Ways, Hartford, Conn.

"The Encompassing Eye: Photography as Drawing," University Art Galleries, University of Akron

"The Neighborhood," A.I.R., Amsterdam

"Anni Novanta," Galleria d'Arte Moderna, Bologna

"Real Fake," Cartier Fondation, Jouy-en-Josos, France

"Outside America," Fay Gold Gallery, Atlanta

"The Fetish of Knowledge," Real Art Ways, Hartford, Conn.

1990

"Non Sculpture," Galerie Barbara Farber, Amsterdam

"Constructed Illusion," Pace MacGill Gallery, New York

"Assembled," Wright State University, Dayton, Ohio

"On the Edge Between Sculpture and Photography," Cleveland Center for Contemporary Art

1989

"De Rozeboomkamer," Beeldenroute Foundation, Diepenheim, Holland

"Wortlaut: Konzepte Zwischen Visueller Poesie & Fluxus," Galerie Schuppenhauer, Cologne

Selected Bibliography

Aletti, Vince. "Constructed Illusions." *Village Voice*, November 20, 1990.

______. "Organized Confusion." *Village Voice*, December 2, 1997.

Baker, Kenneth. "Eccentric and Entertaining Pieces." *San Francisco Chronicle*, April 7, 1990.

______. "Muniz Whets the Appetite for Images in Chocolate." *San Francisco Chronicle*, April 17, 1998.

Barilli, Renato. *Anni Novanta*. Exhibition catalogue. Bologna: Galleria d'Arte Moderna, 1991.

Bonami, Francesco. "Vik Muniz at Stux Gallery." *Flash Art International* (May–June 1993).

Bonetti, David. "The Inevitability of Vik Muniz." *San Francisco Examiner*, April 6, 1990.

______. "Vik Muniz at Rena Bransten." *San Francisco Examiner*, May 10, 1996.

Cotter, Holland. "Three Shows Celebrate the Spirit of Fluxus." *New York Times*, October 23, 1992.

______. "200 Images Leisurely Chatting." *New York Times*, January 31, 1997.

______. "New Photography 13." *New York Times*, November 7, 1997.

Cyphers, Peggy. "Vik Muniz." *Arts Magazine* (May 1990).

Dector, Joshua. "Vik Muniz at Stux." *Arts Magazine* (March 1989).

Faust, Gretchen. "Vik Muniz." *Arts Magazine* (May 1990).

Goldberg, Vicky. "Of Fairies, Free Spirits, and Outright Frauds." *New York Times*, February 1, 1998.

Grundberg, Andy. "Sweet Illusion." *Artforum* (September 1997).

Hagen, Charles. "Mixing Humor with the History of Photography." *New York Times*, March 24, 1995.

______. "Vik Muniz." *New York Times*, February 5, 1993.

______. "The Encompassing Eye: Photography as Drawing." *Aperture* (Fall 1992).

Huitorel, Jean-Marc. "Life Size." *Art Press* (October 1992).

Jouannais, Jean-Yves. "Vik Muniz." *Art Press* (December 1991).

Kahn, Wolf. "Connecting Incongruities." *Art in America* (November 1992).

Kandel, Susan. "Artful Illusions and Serial Masquerades Spring to Life." *Los Angeles Times*, April 4, 1997.

Katz, Vincent. "Vik Muniz at Brent Sikkema." *Art in America* (December 1995).

______. "The Cunning Artificer." *On Paper* (March–April 1997).

Kismarik, Susan. "Vik Muniz, New Photography 13." *MoMA Magazine* (Fall 1997).

Kurjakovik, Daniel. "Wesenchau." *Kunstbulletin* (January 1997).

Leffingwell, Edward. "Through a Brazilian Lens." *Art in America* (April 1998).

Levin, Kim. "Vik Muniz." *Village Voice*, February 16, 1993.

Lieberman, Rhonda. "Stuttering." *Flash Art* (April–May 1991).

Life Size. Exhibition catalogue. Prato, Italy: Museo d'Arte Contemporaneo Luigi Pecci, 1992.

Mahoney, Robert. "Vik Muniz, Sugar Children." *Time Out New York*, December 19, 1996.

Melrod, George. "Vik Muniz, Stux Gallery, New York." *Sculpture* (November–December 1990).

Mesquita, Ivo. *Panorama da Arte Contemporanea Brasileira*. Exhibition catalogue. São Paulo: Museu de Arte Moderna, 1995.

Miller, Kenneth. "Sugar Snaps." *Life* (March 1998).

Morgan, Stuart. "Vik Muniz at Prato." *Frieze*, no. 7 (1992).

Perela, Christina. "Vik Muniz." *Tema Celeste* (Fall 1992).

Princenthal, Nancy. "Vik Muniz at Stux." *Art in America* (April 1989).

Roberts, Lisa. "Expatriate Art: How Brazilian Is It?" *Polyester* 2, no. 8 (Spring 1994).

Rosenburg, Barry. *Assembled*. Exhibition catalogue. Cleveland: Cleveland Center for Contemporary Art, 1990.

Whitney, Scott. "Must Museum." *New York Post*, October 15, 1997.

Shales, Ezra. "Vik Muniz." *Review Magazine*, December 1, 1996.

Smith, Roberta. "Art in Review." *New York Times*, December 13, 1996.

Tager, Alisa. *Detour*. Exhibition catalogue. New York: International House, 1992.

Vescovo, Marisa. "Vik Muniz a Torino." *La Stampa*, April 27, 1992.

______. "Post-Verbum." *Tema Celeste* (June 1993).

Vik Muniz. Exhibition catalogue. São Paulo: Gabinete de Arte Rachel Arnaud, 1991.

Weibel, Peter. *Inclusion/Exclusion*. Exhibition catalogue. Graz, Austria: Kunstlerhaus, 1996.

Wilson, Beth. *Vik Muniz*. Exhibition catalogue. New York: Stux Gallery, 1989.

ACKNOWLEDGMENTS

First and foremost, I must thank Paulo Machline and the Fundação Matias Machline for their generous support of this publication, and Charlie Stainback, whose inspiring enthusiasm and restless perfectionism made this project a reality.

A special note of appreciation must also be extended to James Crump, Bethany Johns, Mark Alice Durant, and Philomena Mariani, who have shaped a chaotic array of documentation into a work of art itself. Many thanks to all the friends and associates who over the years have believed in my work, sometimes more than I could myself: Brent Sikkema, Michael Jenkins, Marcantonio Vilaça, Karla Camargo, Rena Bransten, Tricia Collins, the friends at Chelsea Black and White Photo Lab, David Sembrot, David Leigh, Kim Caputo, Adam Fuss, and finally Marion and Gaspar, my loving teachers of realities and dreams.

This book is dedicated to Ana Rocha.

—VIK MUNIZ

This publication was produced in conjunction with the exhibition of the same title at International Center of Photography (ICP). It would not have been possible without the hard work and support of countless individuals. The book itself, its look and ultimately its perfection, are the result of Bethany Johns's diligence, patience, intelligence, and creative sensitivity. Without her extraordinary ability to pull together many disparate elements, on an unbelievably tight schedule, this publication would be just another book. From Arena Editions I must also thank Elsa Kendall, art director, and James Crump, who were a pleasure to work with. I wish all publishers were like them. Philomena Mariani, who edited all the various texts in the publication, deserves a special note of appreciation for adding clarity and conciseness to all the texts. Lastly, Mark Alice Durant's insightful and delightful essay completes this publication, beautifully.

I would be remiss if I did not thank the following people who, in ways both big and small, have made this entire project a success: Brent Sikkema of Wooster Gardens; Phil Block and Mary Vahey at ICP; Jackie Goldberg of Bethany Johns Design, New York; Rennie Knapp at Skidmore College, Saratoga Springs; Sharon Lignier of Castlerock Entertainment, Hollywood; Jennifer Hartz of the Chicago Historical Society; Pam Stuedemann of the Art Institute of Chicago; David Wilson of the Museum of Jurassic Technology, Los Angeles; David Strettell of Magnum Photos, New York; Bruce Hackney of the McKee Gallery, New York; Virginia Dodier of the Museum of Modern Art, New York; Stephanie Sloane and Richard Solomon of Pace Prints, New York; Linda Fiske of Pace Wildenstein MacGill, New York; Kimberlie Gumz Fixx of the Allen Memorial Art Museum, Oberlin College; Norm Deska, Edward T. Meyer, and Christina Favalo of Ripley's Believe It or Not!, Orlando, Florida; Tim Clifford of John Weber Gallery, New York; Susan Jimison of Weekly World News, Lantana, Florida; Andrew Silewicz of Victoria Miro Gallery, London; Nora Tobbe of 303 Gallery, New York; Meaghan Delmonico of Marian Goodman Gallery, New York; Janet Borden, Madame Gilberte Brassaï, Victoria Clary, Robert Cumming, Vija Celmins, John Pfahl, Felicia Murray, Tom Bridges, Anita Bikowitz, Thomas Demand, Gerhard Richter, Jerry Seinfeld, Mark Sloan, Charles Melcher, Max Stainback, and Eric Stern. A special note of thanks to the Exhibition Committee at ICP, Barbara Foshay-Miller and Chuck Miller, and the Peter Norton Family Foundation for their support of the exhibition at ICP.

Lastly, a heartfelt thanks to Vik Muniz—who can transform an everyday discussion into an amazing journey—for reminding me of how much fun it is to be an artist.

—CHARLES ASHLEY STAINBACK

CHARLES ASHLEY STAINBACK has been involved in photography as a practitioner, educator, and curator for over two decades. He is currently Dayton Director of the Tang Teaching Museum/Art Gallery, and professor of liberal studies at Skidmore College, Saratoga Springs, New York. In addition to being the former director of the Aperture Foundation's Burden Gallery in New York, and the exhibition coordinator for the Visual Studies Workshop, he has worked with the Friends of Photography in San Francisco and been director of exhibitions at the International Center of Photography, New York. Over the past decade, Stainback has published several books and curated numerous exhibitions of some of the most challenging work by contemporary artists and photographers, including *David Levinthal: Works from 1975–1996* (1997), *Science Projects: Taxonomy of Images* (1997), *Jeff Wolin: Written on Memory* (1997), *Special Collections: The Photographic Order from Pop to Now* (1993–94), *Iterations: The New Digital Image* (1993–94), *The Anonymous Other: Photographic Installations by Christian Boltanski, Barbara Bloom, and Alfredo Jaar* (1991), *Bruce Charlesworth: Private Enemy/Public Eye* (1988), and *Portrayals* (1987). In 1995, he curated a special exhibition that toured Russia and Eastern Europe entitled *Along the Frontier: Video Installations by Ann Hamilton, Bruce Nauman, Francesc Torres, and Bill Viola.*

MARK ALICE DURANT has written extensively on the nexus of photography, performance, and cultural phenomena. His essays have appeared in *Art in America*, *Afterimage*, the *Boston Book Review*, *Camerawork*, *Exposure*, *New Art Examiner*, and *SEE: A Journal of Visual Culture.* Recent publications include *McDermott and McGough: A History of Photography* (Arena Editions, 1998); "Lost (and Found) in a Masquerade: The Photographs of Pierre Molinier," in *The Passionate Camera: Photography and Bodies of Desire* (Routledge, 1998); and "The Caliban Codex, or A Thing Most Brutish," in *Jimmie Durham* (Phaidon, 1995). Durant has received grants and awards from the National Endowment for the Arts, the Center for Creative Photography, and Macdowell, among others, and has served on the faculties of the School of the Art Institute of Chicago, University of California, Los Angeles, and the University of New Mexico. He is currently assistant professor in the Department of Art Media Studies at Syracuse University. Durant received his MFA in photography from the San Francisco Art Institute. His photographs and installations have been presented internationally, including showings at the Museum of Contemporary Art, Chicago; Los Angeles County Museum of Art; Museum of Photographic Arts, San Diego; Artist Space, New York; and DeBeyerd Museum, The Netherlands. In 1991, he co-founded the performance duo Men of the World, which has performed public street actions in Chicago, Boston, New York, Washington, D.C., San Francisco, Cleveland, Los Angeles, and Houston.

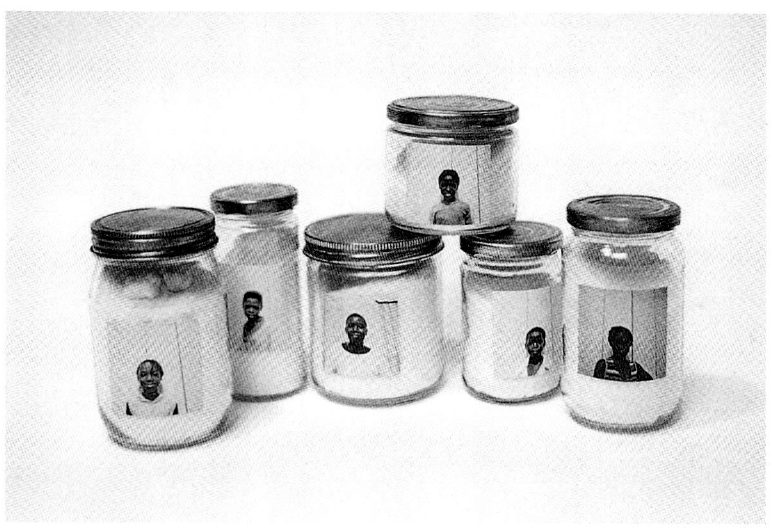

Vik Muniz, *The Sugar Children*, 1996, set of six jars containing the sugar used to produce the portraits, labeled with the original source images for the project. Collection of John Robershaw, New York.